Women, the Environment and Sustainable Development

Towards a Theoretical Synthesis

ROSI BRAIDOTTI   EWA CHARKIEWICZ
SABINE HÄUSLER   SASKIA WIERINGA

Women, the Environment and Sustainable Development

Towards a Theoretical Synthesis

ZED BOOKS

in association with

INSTRAW

Women, the Environment and Sustainable Development
was first published by Zed Books Ltd, 7 Cynthia Street,
London N1 9JF, UK, and 165 First Avenue,Atlantic Highlands,
New Jersey 07716, USA, in association with the
United Nations International Research and Training Institute
for the Advancement of Women (INSTRAW),
César Nicolás Penson 102-A, Santo Domingo, Dominican Republic,
in 1994.

Second impression, 1995.

Cover designed by Andrew Corbett.
Laserset by Rami Tzabar.
Printed and bound in the United Kingdom
by Biddles Ltd, Guildford and King's Lynn.

A catalogue record for this book is
available from the British Library

US CIP data is available from
the Library of Congress

ISBN 1 85649 183 8 Hb
ISBN 1 85649 184 6 Pb

Contents

Foreword

INSTRAW

Conscious that environmental problems affect women in very specific ways, from as early as 1982 INSTRAW has been involved in programmes aimed at promoting the involvement of women in the solutions of problems related to water, sanitation and energy. Since their inception, these programmes were oriented towards promoting environmentally sound use of water and energy sources and at contributing to a new approach through the integration of women's needs as well as their participation in planning, technical operations and projects.

The sectoral focus of these programmes at the time of their development responded to the critical problems that developing countries faced in satisfying their water and energy needs. As the need to establish the link between these sectoral problems and other environmental issues became evident and as environmental issues became important items on national and international agendas, INSTRAW launched a new programme in 1990 on Gender, Environment and Sustainable Development. This programme is concerned with environmental problems related to water and energy, including such specific issues of immediate relevance to women as waste disposal, the effects of pesticide use, and nuclear testing, to name but a few.

The present study is one output of this programme. It was commissioned by INSTRAW with the purpose of compiling a state-of-the-art report on debates around the issue of women, the environment and sustainable development. Due to the complexity and intersecting nature of the topic, an interdisciplinary research team from the Women's Programme in the Humanities at the University of Utrecht, and the Women and Development Programme at the Institute of Social Studies in The Hague, was asked to carry out this project. The result is a highly comprehensive review of the issues and a challenging alternative framework which could hardly have been achieved by a single author.

The project began in late 1990 with a desk-top study. In mid-1991 an interim international workshop entitled 'Women, the Environment and Sustainable Development: Towards a Theoretical Framework' was held in the Netherlands in which activists, researchers and development experts were invited to present their views. A first report presented the various perspectives, views and positions upheld by the major actors in the field of women, the environment and sustainable development. This report was revised and expanded for publication and as well as including a platform for the various positions, it also provides provocative insights for both reflection and action. A framework emerges emphasizing not only mutualism, sustainability, holism, justice, equity, autonomy, self-reliance and peace, but also that the different ways in which individuals approach the topic depends on their own situation. It is a framework that owes much to feminist thought and calls for very specific research methodologies and policy actions. It is a feminist contribution to both science and sustainable development.

INSTRAW is pleased to present this joint publication at a moment in which the future of our planet is at a crossroad and an understanding of the complexity of issues and the resources that can be harnessed for a solution are imperative. This book will be of interest to activists in women's environmental and development movements, development experts and to students and scholars working in these fields. The book's most important contribution to thinking on the crucial topic of environment and sustainable development is the evidence of the total involvement of women worldwide in environmental issues. It is hoped that anyone reading this book will conclude, as we have, that present and future environmental decisions cannot be undertaken without the active participation of women. Their contribution is not just valid, but essential for the future of our world.

The opinions expressed therein are those of the contributors and do not necessarily reflect the views of the United Nations or INSTRAW.

United Nations International
Research and Training Institute
for the Advancement of Women
(INSTRAW)

Preface

Bella Abzug

Like Molière's *bourgeois gentilhomme*, who was astounded to find that he had been speaking prose all his life without knowing it, women around the world — of every colour, class and culture — have been interacting with the environment and the development process every day of their lives without yet realizing, in large enough numbers, that they are key players in determining the future of our planet.

Increasingly, however, as women join in the global environmental movement, their wide range of social and economic situations, their lifestyles and what they do in their homes, communities, nations and international groups are being identified, described and closely analysed, particularly in the epistemological studies of women academics and feminist theorists.

INSTRAW's provocative and intellectually challenging book makes a much-needed contribution to our growing store of knowledge, by seeking to provide a theoretical framework for the diversity of views and activities related to women's complex roles in environment and sustainable development. The contributors evaluate the strengths and vulnerabilities of various theoretical models, including those that link the female sex with Nature, deny the equation of sustainable development with true progress, and question whether women will be corrupted by political power and succumb to male patterns of domination.

While proposing their own syntheses of these theories, the contributors recognize the necessity for connecting theory with action, for seeking bridges between women in the industrialized and the poor nations, and for building coalitions (temporary, ongoing or changing) among the various groups in the women's, environmental, development, indigenous and other social movements, in order to promote their agendas for positive change.

As a lifelong feminist, political activist and participant in the anti-nuclear peace movement, I came into the environmental movement out of a sense of horror at what the unbridled greed and social irresponsibility of multinationals, governments and war machines were doing to the health of our planet. It did not take long for me to find out that, typically, women were the major victims of these acts and also the ones most eager to clean up the man-made messes. From this concern, shared by women in all regions of the world, came the creation of the Women's Environmental and Development Organization's (WEDO) international network and, in November 1991, the World Women's Congress for a Healthy Planet.

The Women's Action Agenda 21, reached by consensus at the Congress, was, as the authors note, 'a major breakthrough and a historical watershed in the global women's movement'. It brought together women from the North and South, some 1,500 women from 83 countries. Professionally, they ranged from full-time activists, agronomists, academics and economists to nurses, parliamentarians, technicians and zoologists. They came from grassroots groups (many attending their first international conference), women's environment, development and religious groups, universities, UN agencies, foundations and the media.

The Agenda was designed to serve as an action guide for incorporating the women's dimension into local, national and international environment and development decision-making, beginning with the UN Conference on Environment and Development (UNCED) and the 1992 Global Forum in Rio and continuing into the next century. As a living document, put together out of the experiences, analyses and hopes of the women present at the Congress, the Agenda covered a range of global issues, from democratic rights, environmental ethics and accountability, biodiversity and biotechnology, nuclear power and alternative energy, and militarism, to women's rights, population policies and health, foreign debt and trade, consumerism and women, poverty, land rights, food security and credit.

Clearly, some issues were of most immediate concern to women of the South and others spoke to such Northern problems as over-consumption, but the unifying theme in the Agenda's preamble was a vision of a healthy and sustainable planet 'contingent upon world peace, respect for human rights, participatory democracy, the self-determination of peoples, respect for indigenous people and their lands, cultures and traditions, and the protection of all species'. It also stated the belief that 'basic human rights include access to clean air and water, food, shelter, health, education, personal liberty, and freedom of information'.

At the core of this vision was a commitment to the empowerment of women, 'the central and powerful force in the search for equity between and among the peoples of the Earth and for a balance between them and the life-support systems that sustain us all'. Recognizing women as catalysts and initiators of environmental activism, the preamble pointed out that, nevertheless, 'policy-makers continue to ignore the centrality of women's roles and needs as they make Fate-of-the-Earth decisions'.

The wisdom and political experience gained from working in UNCED must carry over to the 1995 Fourth World Conference on Women (Beijing, China, 4–15 September). This event will mark the tenth anniversary of the 1985 Decade of Women conference in Nairobi — the historic world assembly that produced the Forward-Looking Strategies, and is widely regarded as the birthplace of a global feminist agenda and of hundreds of new international networks of women.

If the 1995 conference is to make a realistic evaluation of how the lives of the world's women have changed — for better or worse — since Nairobi, how the 1985 recommendations have been implemented, how women in both the developing world and the industrialized nations have been coping with the enormous problems of environmental hazards, worsening poverty, illiteracy, the cancer and AIDS epidemics, violence, denial of their reproductive rights and exclusion from political power, then women from the grassroots as well as from academe and the highest levels of power must be there in large nmbers to speak and act for themselves.

Together, activists and theoreticians can transform existing agendas and power relationships into an expanded vision of what must be done to assure a healthy, peaceful, equitable planet for ourselves and future generations.

Bella Abzug is a former Congresswoman, a lawyer, lecturer and writer. A founder and co-chair of WEDO, she is also UN representative of World Women Parliamentarians for Peace. She was an active participant in all three international conferences during the 1976–85 UN Decade of Women, was presiding officer of the US-sponsored National Women's Conference at Houston, in 1977, and was co-chair of the National Advisory Committee for Women.

Authors' Note

In late 1990, the United Nations International Research and Training Institute for the Advancement of Women (INSTRAW) commissioned a report on women, the environment and sustainable development. In 1992, on the initiative and with the support of INSTRAW, that report was revised and expanded into the present book.

Work on this project was carried out jointly by the Women's Programme in the Humanities at the University of Utrecht, and the Women and Development Programme at the Institute of Social Studies in The Hague. The response to the report had been overwhelming, and stimulated so much debate that we decided to elaborate further the arguments it presented. In the course of almost two years of research on this theme our perspectives evolved — the results of this book. We hope that it will contribute to forging women's and other groups coalitions and strategic alliances and to further global networking in the process of transformations towards pro-environmental changes.

Work on this book finished in late 1992. A lot has happened in the follow-up to UNCED since that time, which cannot be reflected here. The authors are aware of this, but hope that readers will, nevertheless, find much of value and stimulus to fruitful thought.

The INSTRAW report was originally intended as a platform of the various positions which we perceived to be relevant to the issues surrounding women, the environment and sustainable development. In this book we have gone a step beyond that. While the major emphasis of the book still falls on the attempt to disentangle the various perspectives and positions upheld by the major actors in the field of women, the environment and sustainable development, we now make our own perspective much clearer. In the process of researching this theme we realized that many people involved in the women's, environmental and development movements harbour underlying assumptions which are not always made manifest in their writings. We like to see this book as an attempt to uncover these latent assumptions and reveal some of their implicit biases. We hope that this process of clarification will contribute to highlighting the political and theoretical issues that are at stake in the debates on women, the environment and sustainable development. We, the authors, are held together not only by a common interest in the research topic and political practice linked to development issues, but also by the complementarity of our respective differences in orientation and training. We come from different disciplinary fields: Western continental philosophy, non-Western sociology, linguistics, forestry, and development studies. We consider that our respective positions greatly enriched our comprehension of the debates on women, the environment and sustainable development. We all wrote certain sections and contributed generously to each others' chapters. Rosi Braidotti wrote Chapter 3, Ewa Charkiewicz Chapter 8 and the greater part of Chapter 7. Sabine Häusler wrote Chapters 2, 5, 6 and the subchapters 'UNCED and the NGO Global Forum in 1992', 'The Sustainable Development Debate', and 'Population, Environment and Development' in Chapter 7. She also served as editor of the book. Saskia Wieringa wrote Chapter 4 and made extensive inputs into Chapter 8 on ecofeminism.

Inevitably, this working method has given rise to certain differences in style. Instead of following the standard academic procedure that would call for uniformity, we nutured our differences and allowed them to coexist within the same text. This is not only the mark of a multidisciplinary method, but also of a multi-voiced approach which does justice to the complexity of the theme we are discussing. Also, the diversity of positions which each of us represents means that the final text is far more comprehensive than would have been possible had it been written solely by any one of us.

Many people contributed to this book. Apart from INSTRAW, the University of Utrecht, and the Institute of Social Studies which all gave financial and logistic support in various forms, special thanks are due to the Institute of Social Studies Advisory Service which provided a grant to one of the authors to coordinate the reworking of the original INSTRAW report. We are also indebted to the following: Henk van Rinsum and Arie de Ruyter from the University of Utrecht; Ria Brouwers and Tony Dolman from the Institute of Social Studies Advisory Service; Eleni Stamiris and Julia Tavares from INSTRAW; Jan Nederveen Pieterse, Wim Burger, Gina Vargas, Hans Verolme and Maithreyi Krishnaraj from the Institute of Social Studies; Joke Schrijvers, Ange Wieberdink, Philomena Essed, and Heleen van den Hombergh from the Institute for Development Research of the University of Amsterdam; and Lies Wesseling, Christien Brouwer, Anneke van der Meulen and Silvia Koene from the Women's Programme in the Humanities of the University of Utrecht. Our special thanks go to Thanhdam Truong who provided stimulating comments on the different drafts of the book. Rachel Kurian contributed important comments to chapter seven and Loes Keysers to the subchapter on Population, Environment and Development. There are many others who inspired us and shared information generously; they are too numerous to name individually. We would like to thank them here as well and hope that our exchanges will continue in the future. Finally, we dedicate this book to the memory of Joan Davidson.

Rosi Braidotti
Ewa Charkiewicz
Sabine Häusler
Saskia Wieringa

1. Introduction: The Global Crisis of Environment and Development and the Emergence of the Women, Environment and Sustainable Development Theme

It has become increasingly clear in recent years that development, which has been conceived as a Western project to modernize the post-colonial societies, did not bring the promised improvement in the living conditions of people in the South. Instead, the development process contributed to the growth of poverty, to an increase in economic and gender inequalities, and to the degradation of the environment which further diminishes the means of livelihood of poor people, particularly women. The environmental crisis is also a warning signal of the crisis of development in the North. The impacts of the degradation of the environment on health and means of livelihood of populations in the capitalist North as well as in the countries which have abandoned the state socialist system are also serious problems. The processes of chemical and radioactive contamination of soils, air and water, of decreasing biodiversity, an alarming rate of depletion of natural resources, deforestation and desertification have not only local but also transboundary and global impacts which threaten the survival of life on earth.

Capitalist and socialist political systems alike subscribe to the same notions of science and technology as they evolved in Europe over the last three centuries and centre on technology as the motor for development. Both systems fared badly in their use of technology. Need we remind ourselves of the devastating environmental situation due to industrial pollution in Eastern Europe, the contamination of a vast landscape around the Chernobyl reactor, the massive clear felling of old growth forests in British Columbia, or Waldsterben in central Europe? The belief in the limitless manageability of nature with the help of science and technology has by now rendered entire landscapes uninhabitable and beyond repair for the next centuries.

The recognition of limits to development by nature has fuelled the search for sustainable solutions to the crisis. In women's attempts to conceptualize sustainable development the recognition of the connections between the domination of nature and of women provided important insights. In the South this recognition stimulated the debate on women, environment and sustainable development (WED) within the development context while in the North it has given rise to nature feminism and ecofeminism.

In the 1980s the WED theme became an increasingly fashionable topic for discussions, publications and eventually workshops and international conferences of women within environment and development circles. As environmental degradation in the South accelerated, fuelwood, animal fodder and water became increasingly scarce in many areas, and those most severely affected were the women who need to collect these items for the subsistence of their families. In development and other Northern agencies concerned with global environmental problems poor people are often seen as the source of large scale deforestation and desertification in the South. High levels of population growth in the South lead, so they argue, to a global environmental crisis manifesting in such phenomena as depletion of the ozone layer and global warming. These threaten the planet as a whole.

Northern women and development experts, women experts who had moved into professional environmental fields such as forestry, agriculture, water system engineering, and women leaders from the South gradually joined forces and drew international attention to the problems of poor women in the South. A number of women, many of them from movements and non-governmental development organizations (NGDOs) and non-governmental organizations (NGOs) from the South, and from the North, have decisively shaped the WED debate to date. A special role in these debates has been played by academic women across the globe. The publications and activities of such outstanding women as Joan Davidson, Vandana Shiva, Irene Dankelman, Bella Abzug, Shimwaayi Muntembe, Wangari Maathai and many others illustrate the successful efforts to place women's interests on the environment and development agendas globally. Together they created a space for a large variety of women, eventually even women from the grassroots who are most affected, to voice their concerns in international fora which discussed solutions to the global environmental crisis.

In the evolution of the debates on WED since the mid-1980s, there has been a shift in positions and political priorities. While earlier the emphasis was on women as victims of the environmental crisis, it shifted to their roles as efficient environmental managers within the development process in the South. The argument for the increased participation of women in environmental management has been derived from their privileged knowledge and experience of working closely with the environment. A somewhat different line of argument has been advanced by Vandana Shiva and Irene Dankelman, who stress the 'feminine principle' based on the assumption of women's special empathetic and nurturing capacities in relation to nature. The net result of both positions is that women are seen by many people involved in the WED debate as privileged environmental managers, or the source for solutions to the environmental crisis.

By the late 1980s the debate on WED became an established item on the international development and environment agendas. The growing recognition of the connections between the crisis in development, the deepening global environmental crisis, the growth of poverty and gender inequalities opened the way for the integration of social aspects in the proposals for sustainable development. As a result, women's voices have been added to the debates on sustainable development, stressing the social aspects of sustainability.

A global movement, in which some women from Eastern Europe and the former Soviet Union also joined in, emerged within the preparatory process leading up to the Earth Summit, the United Nations Conference on Environment and Development in 1992. In this process, in 1991 at an international women's meeting in Miami entitled 'World Women's Congress for a Healthy Planet', women from all over the world, representatives from different NGOs, NGDOs, government agencies, academia, business organizations, from their respective positions came up with a common position critical of the dominant development model. The resulting document, the Women's Action Agenda 21, represents a consensus of women across the divides of race and class never reached before. Together they outlined what needs to be done to avert the global environmental holocaust that humanity as a whole and the entire planet are heading for if things do not radically change.

Preparation for the United Nations Conference on Environment and Development (UNCED)

The preparatory process that led up to the 1992 Earth Summit in Rio de Janeiro marked a new momentum in the WED movement and the alternative developmental, environmental and ecological movements and debates at large. Within UNCED and the parallel conference, the Global Forum, attended by social movement groups, NGOs, and NGDOs, the business community, churches, youth groups, different UN institutions, and many groups from the South, West and East, many new actors emerged on the environmental scene. These actors had largely differing and often contradictory agendas, as illustrated in the highly contested meaning of the notion of sustainable development employed in their agendas. It needs to be stressed that the non-governmental sector attending the Global Forum comprised a large number of very heterogeneous groups and that to speak of 'the non-governmental sector' fails to reflect this. Women organized a separate event — Planeta Femea — at the Global Forum.

Within the inter-governmental UNCED process the imperative for 'sustainable' development had moved onto the agenda of development agencies, governments, the World Bank, the business community and so on who had to a large extent been responsible for bringing the dominant mode of development to its natural limits. Governments and the development industry at large now also acknowledge the role of 'the non-governmental sector' in bringing about sustainable development. UNCED proceedings speak of 'all of humanity' united by their 'common interest' in surviving in a world with limited and increasingly 'scarce natural resources'. The solutions to the crisis are seen by them to lie within the range of measures that contributed to the environmental crisis in the first place:[1] more economic growth to pay for environmental recovery, more funds for environmental projects, more technology, and altogether better and more management of the environment. 'The non-governmental sector' is asked to bring the UNCED messages down to grassroots level globally. Even though it is true that humanity as a whole is threatened, opinions differ as to how far-reaching are the changes needed to address the problem. Therefore, citizen's movements[2] do not subscribe to the governmental UNCED results. Many of them advocate a radical departure from the present model of development itself.

One of the important shifts at UNCED within mainstream Northern positions, however, was Northern governments' admission that not only the growing populations in the South but also the North itself, with its high levels of consumption of natural resources, has been responsible for the global environmental crisis; the need for more environmental reforms was clearly acknowledged. Southern governments' representatives pressed for more funds to be channelled to the South for environmental projects.

Within the UNCED process an increasing polarization of different actors' positions became ever more clear. Within the preparatory activities of the different groups involved in preparing for the Global Forum, Western, Eastern and Southern social movement groups critical of the development model devised strategies for the future. A treaty-making process parallel to the governmental UNCED-treaty process was organized at the Global Forum. The alternative treaties are meant to lay out future actions for the citizen's movements' NGOs interested in a fundamental departure from the dominant development model. The role of excessive military spending, the dynamics of aid, unjust international trade mechanisms which favoured the rich countries, the effects of structural adjustment programmes, disempowerment of local people and erosion of control over their natural environments, to name but a few, were seen as sources of the fundamentally unsustainable development model. Most of these had been left out in the UNCED agenda. The alternative treaties outline the need for a democratization of the development process in a bottom-up approach, linking democracy with community control over resources, a rethinking of the relationship between humans and nature and of life-styles in general. Integrity and interdependence of all life forms are integral to a new relation between humans and nature.

Other NGOs, such as the international business community, organized their own independent preparatory processes for the Global Forum. Their interest was of course of quite a different nature. They sought for ways to integrate environmental concerns into industry and business in order to secure their stake in the potential market of 'greener' production and consumption in the North.

Planeta Femea, the women's event organized within the Global Forum, was attended by women across the board: representatives of UN agencies, feminist groups and networks, NGOs, NGDOs, academics, women active in consumer and environmental movements, farmers' struggles, and many more. They presented a summary of the Women's Action Agenda 21 (written up in Miami, and as participants at Planeta Femea complained in a watered-down version) to the official UNCED plenary, and the Population Treaty as well as a Women's Treaty to the organizers of the alternative treaty-making process at the Forum.

The logical consequence of the present dominant Western model of development, so women argue in their Agenda 21, has led to the ruthless plundering of the earth's resources and created increasing poverty for most people in the South, and especially women. Women from the industrialized North, and some from Eastern Europe and the ex-Soviet Union present during the drafting process in Miami, criticized the effects of industrialization on the health and well-being of their families. Women across all divides criticized the global economic military and industrial system based on economic growth and a free market ideology as the root cause of the problem. They pointed out that the crisis in development and the environmental crisis were inextricably connected with militarism, the nuclear threat, growing economic inequalities, violation of human rights and the persistent subordination of women.

Even though such collective criticism from across a wide spectrum of women has been a political success and a powerful move, it has not been without problems. As the UNCED process unfolded the two of us who attended the Global Forum in Rio de Janeiro became convinced that even though the women participating had achieved an unprecedented common position critical to the dominant development model and visions for the future, at Planeta Femea they did not always avoid the dangers of reproducing patterns of domination, dualism and reversal of old hierarchies in the process. The question of representation also came up: how representative of women globally was this united position? Did all women in the world 'naturally' 'care' about the state of the environment, on top of all the other problems they are dealing with daily? Implicitly, some women insisted on their privileged position *vis-à-vis* nature and hence their right to be heard when it comes to deciding the planet's future. It seems to us that the consensus between Northern and Southern women had been built upon this assumption. Differences in political positions, based on class, race and geographical origin had been set aside; many women recognized that such a consensus of women globally was most urgent in view of the crisis which threatens the survival of us all. We think that these questions need to be raised if we as women are to influence the direction in which the dominant development model is heading.

In search of theoretical connections: A proposal

This book is an attempt to explore the interconnections between the themes of women, the environment and sustainable development on a theoretical level.

Our search for a theoretical framework for the transboundary theme of WED started early in 1991; we realized that WED as a theme has quite a large potential for criticizing the dominant development model and should be pushed further in this direction. This is the potential to seek for and act upon connections with other actors, such as environmentalists, ecologists and groups and movements who are also critical of the dominant development paradigm, and have an interest in, or are already participating in, transformations towards environmentally sustainable development. The women's perspective adds to many of these positions the recognition that different groups in society (women, members of different classes as well as ethnic groups) should not be left out of their own emancipatory visions for the future. We decided to focus on various critical positions forwarded from within the three fields: women, environment and sustainable development, as expressed by a number of actors. We are consequently discussing the sometimes conflicting, ambivalent and contradictory analyses they provide of their concerns. Our aim in this book is to touch upon the most important debates on these themes, highlighting their strengths and weaknesses, so as to suggest new ways of proceeding in thinking and planning for women's, but also environmental and sustainable developmental concerns. We need to stress here that the predominantly theoretical positions we are outlining are not necessarily taken as a basis of action for different social actors as such. Social actors do, however, use elements of these theoretical positions in their discourses and actions in practice.

Alongside the WED debate we have chosen to explore the following positions: feminist critique of science; feminism; alternative development, environmental reforms from within political, economic and developmental organizations; deep ecology; social ecology; and ecofeminism. This list is by no means exhaustive but we feel confident that we have selected some of the most representative critiques of the dominant development model, emerging from within mainstream development organizations and academia, alternative development thinking and the environmental and women's movements.

In view of the problems of essentialism inherent in a global women's position to the crisis attained in the 1991 Miami Conference,[3] in this book we explore the links between the oppression of women and the degradation of nature. Since the last decades of the 19th century the women's movement has been denouncing women's oppression and advocating women's equality. A central theme in this struggle has been the controversy over whether women's subordinate position has been 'naturally' given or socially constructed. Women's supposed link with nature has been both a justification of their subordination (biological determinism) and a source of inspiration for women in their struggle against their oppression. The debates between women over how to position themselves in the struggles to address environmental degradation and the different strategies advocated by other actors in the debates and struggles has become an important bone of contention. The significant contributions of women in academic circles are of direct relevance to this debate. Especially over the last decades, feminist philosophers have been active in exploring the interconnections between power, sexuality, gender and knowledge. One assumption that guides our work is that this set of issues has a direct bearing on the general need for a critical reassessment of the developmental and the ecological crises.

Although issues of development and the environment in general will be raised, our focus remains on the links between women, the environment (nature), and sustainable development. Some of the questions we ask are: is the intimate link between women and nature due to the fact that both are objectified as 'the Other' of a patriarchal, dominant, supposedly rational subject? Are women, and especially poor women in the South, and nature simultaneously subordinated by a male drive for progress? Are women special victims of the destruction of their environment? Is this linked to their special status as victims of male domination, or does it have more to do with the fact that women are such excellent 'carers', that they turn out to be the experts who are called in to repair the damage? Or are they simultaneously carers and victims because they are trapped in a certain gender-based division of labour? How do these material conditions influence women's sense of their identity, especially their relationship to technology and development? Is it the ideological structure that combines domination with masculinity and women's subordination, that needs to be criticized from a feminist perspective, as well as its epistemological[4] and philosophical underpinnings? What do the new feminist epistemologies have to contribute to analyses of hierarchy and power in general and more specifically in the contexts of issues related to development? These questions are the starting point for our research and form the axis along which we have structured our analysis of the debates around women, the environment and sustainable development.

In our theoretical search we became convinced that the sex of the actors is not the most relevant aspect of the interconnections between women, the environment and sustainable development. Although women are differentially positioned in relation to the use of the environment and the process of development, the relationship between these should be analysed on a more profound level. The way women are affected by the degradation of the environment, and the strategies they employ to counter this crisis, are indeed gender specific, but their position as women alone does not qualify them to manage the environment better than anyone else.

In our proposal for a conceptual framework for WED the contribution of the women's voices in the environment and development debates is indispensable to the search for solutions to the multiple global crisis. But neither women nor any other concerned group can assume a monopoly on providing valid solutions to the crisis. On the contrary, the importance and the magnitude of the task call for alliances of all parties involved in the process of transformations towards pro-environmental changes. It is essential that environmentalists, ecologists and developmentalists do not simply give lip service to women's involvement but fully recognize the interconnections between gender inequalities and the environmental crisis. On the other hand, women, as well as all other actors interested in fundamental transformations of development, should be critical of how they themselves reproduce patterns of domination in their own struggles. It is important to see transformations of development as a process which inevitably engenders new structures of domination as new strategies of power co-emerge. These must be made visible, dismantled and dealt with continually as we move on.

One of the mechanisms by which patterns of domination are spread is the reversal of hierarchy. If, for example, women assert that men must now step back and that it is women who must determine the future, an old hierarchy is simply reversed and no qualitative new relation between women and men comes into being. Therefore, one of our central concerns is to avoid such reversals which are likely to occur when women are perceived as both the privileged knowers and potential saviours of nature. Especially relevant in this respect is the feminist debate on essentialism versus constructivism, to which we shall come in Chapter 4. We do not agree with an approach that sees men as the culprit of the subjugation of women as well as nature, although this position has informed several feminist analyses within the WED debate. It is quite clear to us that men, too, have been victimized by the environmental crisis. But in so far as most institutions worldwide are male-dominated, neither can we disregard the issue of the masculinization of power. Indeed, wider changes in economic, political and cultural power structures are greatly needed. At a deeper level, transformations of values and frameworks of thinking are at stake. Therefore we suggest that safeguarding and recovering the environment cannot be formulated as a project of women alone.

Most positions which inform our theme of WED stress the need for a transformation of knowledge and science. Recent studies on women and development have positively generated the need for critical perspectives on Western science and rationality. We shall return to this point in Chapter 3. It is almost an axiom for feminists that Western science and the technology developed along with it are tools for the domination of people and nature and that their uncritical application threatens to exterminate life on earth. In this respect, the environmental crisis can be seen as the logical outcome of a vision of science and technology that has developed in European history since the eighteenth century, also known as the period of Enlightenment. Scientific and technological progress has been unduly focused on concerns about economic goals and become implicit in ideas about development, and thus introduced in the countries of the South. Feminists across the board, as well as some environmentalists, ecologists and alternative developmentalists argue that what we see today is a ruthless application of technology, especially in the form of big-scale development projects, such as large dams which serve urban and industrial water and power supply and the modernizing economies. These projects displace thousands of people from their land and means of livelihood. Another example is the relentless logging of tropical rainforests where entire population groups have become subject to extermination. Increasing local protests against such projects indicate that 'progress' is accompanied by massive destruction of local cultures and lifestyles, displacing large numbers of people against their will. Small-scale development projects have in essence similar effects as they inherently follow the same logic. There are many parallel Northern examples of people's struggles against such modern large-scale projects as nuclear power plants and highways.

Some protagonists of alternative development, environmentalists, as well as feminists, have pointed out that rationality and progress have come to be synonymous with economic rationality and economic progress as seen from the centres of political and economic power in the North, as well as their satellites in the South.

Western science: the motor of the crisis

Because of our positions as feminists and our concern for the positions of women in the environmental and developmental crisis we have brought to the fore the findings of feminist epistemology about science, power and domination. The production of theory within the framework of Western science is part of the multiple crisis. The way it has been practised and the assumptions on which it has been based are important factors in the crisis of environment and development. Science via its claims to objective truth plays an important role in the way we think and act, and in the way modern societies function. Feminist critics of science point out that in order to effect change, the crucial areas to address are epistemologies, that is the terms for the production of knowledge itself. The growing body of theoretical work undertaken from different positions dismantles the claims of science to objectivity and highlights its crucial role in a particular form of rationality which invalidates all other forms of knowledge. As long as the production of science has been based on these claims, science is perceived to be the source of truth and acquires a totalizing control over reality.

Michel Foucault (1980) reveals that the production of science is intimately linked with power relations. The claim to formulate scientific truths is but the product of power/knowledge regimes, which operate both on the macro and the micro levels. In his writings on power Foucault has pointed out that what is most problematic about the discourses of Western societies is that the centres of truth and the centres of power are identical: the Western institutions and scientifically based discourses they produce have claimed amongst others the 'truth' about development, hence have wielded the power to fundamentally reshape reality globally in the economic interest of the North. Images of modernity and progress, in short 'development' with high-consumption urban life-styles and white collar jobs have penetrated into virtually all corners of the globe with the help of Western media. But as is becoming increasingly clear in view of the environmental crisis, this kind of life-style is neither possible nor desirable for everybody.

Foucault points out that resistance to power starts from the margins where power is manifesting itself in its crudest form. In his 'micro-politics of resistance', Foucault proposes that an acceptance of multiple centres of truth,[5] as opposed to the belief in its central and unique location, is a necessary premise to the political process of resisting the violence inherent in the power of Western science. Part of this process of political resistance is the resurrection of the subjugated vernacular knowledges of local people, which is vital in the context of our concerns in this book. Foucault warns against the construction of any new universal theories because they will necessarily be oppressive.

Although we will rely on the materialist politics of Foucault in our work, we do not mean to posit his theory as a universal panacea; the post-structuralist approach he puts forward is useful in its redefinition of the politics of resistance, but some of its critics have argued that it does not per se guarantee the end of ethnocentrism (Spivak 1988; Slater 1992). Foucault's valorization of the periphery as the location of resistance may result at times in concealing the new and ever more subtle forms of domination that are emerging in the post-industrial world order, where there is no longer one centre of power, but a multi-located system of constant surveillance. As post-modernist writer Donna Haraway points out, Foucault describes the workings of modern power at the moment of its implosion; he emphasizes the large-scale institutions of the hospital, the military, the prison and the school according to the nineteenth century model: 'Our dominations don't work by medicalization and normalization anymore; they work by networking, communications redesign, stress management' (Haraway in: Nicholson 1990:194). Pre-modern forms of power rely predominantly on open coercion and cultural norms of behaviour, modern forms of power function through normalizing mechanisms which aim at reducing heterogeneity, thereby also structuring feelings and desires of the individual, while post-modern forms of power are based on the decentralized, technologically highly sophisticated 'informatics of domination' (Haraway, ibid: 203).

Post-modernism as a movement within academia has been negatively criticized as foreshadowing the end to all theory and a total lapse into relativism. As of now, post-modernism has mainly been a preoccupation of Western artists and intellectuals in academia who have shown little interest in the countries of the South. Jameson demonstrates that there is no longer any place outside the all-encompassing system of domination that can establish a comfortable fiction of critical distance (Jameson cited after Haraway ibid:194). In other words, whether we like it or not, we are already part of and function within this system of domination. Instead of drawing from this a cynical conclusion, we take this analysis as the starting point for a redefinition of political agency as resistance and the politics of transversal coalitions and alliances. Following Haraway's suggestion,[6] we want to take the post-modernist-materialist approach in its potentially enabling sense and apply it to critical development theories.

Science, however, cannot be the only source of solutions to the crisis in development and our role as researchers and 'producers of truth' on the theme of this book on women, the environment and sustainable development is not an innocent venture. Searching for non-dominating ways of doing science we have been inspired by post-modern feminist critiques of science, in particular by Donna Haraway (1989, 1991). In order to create more equitable relationships between scientists as privileged 'subjects' in knowledge production and the 'objects' they study, Haraway proposes a critical genealogy of subjectivity: to disclose the subject's position, to state his/her situatedness (based on sex, class, race) and hence particular bias, in order to hold her/him responsible and accountable for the knowledge s/he produces, and not to obscure the outcomes of research with claims to objectivity.

In keeping with Haraway's notion of 'situated knowledges', we shall therefore disclose our own starting positions. We speak as women and from multiple positions determined by our identities and experiences. Rosi Braidotti, an Italian/Australian educated in France, positions herself in this project from two different angles: feminist epistemology and critiques of science, and non-Western women's studies and more specifically issues of development. Since her working days at UNESCO she has cultivated an interest in global feminism and has grown aware, both intellectually and emotionally, of the problems involved in cross-cultural translation. This awareness has fed into her assessment of the political and theoretical implications of post-modernism and more specifically post-structuralist philosophy. She is currently professor of Women's Studies at the University of Utrecht.

The views of Ewa Charkiewicz on ecological and social change are grounded in her experiences of animating an alternative ecological movement under the conditions of Polish authoritarianism. She has been living in all three worlds and has been moving from farm and factory to journalism, motherhood and university work. These diverse experiences in accommodating differences and in translations from one reality to another made her value non-violence and equity in ways of thinking and social relations and informed her input into this book. She has been involved in the NGO preparatory process for UNCED. Currently, she is teaching on ecology at the Institute of Social Studies and working on her Ph.D thesis on the epistemologies for transition and politics of sustainable development. Ewa Charkiewicz and Sabine Häusler together studied Politics of Alternative Development Strategies at the Institute of Social Studies in the Netherlands.

Sabine Häusler from (West) Germany worked as a forester for four years in integrated rural development projects in Nepal. There she was confronted with the highly complex and interrelated nature of environmental degradation in the Himalayas and the practical problems of involving rural people, particularly women, in forestry work. Seeing the need to clarify conceptually the multiple and interrelated political, economic, social and natural dimensions of environmental degradation in the Himalayan region and the inadequacy of addressing these highly complex and interrelated problems within the framework of development projects she returned for further studies to Europe. Since her participation in Planeta Femea at the Global Forum in Rio de Janeiro she has become involved in organizing an international interdisciplinary research project on Women, the Environment and Sustainable Development. At the same time she is preparing her Ph.D. thesis. Her main interests lie in sustainable development and global feminism, in particular the interface between new epistemologies and post-modern politics in relation to the post-UNCED process.

Saskia Wieringa is from the Netherlands and has been active in the Dutch women's movement since the early 1970s. She was among the first to establish cross-cultural women's studies in the Netherlands. By training she is a non-Western sociologist and lectures in the Women and

Development Programme at the Institute of Social Studies. She has a wide international experience and was co-ordinator of a research project on the history of women's movements and organizations in the Caribbean, India, Indonesia, Peru, Somalia and the Sudan. This experience convinced her of the need to build cross-cultural links between women's movements. It also taught her the value of respect for differences and pluriformity.

Having clarified our starting positions, we hope the reader can envisage our biases, our investments and the expectations that we carry into this project. We want to attempt to establish a more equitable relationship between ourselves and the theme we study: we are neither disembodied nor disembedded researchers, but situated ones. Our location covers multiple positionalities determined by our experiences, theoretical inspirations and knowledge. This multiplicity is the groundwork for our claims to knowledge in that it makes each of us accountable for her statements and beliefs. However, we do acknowledge that we cannot claim to be entirely on an equal footing with the activist and academic positions which we study, learn from and converse with in this study, due to the privileged positions we occupy as white, academic women. Thus, we state our own biases and want to be held accountable for what we are seeing from our situated positions. This is the sort of materialist ethics that Haraway proposes when she suggests that we replace the previously asymmetric, hierarchical and impersonal relationship between the knowing subject and the object of investigation with one that rests on affinity and empathy. This redefinition opens the way to a redefinition of scientific objectivity in terms of compassionate ways of learning, which Haraway describes as 'passionate detachment'(Haraway 1991, quoting Kuhn 1982). Haraway's approach opens up new possibilities, not only for positive critiques of science, but also, for a post-modernist redefinition of political agency. We see this as a fruitful approach to our theme which we will employ when we discuss the positions of actors in the various fields that we have selected to include here.

Transformations of development: different suggestions

Faithful to our premise of accounting for as wide a variety of positions as possible, we will analyse arguments developed by academics, some by development institutions and different citizen's movements. These different actors analyse problems of development from different angles: many aim at elaborating more effective policies; others focus on the need for a new kind of science; some stress the acceptance of other epistemologies and other ways of producing knowledge, whereas others are satisfied with simply revalidating traditional female ways of knowing.

Problems are analysed and solutions sought also on different levels: on the level of epistemology, feminist critics of science make suggestions for transformations in the production of knowledge which we consider indispensable for sustainable development styles conceived in holistic terms. But also alternative developmentalists and deep ecologists take critical stances towards Western science. Other critics suggest changes on the levels of theory, policy or practice. Some on all these levels, others only on one or the other level. All of these positions taken together make up a broad movement of many facets.

As we engage in dialogue with these positions, we try to include some of the criticisms that we and other actors are making to specific lines of argument. We also distinguish approaches to the crisis which aim at reforming the system from within by using a range of measures geared at better and more effective management from suggestions for deeper epistemological transformations.

The multiple crisis in environment and development demands a complex process of simultaneous and interdependent transformations on different levels, both within and outside mainstream development and political institutions. Patterns of domination are reproduced in all the positions we describe. Even though we are convinced of the need for far-reaching transformations, for strategic reasons we also support reformist attempts for change from within these institutions. Individuals produce liberatory ideas and proposals within them, but also radical ideas from other actors are continuously co-opted by the mainstream institutions and thereby their liberatory potential is diminished. Diverse inputs of positions from within mainstream development institutions and those which come from outside of the institutions, from for example academics, NGOs and social movements, have already been interacting in a process of incorporation and co-optation of ideas and concepts. Even though this process leads to confirmation of the primacy of the mainstream organizations' position it is their constant change from within that needs to be fostered to maintain a transformative momentum towards pro-environmental changes.

In this process of engaging in dialogues with different positions, we do not claim to have a 'correct' view on the vast field we are travelling through; neither do we want to propose yet another totalizing map. We are the first to be acutely aware of the complexity of views expressed by different actors and the large variety within their fields of study and action. In this respect, we would like to stress that we see this large diversity as a source of strength and that the transformational power of the broad movement towards environmental changes lies in its multiplicity. At the same time, this implies as already noted, that none of these positions alone can establish a privileged position from which to search for transformations.

Consequently, what we are outlining should be regarded as suggesting potentially useful propositions for people interested in transformations of development. We do not provide a blueprint for change, nor separate 'the true and untrue, good or bad' positions, but rather show paradoxes, pose questions, and highlight commonalities. We not only show the complementarity of inputs but also highlight and stress the importance of differences and indicate ambivalences and ambiguities. We shall demonstrate how the respective positions relate to each other, and what are the possible points of convergence between and among them.

What we suggest is not a homogenizing platform of all of these positions because they are backed up by largely varying positions of power based on their institutional investment, but we suggest that these different positions do fruitfully inform each other. As they engage in dialogue, exchange and even co-optation of ideas they become part of a broader transformative movement.

As to the structure of the book, in Chapter 2 we will give a brief description of the nature of the crisis in development. In Chapter 3 we will explore different positions within feminist critiques of science as they provide important insights into the reproduction of domination and suggest some important proposals for transformative epistemologies and politics based on multiple subjectivities. The debates in feminism on the relationship between women and nature outlined in Chapter 4 help us to highlight the potential pitfalls for women identifying themselves with nature and on this basis assuming a privileged position in the movement towards environmental changes. We shall discuss the field of WID, give a historical overview and describe the main ideas circulating in the field of WED at some length in Chapter 5. Chapter 6 introduces alternative proposals to development, including the one provided by Development with Women for a New Era, DAWN, a Southern women's network. Environmental reforms from within mainstream political and developmental institutions and changes within the field of economics towards sustainable development, a discussion of the concept of sustainability as well as a section on the interrelation between environment, development and population are presented in Chapter 7. Deep ecology, social ecology and ecofeminism as proposals for epistemological changes and a re-evaluation of the human/nature relation are described in Chapter 8. By way of a conclusion, we attempt to synthesize our findings and make some concrete suggestions for future action.

Notes

1. See Chapter 7
2. The term citizen's movement was adopted by environment, alternative

development, solidarity, women's and other people's movements involved in the process of preparation for UNCED. The purpose of adopting this term was to stress their identity as NGOs which represent grassroots people's movements *vis-à-vis* the NGO sector in general at UNCED. In recent years the term NGO has been used by all kinds of organizations: from transnational corporations, (TNCs), business and industry, to profit-oriented development agencies (in our text called non-governmental development organization, NGDOs), as well as organizations which genuinely represent people's movements. Please note that in this book we use the terms NGO and citizen's movements interchangeably. When referring to business-, industry- and other NGOs which do not represent any people's movements organization we indicate the specific group referred to.

3. See Chapter 5 for a discussion of the outcome of the 1991 Miami Conference 'World Women's Congress for a Healthy Planet'.

4. Epistemology looks at how knowledge is produced. Questions asked are: who is legitimized to be a 'knower', what is the object of his inquiry, the 'known', and how does the process of arriving at knowledge take place?

5. See also polycentric and polyphonic developments as advocated by Nederveen Pieterse (1991).

6. See Chapter 3 for Haraway's full argument for the use of post-modernism in an enabling sense.

2. Developmentalism: A Discourse of Power

This chapter provides a brief introduction to the nature of the crisis in development we face today. As the subject has been widely discussed elsewhere (Sachs 1992; Nederveen Pieterse 1991; Mathur 1989) we shall focus here only on aspects of developmentalism which are of specific relevance to this book. This chapter is not meant as an exhaustive analysis but rather a descriptive overview which will serve as an introduction and point of departure for the chapters following. Women as a subject matter are not very prominent here; their roles in and perspectives on development will be addressed in the subsequent chapters.

The development decades: their impact on the South

The United Nations development decades have encompassed several stages. First the goal was rapid economic growth, then redistribution with growth, followed by satisfaction of basic needs and structural adjustment. Recently, Human Development has been postulated by UN institutions.[1] Whereas in the 1960s, the first UN development decade's goals focused on the industrialization of the South's post-independent countries, involving large-scale projects in order to foster fast economic growth which would eventually benefit the entire populations, the second development decade's goal took heed of the fact that the expected 'trickle down effect' did not take place.[2]

It was in the spirit of the development strategy of the Second UN Development Decade, the 1970s, to stress the development of people as a prerequisite for sustained economic growth. The idea was to go beyond mere capital investment towards investment into 'human resources' in the form of equitable distribution of wealth and income, social justice and improvement of facilities for education, health, social security and so on as salient features. Growth policies were coupled with distribution policies in an attempt to increase the productivity of the poor. The World Employment Conference held by the UN International Labour Organization in 1976 (ILO 1976) was decisive in launching the concept of Basic Needs, the operational term for human development. The Basic Needs approach was adopted by the World Bank as a condition for its lending activities; multilateral, bilateral and non-governmental development organizations subsequently endorsed the approach.

The era of concern with equity and Basic Needs was, however, short-lived in the light of developments within the global economy. The oil 'crisis'[3] in 1973, deteriorating terms of trade, slowly growing export markets, net capital outflows from the countries of the South and increased interest rates on large-scale loans taken up earlier by governments in the South from Northern governments and banks for development programmes, led to the debt crisis and generally a deteriorating economic situation in the South. This situation was matched with a slow down in growth in the Western economies and budgetary constraints for aid allocation due to stagnation and recession. A more rigorous and economistic approach to development was the result of these changes. The neo-liberal school of economics[4] questioned the usefulness of explicit development policies altogether and gave rise to a liberal and free market style of development. Emphasis on short-term economic management in response to the crisis replaced a coherent development strategy for the Third Development Decade in the 1980s and led to a neglect of the human development idea of the 1970s.

Structural adjustment policies were implemented in many countries of the South in order to speedily remove external imbalances of payment in the debtor countries. Emphasis on debt repayment shifted the priorities for government spending away from the public sector and social services such as health, education and food subsidies to areas where production for internationally tradeable goods could be stimulated in order to produce goods in exchange for foreign currency. Debtor governments were advised to withdraw as prime movers of development in favour of the private sectors of the economies in line with the neo-liberal creed of economic thinking. This approach postulated the need for free market mechanisms and the importance of the private sector as providers of the dynamics for economic growth.

Government expenditures for social services were severely reduced with serious consequences for poorer peoples of the South as well as the natural environment. It is widely documented how poor women in particular had to compensate for the cuts in social services by an increase in their work (Elson 1990; UNICEF 1987; Commonwealth Secretariat 1989). This situation led to a standstill and even regression in social development in many countries of the South; poverty was increasing, and the natural resource base came under heavy pressure to compensate for the tightening situation. Natural resources in the South were increasingly exploited for debt repayment while satisfaction of local needs for fuel, water, fodder and other essentials became more and more difficult. The 1980s are therefore frequently referred to as the lost decade.

In order to minimize the negative effects of structural adjustment programmes, UNICEF proposed an 'Adjustment with a Human Face' (Cornia, Jolly and Steward 1987), in which some selective policies aimed at protecting the poor during the period of adjustment were included in the economic policy package worked out by the World Bank for each respective country. However, the practice of structural adjustment as a disciplinary measure was not fundamentally questioned by UNICEF. The process of structural adjustment steered the affected countries further into the direction of export-led growth, vulnerability to world markets and to stimulate investment by TNCs with their questionable practices in search for quick profits.

The constantly deteriorating situation in many Southern countries gave rise to a new effort to deal with increasing poverty. The recently re-emerging concept of Human Development focuses on indemnifying past failures of development practice and denotes a human needs-oriented development model which encompasses more humane values and respect for human life. As the framework for new development policies Human Development revolves around two main themes: investment in people, and human-centred development. The concept has been promoted mainly by the World Bank (World Bank 1990 and 1991) and the United Nations Development Programme UNDP (UNDP 1992). Women, however, hardly figure in these reports. If they are considered, they are seen in an instrumental role to the development process at large (Lycklama à Nijeholt 1992).

Truong (1992:8) pointed out that the World Bank's new strategy of Human Development to alleviate poverty basically contains all the elements of the Basic Needs strategy launched by ILO a decade earlier, with the exception of including environmental issues. The Human Development strategy remains firmly committed to economic growth as the central objective of development policies. UNDP's conception goes further by seeing economic growth only as a means to achieve human development, not an end in itself (UNDP 1992). For UNDP Human Development encompasses a range of objectives beyond economic growth which are intended to enable people to participate actively and creatively in the development process. It also takes into account the wider issues of environmental degradation, militarization and unequal North/ South relations. Institutional changes, policy dialogue and changes in production processes are deemed necessary. Truong (1992:9) draws attention to the fact that UNDP's definition of Human Development provides scope for transformations because it does not start with a pre-determined model as does that of the World Bank, but '...draws its inspiration from the long-term goals of a society. It weaves development around people, not people around development' (UNDP 1992:2, cited after Truong 1992). UNDP's strategy for Human Development includes such economic measures as the increased investment in human capabilities. Institutional changes, such as restructuring the World Bank and the International Monetary Fund (IMF) and creating a UN Development Security Council are also proposed. Yet, how the top-down approach is to be transformed into a bottom-up, people-centred one is not addressed in concrete terms. The inherent gender blindness is also eluded.

These changes from within some of the mainstream development institutions indicate a move towards incorporating reformative elements and thus imply a recognition that far-reaching changes in development practice are necessary. Internal reforms within the development industry in the North, however, have to be seen in the global context of the 1990s. They mark an important shift in the international economic and political landscape after the collapse of the Eastern bloc with important implications for Southern countries and their economic development. The European countries, the US, Canada and Mexico as well as the Asia/Pacific countries are uniting in separate economic blocs. These changes give rise to new constellations of economic power. As industrialized countries join into economic blocs to strengthen their internal relations and defend their wealth, Africa, Latin America and large parts of Asia are becoming increasingly uninteresting for the countries of the North as targets for development assistance. In the context of development assistance the North's interest in the South largely gravitates towards the issues of global environmental degradation and population growth. Willy Brandt (1990) and many others have pointed out that these two issues will be the major challenges for development in the decades to come. Northern interests in development in the South are motivated mainly by self-interest, be they of an economic nature or for a safe global environment. Addressing human misery and increasing poverty in the South, even though included in the discourse of mainstream development institutions, hardly figure as reasons in themselves. The imperative of economic growth for the Northern economies dictate the terms of the development discourse.

The theoretical assumptions of developmentalism

Nederveen Pieterse (1991) has pointed out that developmentalism understood as a theory of linear progress 'has taken several forms — evolutionism, modernization theory, development thinking — which correlate with different epochs of western hegemony'. He unmasked developmentalism as universalist, ahistorical and ethnocentric; it has incorporated non-Western societies into the dominant mode of development in which the terms of discourse are shaped by Western thinking.

Developmental discourse was conceived in the aftermath of the Second World War with the aim of providing an alternative to Communism for the decolonizing countries of the South. The tripartite post-war order was based on the construction of the First World, the modern, 'developed' 'self', that is, the capitalist West, in opposition to the 'other', the Second World, the socialist East, which was subsequently left out of the development discourse altogether. The Third World, the 'underdeveloped' South, became the residual category. The large variety of societies living in the South were subsumed under this unitary category: the Third World. Their main line of differentiation became their political alliance to either the capitalist West or the socialist East as development models. It is important to note that this arrangement which has become of paramount importance in organizing and shaping realities in the South and globally was in its inception a political move. The goal of this move was to set up ideological opposition between capitalism and socialism as two different roads to progress.

Using Michel Foucault's conception of power, Escobar demonstrated that an understanding of how development was put into discourse is indispensable in order to unmask how '. . . the Western developed countries have been able to manage and control and, in many ways, even create the Third World politically, economically, sociologically and culturally . . .' (Escobar 1984-85:384).

In 1949, the then US President Harry Truman, in his important speech before the US Congress postulated the larger part of the world as 'underdeveloped' and thereby set the frame for development assistance directed from the North to the South. The United States as the epitome of the 'developed' world embodying modernity, progress and a political model that was conducive to the unfolding of individual well-being and freedom played a decisive role in the enunciation of the development discourse and figured as a yardstick by which all other countries came to be measured. All countries were supposed to follow the same track with the unitary goal of development and progress as exemplified by the US. Technical assistance together with the introduction of Western-style institutions, most importantly the nation state as the prominent institution to administer development, were devised as strategies to overcome the suffering and destitution of the South's 'masses' and, more importantly, to curb Communist insurgence. The Communist model of development orchestrated from Moscow had inherently the same objectives as the US model: to move the 'underdeveloped' countries from the 'dark age' of traditionalism to one of modernity and technological progress — only the ideological garb differed.

Development practice became the instrument to organize the post-colonial, 'backward' societies, thereby devaluing non-Western systems of knowledge, cultures and social arrangements. Western-educated political and economic elites of the developing countries, having been initiated into Western patterns of thinking, functioned within the newly independent nation states as prime movers of Western-style economic development, which they had learned to see as a prerequisite for progress in their own countries. The introduction of the modern nation state rendered 'backward' societies and their populations manageable. Previously smaller societies were agglomerated, subjected to social engineering (Nederveen Pieterse 1991) and subsequently incorporated into the global economic system. The South entered the race to catch up with the North. Economic development and increased levels of production for the global market became imperative in order to attain the desired goal of development. A profound shift in worldview accompanied these changes: economic indicators such as gross national product (GNP), economic growth rates, export rates, and so on, became all-important in evaluating the well-being and state of development in any given country. Poverty was defined as a lack of consumable goods based on the Northern experience of commodity-based needs. Subsistence economies were by definition 'underdeveloped'.

The central thesis of developmentalism is that changes occur in pre-established patterns whose logic and direction are predictable. Modernization theory, as postulated by Walt Rostow after World War II, describes this foretold pattern of change from tradition to modernity in four stages: 1) tradition with backward beliefs and technology; 2) introduction of modern technology; 3) take-off towards modernization; and 4) stage of modernity with mass consumption.

The evolutionary, linear concept of progress was also shared within Marxist discourse, albeit with different stages: primitive communism, slavery, feudalism, capitalism, socialism. Science and technology, industrialization, bureaucratization and the concept of the nation state were also seen as central to the Marxist/socialist concept of development. Despite variations one can therefore speak of the dominant mode of development as practised within the (ex-)socialist as well as capitalist systems — both subscribing to the idea of modernization and progress brought about with the help of Western science and technology. Additionally, both contain a male bias; policies for change are devised by male planners/revolutionary leaders.

The development discourse was shaped within the newly emerging institutions specifically founded to administer and implement the development of the nations of the South: the World Bank, the International Monetary Fund (IMF), the United Nations institutions and US state departments, and the national development ministries and departments. The new professionals, the development experts working in these institutions, gathered large quantities of data in the countries of the South as well as the North and devised statistics which served as a basis for the comparison and hierarchization of realities in the countries of the world. On the basis of such data development plans, that is, reform measures were drawn up for the Southern countries.

The discourse produced from within these institutions on the basis of hierarchal observation systematically formed the objects of which it spoke: the populations in the countries of the South. It grouped and arranged them in certain ways and gave them a unity of their own (Escobar 1984-85:386). Birth rates and infant mortality were identified as 'too high', literacy rates as 'too low' and so on, with the effect that the objects of the development discourse came to see themselves along the lines set out for them by Western development experts: 'underdeveloped' and 'backwards'.

With the help of the discourse on development new practices of intervention in the developing countries were introduced and thus new mechanisms of control became possible. Escobar (ibid:387-90) identified three major strategies which have greatly extended the power of the discourse:

- The progressive incorporation of more and more issues into the framework of development problems consequently led to the emergence of new fields of intervention for development experts.

- The professionalization of development into new fields of knowledge, disciplines and careers resulted in establishing the nature of the Third World, to classify it, and to formulate policies for a future designed within the logic of Western economic rationality.

- The institutionalization of development on global, national, regional and local levels with the respective development institutions as implementors of centrally devised development policies had the effect of creating a tight network and system of regulatory controls down to village level in the South.

Applying these three strategies 'development has been successful to the extent that it has been able to penetrate, integrate, manage and control countries and populations' (Escobar, 1984-85:388). The problem of 'underdevelopment' was segmented into different fields of intervention such as economics, public administration, regional planning, agriculture, industry and so on. Thus the underlying political character of the whole development enterprise was cast in the language of science and effectively transformed into a technical problem.

Development is to be seen, 'not as a matter of scientific knowledge, a body of theories and programs concerned with the achievement of true progress, but rather a series of political technologies intended to manage and give shape to the reality of the Third World' (Escobar, 1984-84:388).

It is important to note that the control of population growth, particularly in the South, was part and parcel of the development package from its inception. Acceptance of population control programmes within the development aid package became mandatory for the recipient governments. Northern authors' great concern about unprecedented population growth rates had been reflected in books with value-laden titles, for example Osborn's *Our Plundered Planet* published in 1948. In his discourse, women in the South became reduced to their function as breeders of 'too many' children, hence the need to control 'excessive' birth rates. It was seen as imperative by the development establishment to plan centrally the matching of population size and food supplies globally in order to avert political crisis. We will return to this discussion later. The UN Food and Agriculture Organization (FAO) and the Economic and Social Council (ECOSOC) were given the task of monitoring and securing food supplies to the Southern countries; the United Nations Fund for Population Assistance (UNFPA) took up the role of monitoring and managing population growth.

Even though developmentalism has not delivered its promise of leading every nation of the globe to the land of freedom and plenty, the development industry (development experts, agencies, development studies institutions, consultant firms and so on) are thriving.

Development, as Escobar (1984-85: 388) argues, has created a type of underdevelopment which so far has been politically and economically manageable. Despite the postulated crisis in development the primacy of the concept of development itself has been preserved largely intact. Our intention here is not to subscribe to an anti-development position or to romanticize times before the rise of developmentalism; subsistence economies have their own problems such as the need for hard physical labour for both people and animals. Yet, the underlying assumptions of developmentalism as outlined above, coupled with increasing centralization of management and planning alongside the widespread destruction of local lifestyles, knowledges and cultures that accompanied development, need to be fundamentally questioned. They have consistently eroded people's control over their own lives and use of natural resources. National power structures have been strengthened to the detriment of local people. Development has been an instrument in wider economic changes that resulted in transforming both people and nature into 'resources' to be traded on global markets.

Within the global economic system, economic development replaced colonialism in the post-World War II era. Sustained net transfer of capital from the South to the North has been maintained since colonial times. Even the aid flows of well below one per cent from industrialized countries' GNPs largely flow back to the donors as payment for expert advice and technical equipment.

Development in the 1990s

A major criticism of development practice is its neglect of the increasing environmental destruction. This neglect led to the organization of the United Nations Conference on Environment and Development (UNCED), the Earth Summit in 1992. Within the preparatory process leading up to the Conference, the global dimensions of the environmental crisis and the interconnections between development and the environment were clearly recognized by governments and mainstream economic and political actors. Market mechanisms alone will not suffice to address the crisis in progress. Within the UNCED proceedings Northern governments acknowledged the need to change the North's production and consumption patterns. The need for 'greening' the present global economic system was clearly acknowledged, yet, the need for fundamental changes in the prevailing power structures are carefully excluded from the emerging eco-cratic discourse.

The environmental limits to an unquestioned expansion of the Western economic growth model is symptomatic of the global crisis. It may be misleading to speak of 'the global crisis of environment and development' as such without differentiating how it affects different groups of people in different regions or qualifying which particular problem one is referring to in a particular context. The flip side of increasing poverty of large parts of the population in the South is economic growth and prosperity for parts of the population in the North. In fact, casting the multiple and complex problems of environmental degradation, resource depletion, industrial and nuclear pollution, and loss of biodiversity into the mold of 'the global environment and development crisis' that 'humanity is facing today' has given rise to the image of a unitary world system facing common constraints. Thereby large-scale inequalities and the role of global economic and political processes mainly operating in favour of the Northern countries and elites in the South are often evaded. The way for simplistic solutions to complex problems is opened up. The renewed drive for population control aimed at the South as a major strategy towards sustainable development is a case in point. Even though population growth is a problem, a fundamentally unsustainable global economy aimed at maximum economic growth rates in the North is at the root of the multiple crisis which manifests itself in regionally specific forms.

The ecological limits to economic growth and the imperative to fundamentally rethink the premises upon which the development model has been built, alarming levels of industrial pollution, serious health hazards and increasing loss of human well-being are symptomatic for the environmental dimension of the crisis in the West and even more so in the ex-socialist East. The environmental and social limits to the expansion of the present model of development have to be seen in the context of over-consumption by the few and marginalization of many. Eighty per cent of resources are used by 20 per cent of the world's population, most of them living in the North. The Eastern and Southern elites match their Western counterparts in the adoption of consumerist lifestyles. Global natural resources simply cannot sustain a lifestyle of over-consumption as a norm for all people. TNCs' role as major actors[5] on the global economic scene which are not controlled by any international, national or other mechanism is often completely neglected. The effects of their operations on people, and especially many women in the South who serve as a cheap, 'throw away labour force',[6] and their use of environmental resources cannot be stressed enough. As Wolfgang Sachs suggests: 'Calls for securing the survival of the planet are often, upon closer inspection, nothing else than calls for the survival of the industrial system' (Sachs, 1992:35).

In a move to limit environmental pollution Western countries export redundant, highly polluting production technologies to Eastern countries and the South in exchange for hard currency. It is ironic that some Western development experts have declared Southern countries as 'underpolluted' and the import of nuclear and other toxic wastes as a useful activity to generate hard currency in exchange.

In the South the crisis of developmentalism has left large parts of the population worse off now than a few decades ago. The drive to catch up with the North has led to large debts, resulting in structural adjustment and economic austerity measures. The main beneficiaries of the development process are the urban middle classes; dual societies with unprecedented economic inequalities have been created. Cuts in public spending lead to a marginalization and impoverishment of increasing numbers of people, particularly women. The unquestioned over- and misuse of natural resources in the name of economic development can no longer be maintained without jeopardizing the regenerative capacity of entire landscapes.

Not only Southern but also Western economies are heavily burdened by increasing debt, declining growth rates and recession. The formation of larger economic blocs such as the European Community, or the US, Canada and Mexico, will lead to new constellations of economic and political power. Northern interest in what used to be the 'Third World' will steadily decline in the next decade; Northern government spending on development co-operation will diminish. The need for delinking from the North and increased South/South co-operation, advocated by dependency theorists two decades ago[7] as a liberatory strategy will become a matter of survival for many Southern countries. A transition towards a new economic and political order comparable in proportion to the one set in motion after the Second World War is underway.

Another contributing factor to the global crisis of development and environment has been the collapse of the ex-Eastern bloc and the subsequent crumbling of the post-World War II tripartite world order. It has unleashed an unprecedented scale of armed conflicts, ethnic violence, a rise of religious fundamentalism, the disintergration of nation states in the East as well as the South, and mounting problems of immigration into Western countries. A political shift to the right within European countries and widespread outbursts of violence has been the result.

The development crisis is matched by a crisis in development theory. These theories, developed mainly in the North, have failed to adequately predict the development process, let alone prescribe effective measures to improve the economic situation of most people living in the South. In fact, the application of development theory translated into development strategies and policies has been identified as part of the problem. There is an urgent need for new ways of looking at the developmental crisis as well as new forms of co-operation to deal with the problems at hand.

The role of the West as a global example for development is being challenged on many levels and in many forms: both from within the West in academic and developmental institutions, by the environmental, developmental, and women's movements; and by women's, environmental and other social movements in the South.

In the West the end of modernity has been announced by post-modernist writers. They have postulated an end to linear progress based on European Enlightenment rationality by deconstructing the foundational myths of the West: universalism, reductionism, dualism and hierarchialism, as well as the myth of the unitary subject. Post-modernism implies a rupture in modernity within post-industrial, complex societies. The spread of new forms of technology and information are seen as indicative of this rupture; a shift from a productive to a reproductive social order in Western societies is underway (Featherstone 1991).

What makes post-modernism an interesting field to examine further is the fact that marginality has been validated, the stress is on difference, plurality, locality, and the question of culture. As of now, post-modernism has mainly been a preoccupation of Western academic intellectuals who have shown little interest in the countries of the South. Some post-modern theorists have provided useful suggestions for new political strategies in view of these recent changes. For us the most fruitful strategies come from feminist proponents of post-modernism whose ideas will be presented briefly in the next chapter.

Development theorists are becoming increasingly interested in the phenomenon of a forceful emergence of a variety of people's movements, mounting criticisms of intellectuals and development critics in both the North and the South and the alternative realities that these movements are creating. David Slater (1992), reflecting on the relevance of post-modernism in the Third World, suggests using the term in a constructive, enabling sense. He sees social movements in the South in all their complexity as speaking in post-modern voices. '[T]hey enter the national and international political arena speaking the language of localism and regionalism' (Aronowitz, cited after Slater ibid:303). 'The struggles for democratic transformations take many forms, connecting inter alia ecological, women's, urban, ethno-regionalist and human rights issues' (ibid:311).

But also in the North powerful citizens' movements, development critics and academics are raising similar issues. Within the preparatory process for the NGO Forum held during UNCED in 1992 many of these groups North and South developed closer connections and increasingly interact; we shall return to this point in several chapters of this book.

Notes

1. Especially by the United Nations Development Programme UNDP, see UNDP 1992.
2. The United Nations have proclaimed four development decades to date, the first of which started in 1960. These correspond with internationally adopted development strategies which were revised in view of the previous decade's experiences. There are a number of attempts to analyse the UN development decades. An interesting review has been provided by Uner Kirdar in Haq, Khadija and Uner Kirdar, (eds) (1989) *Development for People, Goals and Strategies for the Year 2000*, North/South Roundtable and UNDP Development Study Programme.
3. We stress that what has been termed as the oil 'crisis' was not a crisis of shortage of oil *per se*, but a move by the oil producing countries to limit oil production in order to increase oil prices.
4. For an example of neo-liberalism in economics see Deepak Lal (1983).
5. The annual turnover of Shell in 1984/1985 for example was US$84 billion, while the GDP of the entire Netherlands in that year was US$171 billion (J. Harrod (1990) The Politics of International Economic Relations, The Hague: ISS, lecture notes).
6. Harrod, J. (1989) *The World Social Economy in the 1990s*, The Hague, p. 66.
7. See Chapter 6 on alternative structuralist approaches to alternative development.

3. Feminist Critiques of Science

In this chapter we shall attempt to outline the extent to which feminist critics of science attribute responsibility for the current crisis to Enlightenment-based ideas of scientific and technological progress. We shall describe different positions within the field of feminist epistemology, and try to assess what we see as their central contribution to the project, namely that of formulating a participatory theory of development from different positions. It is our opinion that, while there seems to be widespread agreement on the importance of women's role in dealing with environmental problems, in both the practice of political struggles and the intellectual efforts that accompany them, connections between feminist activists and environmental activists (even though they were made within the UNCED process), need to be worked out much better. At times, a common ground for coalition between environmentalists, ecologists and feminists seems hard to find. The difference between these groups is often only a matter of priorities. For example, whereas environmentalists and ecologists do not realize the full implications of giving women an equal voice in political struggles, women may see patriarchy itself at the source of environmental destruction. Often, too, feminists do not regard 'cleaning up the mess' of environmental destruction as women's responsibility on top of all the other problems they face in living in patriarchal societies. We hope that our work can contribute to better elucidating possible common grounds and thus work towards making possible new political coalitions between these and the many other actors involved in transformations towards pro-environmental changes.

As stated in our introduction, our positions as white women academics may show particularly in dealing with epistemological issues. And yet, the simplistic opposition between theoretical and activist feminism has come under increasing criticism from women across the board. As bell hooks puts it in an article pointedly entitled 'Post-modern Blackness': 'Racism is perpetuated when blackness is associated solely with concrete, gut-level experience, conceived as either opposing or having no connection to abstract thinking and the production of critical theory' (bell hooks 1990:23).

We shall not speak pidgin just to please our colonizers: in the age of in-depth questioning of identity and of the structure of subjectivity, a radical post-modernist practice of differences can serve struggles against neo-colonialism, exploitation and marginalization.

Feminist thought on science

How does feminist thinking about science go? Feminist scholarship argues that mainstream science is customarily portrayed as universal, value-free and neutral in its pursuit of truth that is deemed valuable for all. For feminists, however, the production of knowledge is best described as a social activity embedded in a certain culture and world view. Science aims to explain reality, but the experience of this reality, of one's perceptions and interpretations of it are a product of human thought determined by culture. For feminists as for other radical epistemologists, universalism is a false perspective that is best assessed as the ideological expression of white, male, supremacist, hegemonic thinking. In this perspective, thinking is neither neutral nor value-free but highly contextualized or situated. Thus, there is no such thing as 'mankind', but only specifically situated humans, whose condition can be analysed by reference to concrete material and semiotic variables, such as: gender, class, race, ethnic identity, lifestyle and so on. Ruth Bleier has pointed out that the world view and consciousness that people develop within a certain culture provide a framework for categorizing and interpreting human experiences which in turn come to confirm the world view of which they are in part the product (Bleier 1987).

Feminist critics of science have pointed out that the Western world view and Western science as they have developed since the Enlightenment period are overdetermined by political, economic and social conditions which can be explained by reference to a patriarchal order. Thus, women were not only systematically excluded from the actual activity of doing science, but patriarchal scientists declared them to be unfit for the usage of reason. In patriarchal ideology, women's social situation, that is, living in the household — the private sphere as opposed to the male domain of the public sphere — was designated a second 'nature'. Women were consequently both defined as and compelled to be closer to a private realm that was seen as synonymous with nature, feelings and emotions, and caring for others. Conversely, men were defined as those best suited to the usage of reason and consequently fit for public life.

Patriarchal thinking therefore affects individuals' sense of their identity and of the world they inhabit, whether they are men or women. In Western languages, the experiences of reality and of identity are framed by relations of dominance and dualities which go back to the basic male/female opposition. This dualistic ordering of reality is also hierarchical: the principle of male over female, mind over body, culture over nature, subject over object, and so on. Male, mind, culture and subject are categories which exercise hierarchical control and domination over female, body, nature and object. In Western thought the principles of hierarchy, domination and control are deeply inscribed in patterns of thinking, yet made to appear 'normal', 'natural' and altogether neutral.

> The organization of knowledge as we know it has been undertaken by men who have translated a male view of the world into universal categories...they have internalized their supremacy over women as part of the natural order of things (Marks (1979) cited in Bleier (1987:198-9)).

Dualism, in the masculinist hegemonic thinking that marks the production of Western science, is a system of exclusion of 'others' from patriarchal subjectivity. The very definition of 'the scientific mind' is coterminous with rationality, masculinity and power. The scientist as model for the subject of knowledge is therefore defined in a set of hierarchical relations to others: the non-scientists. Feminists have criticized scientific discourse as an account of the world that systematically devalues every category that is 'other' than the male, Western, bourgeois self: women, children, other races, foreign cultures, lower classes, handicapped people and nature.

Philosopher and historian Caroline Merchant's contribution to the analysis of the history of Western science (1980) documents the history of science from women's point of view. Her analysis highlights not only the problems due to the exclusion and domination of women, nature and all 'others' from the dominant view of the subject, but also stresses the depth of the crisis internal to Western culture and civilization themselves.

> In investigating the roots of our current environmental dilemma and its connections to science, technology and economy, we must reexamine the formation of a world view and a science that, by perceiving reality as machine, rather than a living organism, sanctioned the domination of both women and nature (Merchant 1980).

Merchant singles out the point which can be seen as the key issue in feminist critiques of science, one that can best be described as an intersection of many lines of questioning: the intersection of the practice of domination of the environment for the purpose of economic gain; the social domination of underprivileged groups, (women, ethnic minorities, the disabled and so on) and the psychological domination of some over others. Our argument is that in all these material, social and identity-related issues, gender relations play a central and paradigmatic role as locations of power.

From a different angle, radical post-structuralist epistemologists such as Foucault (1980) have pointed out that science has been used not to explain reality, but to produce, control and normalize it. Thus highlighted, the problematic connection between power, knowledge and truth proved fruitful for feminists. Scientific discourse is the outcome of a network of power relations, structures and related procedures that determine which statement is to be assigned the status of a scientific truth and which is not. This network of dispersed and all-regulating power relations transforms the activity of producing knowledge, and the institutions that regulate it, into a highly politicized field. In this framework, the political question is the legitimation of scientific truth itself, that is to say: what is allowed to be named, counted, accepted, canonized and financed as scientifically valid.

Feminist critiques of science consequently have a double edge (de Lauretis 1990): on the one hand they display a critical pull and on the other a creative approach. More especially they focus on gender roles and the construction of woman as the 'other' of scientific discourse. Woman as a category has been constructed as 'other than' not only as different from but also in opposition to Man, the subject of patriarchal discourse, in order to reconfirm his position as superior, rational and standard. The human subject in scientific discourse is male; that is to say, he is a projected image of bourgeois, white, Western masculinity. Rationality and theoretical reason, as expounded by the male subject has been unmasked by Simone de Beauvoir (1949) as an instrument of male domination over women (and all others). From a feminist point of view there is a close link between masculinity, rationality and violence. This position remains important although, as we shall see later, de Beauvoir will eventually come under attack for her silence on issues of racial and ethnic differences (Spelman 1989).

In the light of these assertions the value-neutrality of rational, scientific discourse crumbles and reveals its mythical character. De Beauvoir has laid the ground for feminist theorizing by a female subject. Women, hitherto confined to irrationality and passivity in scientific discourse, posited themselves as active agents in the production of knowledge. The starting point is the assertion that a woman is other than a non-man, that is to say that knowledge about women has been overdetermined and distorted by masculine projections, fantasies and myth-making. Feminists argue that the definition of female subjectivity must be based on women's real life-experiences, so as to legitimate women-based ways of knowing. Feminist social and natural scientists, philosophers and others often feel like strangers in their own fields of expertise because their experiences and identities as women place them in a conflictual position with the expectations, modes of behaviour and forms of social interaction at work in mainstream scientific practice and discourse. Researching and theorizing within male categories is often problematic for feminists. Although they have criticized mainstream science from different perspectives and on different grounds, they all agree about the patriarchal nature of scientific inquiry. Feminist criticism of science rests on the assumption that traditional epistemologies are androcentric because they systematically exclude women from being knowers. As Patricia Hill Collins put it:

By following strict methodological rules, scientists aim to distance themselves from the values, vested interests, and emotions generated by their class, race, sex, or unique situation. By decontextualizing themselves, they allegedly become detached observers and manipulators of nature (Collins 1990: 205).

A recent issue of the journal *Hypatia* (1991) devoted to eco-feminism stressed that feminist critiques of science raise not only epistemological but also ethical issues and questions about the structures of identity and subjectivity. The starting point for feminist critiques of the sexism of science was a quarrel with the natural sciences, especially biology, as a discourse that perpetuates beliefs about the 'natural' inferiority of women. Apart from denouncing the tendency to use science to legitimate social injustice and oppression as discriminatory, feminists also raised larger issues about the very foundations of scientific discourse and the practice of science.

Fox-Keller (Fox-Keller, 1983a, 1983b, 1985) was among the first to question the instrumental relationship that Western science conducts with 'nature' as its immediate environment. She argues that ever since Bacon, the natural environment has been conceptualized as brute matter (the Cartesian *res extensa*), without logic or intelligence of its own. In turn, this implies a view of the scientist as the knowing agent with the competence and the power to attribute meaning to nature by penetrating its opaque structure. Keller emphasizes not only the instrumental or colonizing view of scientific reason at work here, but also its highly sexualized connotations: the metaphor of penetration is significant in this respect, as is the vision or scientific gaze as the instrument of penetration. Both the masculinity of the gaze and the flight from femininity have been extensively commented upon by feminists who have traced them back to the rationalist dualism of the seventeenth century French philosopher Descartes, whose dislike for the body, the senses and the emotions has come under criticism (Lloyd, 1984; Bordo 1986).

This point was also developed, quite independently, by French philosopher Irigaray (1977) who sees the man/nature relationship as a prototypical rendition of man's inability to deal with difference other than in terms of power and domination. Male control of natural resources reduces women to merchandise to be exchanged and circulated in a male-dominated economic system. Irigaray (1974) also emphasizes the role of vision as the hierarchically 'noble' sense, which is synonymous with intelligence and reduces other forms of perception to a lower epistemological status.

The main thrust of these critiques is the inter-connection between domination and the rejection of difference, especially sexual difference. Plumwood (1991) also stresses the point that Western science has emphasized difference in the sense of dualistic opposition; thus, what counts in the man/nature relationship is all that differentiates, that is: separates the one from the other. The subject is set up against his 'others', he is legitimated dualistically and oppositionally. His differences from nature, women, other races, and animals are marks of his superiority over these 'other' beings.

Considering this logic of systematic deprecation of differences, the critique of scientific rationality in feminist texts also encompasses the questioning of the rationalist concept of the subject of knowledge: that male, white, middle-class 'owner' of knowledge who is alternatively defined in terms of 'rational egoism' (Plumwood 1991); 'structurally a rapist' (Brownmiller 1979); 'transcendental narcissism' (Braidotti 1991); 'blind to the positivity of differences' (Irigaray 1974) and 'unduly anthropo- and androcentric' (Haraway 1990).

The question that then arises is: can these oppressive features be changed or are science and technology necessarily and inevitably oppressive? We shall return to this question.

Historical analysis of feminist epistemology

Whereas comments on the sexist bias of scientific discourse are present in the very early texts of the second feminist wave, the elaboration of a feminist theory of knowledge is a more recent phenomenon.

The three central questions of epistemology, the theory of knowledge, are: 1) who can be a 'knower', that is to say, what structures and mechanisms are at work in the empowerment of certain subjects of knowledge? 2) what are the processes that determine and legitimate the practice and the act of knowing? and 3) what can be 'known', that is to say, what factors affect the establishment of adequate objects of knowledge? Epistemological assumptions about these three questions have deep political implications: feminist scholars have singled out the male bias as a factor at work in each of these three levels of enquiry. This way, feminists function as 'knowers' by 'changing the subject', from a male-biased vision into one that is more widely applicable, because less discriminatory.

Feminist criticism has also contested the pervasive androcentrism in the formulation of problems, theories, concepts and frameworks of research. The ways in which the object of research is positioned as passive and silent *vis-à-vis* the (male) subject as active agent of knowledge, capable of neutral, 'value-free' observation has also been questioned. This model has been criticized not only for its dualistic opposition of an active agent to a passive object of knowledge, but also for the genderized nature of this opposition. Feminists have shown that theory is written from the point of view and socio-political experience of white, Western, bourgeois men living in patriarchal societies and that the voices of natural, as well as social scientists are male. The texts of Western science, philosophy, history and religion have been handed down through generations as irrefutable truths. In their criticism of these 'truths', as a male-biased structure of thought, feminist epistemologists are indebted to the work of feminist literary critics (Showalter 1985; Miller 1985; Christian 1988).

The epistemological turn taken by feminists is often called the 'meta-discursive' phase of feminist theory, in that it stresses the need for self-reflexive analysis of the central notions of feminist practice (Flax 1983; Kristeva 1982; Spivak 1988). This phase also coincides with the institutionalization of the many feminist ways of knowing, ranging, for example, from formal women's studies courses and research institutes to autonomous women's centres, especially outside the Western world.

Recent feminist scholarship has subjected the central feminist ideas to critical scrutiny and serious methodological and theoretical revisions (Harding and Hintikka 1983; Harding 1986, 1987, 1991; de Lauretis 1990; Haraway 1990; Butler 1990; Braidotti 1991). Special attention is paid to evaluating the central notions, the ruling concepts, the criteria for interpretation and evaluation and the methodological frameworks that sustain and govern the production of feminist knowledge, thereby also advancing the claim that the women's movement has produced its own specific epistemological categories.

This claim to epistemological specificity has not gone unchallenged either within or outside the women's movement. Within, the critical comment was made that this proliferation of theoretical discourse in the Western world coincided with the reflux of political activism in the generally conformist political climate of the 1980s. In some ways this criticism resurrected and reformulated the old-fashioned opposition between feminist activism and feminist intellectuality. Not surprisingly, therefore, one of the main issues at stake in the elaboration of feminist epistemologies turned out to be the relation between theory and practice, ideas and actions, thought and politics. Central to this discussion was the emergence of autonomous feminist texts by non-Western women, who proceeded to redefine the theory/practice debate in different cultural contexts (Walker 1984). As Collins put it : 'reclaiming the Black feminist intellectual tradition also involves searching for its expression in alternative institutional locations and among women who are not commonly perceived as intellectuals' (Collins 1990:14).

A second and equally important challenge came from outside feminism: in the Western world, the 1970s and 1980s were marked by post-modernist or post-structuralist discussions about the social role and the political function of the human and social sciences, including philosophy. In this context of critical discourse, the question was raised as to the viability of theoretical discourse as an instrument of liberation or even of structurally lasting reform (Foucault 1971, 1977; Deleuze 1972,

1980; Bourdieu 1979). Under the influence of deconstructive philosophies (Derrida 1978, 1987) the limits of theoretical discourse were questioned and the issue of the richer potential of literary or poetic language as an instrument of liberation was raised.

Within feminism, this point had already been argued quite passionately by feminist poets (Rich 1979, 1987; Lorde 1980) and the literary critics quoted above, but only at a later stage moved into the heart of the theoretical discussions. This point is particularly significant if one keeps in mind that one of the central notions in feminist epistemology is 'experience', that is: the inextricable unity of thinking and living, theory and practice, intellectuality and politics. Considering the polysemic nature of the word and the complexity of the notion of 'experience', it is not surprising that recent publications have attempted to define it in a feminist perspective, either by historicizing the notion or by setting it in a narrative framework (Flax 1990).

The emphasis on narration or story-telling as the most appropriate theoretical style for feminist theories of knowledge has gained in impetus of late (Snitow 1990; Gallop 1991); see also the trend towards 'personal criticism' (Miller 1985, 1991; Ward 1991 and others). We consider that it is important to set these attempts at clarification of the central tenets of feminist theory alongside more conventional and therefore more academic works. Prominent among the feminists who favour the 'story-telling' approach are women from non-Western cultures, who try to analyse theoretical terms such as 'gender' as a set of relations that allow us to think of both the interdependence and the simultaneity of different variables of oppression such as race, age, culture, life-style and others. We shall return to these later.

Central to the metadiscursive or epistemological turn is the notion of 'gender' as a foundation stone of feminist theory. A brief overview of this notion is necessary because of the rich and complex theoretical history of the term (Scott 1988, 1990).

The starting point for this overview is the awareness that, in Western feminism, the metadiscursive turn in feminist theory, which accompanies the claim to a specific feminist epistemology, is simultaneous with a reshuffling of theoretical positions which had reached a stalemate in feminist theory, most notably the opposition between on the one hand 'gender theorists' in the Anglo-American tradition and on the other, 'sexual difference theorists' in the French and European tradition (Duchen 1986). The polarization of feminist positions was reshuffled also thanks to the increasing awareness of the culture-specific forms taken by feminist theory. It became apparent in fact that the notion of 'gender' is a vicissitude of the English language, which bears little or no relevance to theoretical traditions in the Romance languages (de Lauretis 1988). As such, it has found no successful echo in the French, Dutch, Spanish or Italian feminist movements and, therefore, makes little epistemological or political sense in many non-English, Western European contexts, where the notions of 'sexuality' and 'sexual difference' are currently used instead (Bono and Kemp 1991).

For the sake of precision we will therefore define gender as a notion that offers a set of frameworks within which feminist theory has explained the social and discursive construction and representation of differences between the sexes. As such, 'gender' has been the feminist answer to the universalistic tendency of critical language and of the systems of knowledge and scientific discourse at large. Attention to 'gender' results in renewed emphasis being placed on the situated, that is to say local structure of knowledge; that one cannot speak on behalf of humanity as a whole, that the scientific position cannot claim to represent universal values, but rather extremely specific ones. Today, it is an historical aberration to speak on behalf of 'mankind', without recognizing that this term fails to account for people other than white, adult, professional, Western males.

We wish to state most emphatically that recognition of the partiality of scientific statements, their necessary contingency, their reliance on concrete mechanisms which are overdetermined by history and socio-economic factors, has nothing to do with relativism. Rather, it marks a significant change in the ethical style of research. The rejection of universalism in favour of paying greater attention to the complexity of differences and of 'situated knowledges' calls for more flexibility in the making of knowledge and of scientific discourse. It also requires a positive approach to differences. Differences of class, race, sex, age, culture and nationality require an intellectual or academic recognition that the old style universalist mode does not permit.

Universalism, as we noted earlier, consists in conflating the masculine viewpoint with the general, 'human' standpoint, thereby confining the feminine to the structural position of 'other'. Thus, the masculine qua human is taken as the 'norm' and the feminine qua other is seen as marking the 'difference'. The corollary of this definition is that the mark of sexual difference falls upon women, marking them off as the second sex, or the structural 'other', whereas men are marked by the imperative of carrying the universal. Simone de Beauvoir observed 50 years ago that the price men pay for representing the universal is a kind of loss of embodiment; the price women pay, on the other hand, is a loss of subjectivity and the confinement to the body. The former are disembodied and through this process gain entitlement to transcendence and subjectivity, the latter are over-embodied and thereby consigned to immanence. This results in two asymmetrical positions and two opposed problem areas.

Such symbolic division between the sexes, which the term 'gender' helps to explain, is the system set up by 'phallogocentrism', which is a critical term to describe the inner logic of patriarchy. It is based on a systematic asymmetry between the sexes, which operates to the detriment of women. In other words, this system is neither necessary as in historically inevitable, nor rational, as in conceptually necessary. It has simply become the powerful foundation of a system in which we are all constructed as either men or women by certain symbolic, semiotic and material conditions. We will argue that effective political work by feminists requires serious examination of these conditions, so that their analysis can lead to constructing identities differently, that is: in a manner that is politically enabling and conducive to resisting domination.

The central terms of reference for the debate on gender, devised by feminist theory in the early 1970s under the inspiration of de Beauvoir, developed mostly in such fields as history, anthropology and sociology and only came to the natural sciences much later. Thus, Rubin's classic reading of the sex/gender distinction in the light of cultural anthropological analysis about the exchange of women was to have enormous consequences for the feminist analyses of science (Rubin 1975).

Following Lévi Strauss's work on kinship structures, Rubin studied the material and symbolic function of women as objects of exchange among men. This indicated that the social order as it exists is a male homosocial contract. In other words, the gender-system, which constructs the two sexes as different, unequal and yet complementary, is in fact a power system that aims at concentrating material and symbolic capital in the hands of the fathers, that is to say older men who control younger men and the women. The family is thus the power unit which seals the wealth of (older) men and establishes heterosexuality as the dominant political economy.

By emphasizing the cultural and social construction of differences between the sexes, Rubin's rereading of de Beauvoir highlights the importance of human sexuality as a location of power. She shows how central is the objectification of women to the material but also symbolic maintenance of the patriarchal system and the forms of knowledge, representation and scientific investigation which the system perpetuates. Institutions such as the church, the university and the parliament merely reflect the same logic of domination and exclusion of women. The theological, intellectual, mythical and legal systems they produce do exactly the same.

It is with Rich (1986) however, that the analysis of the political role of sexuality comes to the fore. Rich's standpoint stresses the idea of the 'politics of location'. The feminist subject is, for Rich, marked by a specific location in space and time: the primary location is the female body, that is: the morphological and political space of the female embodied subject. Rich has the merit of emphasizing both the positivity of the difference that women embody and also of stressing the many differences that separate women among themselves, first and foremost differences of race and ethnicity. The commonly accepted portrayal of a culturally-determined position that unites women as 'the second sex' is consequently overlaid by powerful variables that act like axes of differentiation. The issue of embodiment as the grounding of female subjectivity is therefore not a one-way road towards an essentialized female entity, but rather a bio-cultural situation that helps identify differences among women.

This approach gained momentum in the early 1980s under the joint impact of semiotics, structuralist psychoanalysis and autonomous developments within the women's movement (Eisenstein 1984). Central to this new approach is a shift away from the mere critique of patriarchy, to the assertion of the positivity of women's cultural traditions and range of experiences.

Highly significant for this shift of perspective is the new emphasis and value placed on language and consequently representation as the site of constitution of the subject. One of the most striking forms of this new development in feminist scholarship are the French theories of 'sexual difference', also known as the *écriture féminine* movement. The conceptual foundations of this movement are drawn from linguistics, literary studies, semiotics, philosophy and psychoanalytic theories of the subject. The sexual difference theorists innovated the feminist debate by drawing attention to the social relevance of the theoretical and linguistic structures of the differences between the sexes. In other words, this school of feminist thought argues that an adequate analysis of women's oppression must take into account both language and materialism and not be reduced to either one or the other. Science is a construct made of language (Cixous 1985,1987,1988; Hyvrard 1988), it is an institution in the Foucauldian sense, that is, a material and linguistic construction. Theorists of difference are very critical of the Anglo-Saxon notion of 'gender' as being unduly focused on social and material factors to the detriment of the semiotic and symbolic aspects.

Opposed to 'woman-based' knowledge, such radical thinkers as Wittig (1991) developed a critique of the very notion of 'woman'. In her polemical opposition to the valorization of sexual difference, Wittig argued that this notion is a constant factor of the male imagination and of a social system that is dominated by men. As such, it is imbued with masculine projections and imaginary expectations; it is therefore epistemologically unreliable and politically suspicious.

In a move of radical rejection of all identities created in the patriarchal system, Wittig opened the era of suspicion about the very notion of 'woman' which is taken as the ideological construct of a male-dominated gender-system, from the angle of lesbian experience, while others did so from the standpoint of race and ethnicity or of post-structuralist theories (Riley 1988). Wittig argues that in patriarchal ideology 'woman' stands for a normative model of reproductive heterosexuality: she stands for nature, white motherhood, the male-dominated family. Such notions are essentialist because they are passed off as natural and therefore as inevitable or unchangeable conditions that are in fact socially induced and culture-specific.

By the 1980s, therefore, the gender system was no longer seen as the cultural re-coding of a biological reality, but rather the expression of a patriarchal ideology that requires binary oppositions between the sexes in order to assert male dominance (Butler 1990). It is gender that produces sexed identities and not the other way around. These identities serve the purpose of providing an essentialist basis to patriarchal power, that is to say, they comfort the social system with the belief in the 'natural', that is to say biologically founded and historically inevitable structure of its institutions, values and modes of representation, especially its vision of the subject, thereby providing the material and symbolic means of perpetuating its white, middle-class, masculine consciousness. By the same token, feminists following de Beauvoir perpetuated the rejection of psychoanalysis on the grounds of its essentialistic, that is, biologically deterministic, view of women. They opposed to its emphasis on desire a political theory based on the will to change, where the idea of socio-cultural influences, as opposed to the biological construction of differences, plays a crucial role. Their critique joined with that of many non-Western women who questioned the 'whiteness' of psychoanalysis, while not altogether rejecting it (bell hooks 1990).

The debate between sexual difference and gender theorists in the 1980s resulted in two quite contrary forms of reductivism: on the one hand an idealistic form that reduces everything to the textual and on the other hand a materialistic one that reduces everything to the social. These led to two extreme versions of 'essentialism' (de Lauretis 1988; Schor 1988; Fuss 1990; Braidotti 1989, 1992).

The term 'essentialism' becomes the most widely operational in feminism in the controversy that opposed the new theorists of sexual difference to the de Beauvoir-style radical materialists; it entered English-speaking feminism through the influence that both schools of thought exercised in the late 1970s. Some have argued that what is really at stake in this controversy is firstly culture-specific and therefore variable understandings of gender; and secondly, different definitions of the very concept of 'materialism' (Braidotti, 1989). In our opinion, however, what is primarily at stake is the way in which a deconstructive approach to feminist epistemology, which implies the rejection of essentialism meant as biological determinism, can result in fruitful political standpoints for feminist activists. As a consequence, issues such as the body, the structure of identity and desire are linked to the notions of historicity, change and political agency. In the next chapter we shall return to examining this position.

In this respect should be mentioned a number of other feminist groupings which also challenged established ideas of subjectivity and knowledge within the Western world. Among them are the feminists inspired by critical theorists in the German tradition, united in their adherence to the Frankfurt school tradition (Benhabyb and Cornell 1987; Benjamin 1990; Flax 1987). Then the Italian group: through the traditional links between the women's movement and the organized left-wing politics, Italian adaptations of Irigaray produced a highly politicized version of sexual difference in terms of a social and symbolic alliance of women (Bono and Kemp 1991).

Of greatest relevance are the ethnic, Black and post-colonial thinkers: in North American feminism the race issue had been present from the start, but it took a long time for ethnicity and race to be recognized as central variables in the definition of feminist subjectivity: the whiteness of feminist theory becomes the central target, overruling all other differences, including the previous polemical gap between 'gender' and 'sexual difference' theories. Accordingly, as suggested earlier, de Beauvoir is taken to task because of her 'colour-blindness' and lack of sensitivity to the issue of ethnicity (Spelman 1989). The pioneer work of Black women writers (Lorde 1984; Walker 1986; Morrison 1985) and of many other Black theorists (Moraga 1981, 1983) was followed by more systematic methodological critiques of the whiteness and the ethnocentrism of feminist theories of gender and sexual difference, (Spivak 1990; Mohanty 1987, 1988; Smith 1985, 1983; Trinh Minh-Ha 1989; Hooks 1990). Contemporary Black feminist epistemology has also moved beyond its critical orbit to develop schemes of thought of its own (Collins 1990).

One of the points of real, that is to say conceptual difference between these schools of feminist thought, is the question of how to identify points of exit from the universalism implicit in the patriarchal or 'phallogocentric' system and from the dualistic or binary way of thinking that characterizes it. Whereas sexual difference theorists argued for the process of working through the old system, through the strategy of 'mimetic repetition' (Irigaray 1974; Braidotti 1991; Whitford 1991), gender theorists resorted to the 'critique of ideology'. On the one hand this resulted in the investment of the 'feminine' pole of the sexual dichotomy in order to create different meanings and representations for it. On the other hand, it led to the rejection of the scheme of sexual bi-polarization, in favour of a de-sexualized and gender-free position. The argument that one needs to redefine the female feminist subject, which is reiterated by sexual difference theorists, is met by the contradictory claim of gender theorists, that the feminine is a morass of metaphysical nonsense and that it is better to reject it altogether in favour of a new androgyny.

These positions also lead to different epistemological positions: on the one hand the elaboration of woman-identified systems of knowledge, on the other a new form of gender-free knowledge. Instead, theorists from the Black and post-colonial perspective advance the idea of the simultaneity of the levels of oppression, which makes the variable 'gender' interact with other, equally powerful axes of differentiation, such as race, class, and sexual preference. This approach results in identifying as the 'point of exit' from phallogocentrism an interactive alliance of people situated within any of these axes. The idea of coalitions emerges as central to this approach.

An attempt to take this insight seriously is provided by Joan Scott (Scott 1988, 1990). In one of the most authoritative early essays on gender, Scott had argued that 'gender' as marking a set of interrelations between variables of oppression could help us understand the intersection of sex, class, race, lifestyle, age, as fundamental axes of differentiation. In a more recent essay, she goes further and argues for a definition of gender as marking the intersection of language with the social, that is: the semiotic with the material. Quoting Foucault's notion of 'discourse', which she defends as one of the major contributions of post-structuralist thought to feminist theory, Scott suggests that we reinterpret 'gender' as linking the text to reality, the symbolic to the material, theory to practice in a new, powerful manner. In Scott's reading, feminist theory in this post-gender phase politicizes the struggle over meaning and representation.

What emerges here is a radical redefinition of knowledge and of theoretical practice away from the dualistic mode; the text is now approached as both a semiotic and a material structure, that is to say not an isolated item locked in a dualistic opposition to a social context. The text must rather be understood as a stage in a process, that is to say a chain reaction that takes place in a web of power relations. What is at stake in the textual practice, therefore, is less the activity of interpretation than that of decoding the network of connections and effects that link the text to an entire socio-symbolic system.

Our central hypothesis in proposing such a reading of feminist ideas about the subject of knowledge is that the feminist theorists of today are a new transdisciplinary and transnational generation of thinkers, firmly anchored in the humanities, philosophy, social sciences, anthropology, history, semiotics and literary studies; they are multi-layered thinkers who transcend disciplinary boundaries. They have been cross-influenced by different theoretical traditions and are less likely to take for granted such misnomers as 'French feminism', or 'Anglo-American feminism', mostly because they have their share of false polemics generated by post-structuralism and its feminist adaptations. Most importantly, these feminist epistemologists are politically motivated. They take as their starting point the decline of the false universalism of patriarchal thinking, without falling into relativism.

The feminist post-modernist agenda is a radically materialist epistemology aimed at legitimating political and theoretical action not with reference to universal values, but to specifically situated and therefore accountable positions. As Collins put it, quoting Haraway explicitly and Foucault implicitly: 'As epistemological stances, both positivist science and relativism minimize the importance of specific location in influencing a group's knowledge claims, the power inequities among groups that produce subjugated knowledges, and the strengths and limitations of partial perspectives' (Collins 1990:235).

In other words, emphasis on differences among women, far from being relativistic, anarchical or nihilistic — as the critics would have it — lays new grounds for negotiating interconnections and alliances among women of different subjugated groups, united in the common claim to legitimation for their specific knowledges. It also opens the way to make similar alliances with non-hegemonic-minded men whose claims to situated knowledges may focus on gender to a lesser extent than those of the feminists and yet be equally committed to deconstructing the false universalism of Western theoretical practice.

Theoretical analysis of feminist epistemology

In what has since become a standard reference, Sandra Harding (1986) distinguishes three streams of feminist theories of knowledge: feminist empiricism; feminist standpoint; and feminist post-modernism.

Feminist empiricists basically accept mainstream science's notions of the existence of the world independent of the human knower and the primacy of the senses as the source of knowledge about the world. They maintain that sexism and androcentrism are identifiable biases of individual knowers and can be eliminated by a stricter application of the existing methodological forms of scientific inquiry. From this position the way to arrive at the truth about the phenomenal world is by controlling the strict adherence to neutral procedures by the observer/subject. The eradication of the misogynist bias of the researcher is the precondition for the achievement of objective knowledge. This step ensures the acquisition of an unmediated truth about the world, free from the distorting lenses of the particular observer.

In this position the question of who asks which question and for what purpose, which is decisive for the outcome of research, that is, the political nature of the process, the exertion of power, is not addressed. This begs the question of implicit biases in the very formulation of scientific problems. The aim to be pursued is value-neutrality, as opposed to androcentric biases, and this can be achieved by reforming the procedural aspects of research. The oppressive nature of the subject-object relation remains unchanged.

In this framework, the Eurocentric nature of Western science is obscured, a particular type of rationality developed in the period of Enlightenment in Europe is implicitly universalized as the only valid way to arrive at 'truth'. There is no room for sciences developed in different cultures and no other ways of elaborating knowledge. This position is therefore of limited use in our search for alternative ways of developing non-dominating knowledge.

Feminist standpoint theory rejects the notion of an unmediated truth, maintaining that knowledge is always mediated by the individual's position and identity according to race, class and gender in a particular socio-political formation and a certain point in time. Yet, feminist standpoint theorists do not reject the notion of truth altogether. They argue that certain social positions like that of the oppressors produce views of reality distorted by ideology. Other social positions, those of the oppressed, can overcome ideological biases and attain a valid knowledge and understanding of the world. Women's oppression constitutes a privileged position in the pursuit of knowledge; this position is the basis for a feminist 'successor science' to replace masculinist science. Feminist standpoint theory can be related to the Marxist concept of the privileged position of the working class in the search for a kind of knowledge that is free from ideological biases.

The important contribution of feminist standpoint theorists is the stress on the positionality of an observer and its effect on what she/he sees. Stressing the privileged nature of the view 'from below', however, is somewhat problematic. It is easier to see from below, but these standpoints cannot provide an absolute, universal 'truth'. The feminist standpoint position claims truth by implicitly reversing the positions of the 'knower' and the 'known'. The DAWN group[1] adheres to this contention. Women researchers from the South enter the development debate by bringing in the view of non-Western women. The ensuing research results are useful and important as they bring in the perspective situated on the margins of power. The need to deconstruct scientific discourse from its white, male, middle-class biases is thus addressed. Yet, not all women's experience is the same. The perspectives of women scientists from the South from a bourgeois, urban background may differ considerably from those of illiterate rural women; the issue of power relations between women researchers/subjects and women as objects of research cannot be neglected altogether. Futhermore, there is a distinct danger of romanticizing the position of the 'poor Third World woman', the ultimate other to patriarchal self, as the only one who can come up with 'the truth on development and know the solution for all', a tendency that can be observed in parts of the WED debate. It is precisely this claim that is so problematic in the mainstream science as well and one which only reverses established hierarchies (Mohanty 1987, 1988).

Feminist post-modernism, according to Harding, totally rejects the notion of 'a' truth about reality and thus goes further in the critique of mainstream science than the two previous positions. By using the situatedness of each observer in a particular social, historical, and political context, feminist post-modernists challenge the claim of any perspective on knowledge and reality to be impartial. Starting from the disparate conditions that shape individual realities, they question the notion of a unitary consciousness of the human species. They consider knowledge to be the result of invention, that is, the imposition of form on the world rather than the result of discovery. Universal claims about existence, nature, and the power of reason are thus treated with suspicion. Feminist post-modernists stress plurality and difference.

It is in so doing that they challenge mainstream science on a more profound level than the two previous positions. In our search for suggestions for a pluralization of scientific discourse, feminist post-modernists' contributions seem most useful, as they contribute to dismantling the power relations implicit in the production of knowledge. The often-voiced criticism of post-modernism as falling into complete relativism is a reductionist and unjustified reading which fails to take into consideration the impact of post-modernism as a politics based on the respect of differences. Relativism and stress on the relativity of a particular position are not the same: there can be different truths depending on what position one is taking. Feminist post-modernists have introduced the question of how to think differently, beyond dualism and hierarchy, how to produce knowledges that could be less prone to domination, and what a feminist definition of rationality and objectivity could be (Flax 1990). More importantly, they have attempted to translate this into a political standpoint (Cornell 1991; Collins 1990; Braidotti 1991; bell hooks 1990; bell hooks and Childers 1990).

Of Harding's threefold classification we shall concentrate on post-modernism and its positive potential as a new philosophy of development based on situated subjectivities and partial claims to knowledge. It seems to us that what is really at stake in this debate is how to assess the tradition of the Enlightenment, that is: the grand rationalist tradition that wove together, in a teleological process, reason, history and the ideal of social progress. In other words, the great theoretical dividing line in feminist epistemology seems to be between those who claim that feminism is a 'successor science project', capable of enlarging the scope of scientific rationality, and those who believe that meaningful change can come only by down-playing the very notion of reason. Are feminists closet humanists — wanting to rescue what is left of rationality, needing some realist theory of discourse, an alternative female religion? Or should we adopt a radical form of epistemology that denies access to a real world and to a final truth, attempting to approach discourse analysis in a problematic mode? We shall devote more attention to the latter.

For radical feminist epistemologists, the notion of progress and liberation through an adequate use of reason is to be re-examined in the light of history — particularly in the light of extreme phenomena in contemporary Western history, such as totalitarian political systems, genocides, colonialism, slavery, domination and the environmental crisis. Emphasis on the political need for a revision of the Enlightenment as the 'myth of liberation through reason' is particularly strong in recent feminist texts. In this perspective, faith in the self-regulating power of reason lacks validity as a theoretical, political and ethical position. It must be replaced by a more radical critique of reason from within, that is: an analysis of its structural limitations as a theoretical and human ideal. Critical theory is an ethical approach that takes the production of knowledge as its central concern (Code 1991; Merchant 1980; Lloyd 1984).

Furthermore, as Evelyn Fox-Keller pointed out, the historical context in which feminism has emerged as theory and practice rests on structural conditions that are conducive to the revision and the extension of the meaning of reason and of scientific rationality. In other words, if modernity entails a package deal — industrialization, progress via science, liberation via the rational use of reason and the emancipation of women — and if modernity has now come to a crisis point, then post-modernity consists in the decline of the whole package deal that went with modernization, including its underlying rationalist and emancipatory paradigm. Furthermore, if the emancipation of women, as theory and practice, is historically and conceptually built into the modernist project, then the crisis of modernity, or post-modernism, marks the emergence of feminism as an autonomous discourse, different from emancipation and capable of pointing women to specific ways out of the crisis (Braidotti 1991; Cornell 1991).

In other words, there is little scope within the feminist framework for nihilism or cynical acceptance of the state of crisis as decadence. On the contrary, this crisis is perceived by women as the opening-up of new possibilities and potentialities. It leads women to rethink the link between knowledge, identity, power and the community. It allows them to ask: what does it mean to be a human subject today, that is to say, a civilized, socialized member of a community in a post-metaphysical/industrial/modern world?

In this era of crumbling certainties and dissolving identities, how can women assert the positivity of the difference that women can make, while recognizing the fragility of what we call 'civilization': a network of multiply differentiated, interacting subjects, functioning on a consensual basis? (Braidotti 1991)

Our argument here is that this brand of feminist epistemology takes up, like structuralist thought, the conceptual challenge of philosophical modernity. It takes on the question of the crisis of metaphysics and the decline of the classical system of representation of the subject as self-reflecting consciousness. As a consequence, feminist critical thinkers stress the importance of positive difference as a fundamental category of thought and strategy of action. Our argument also deals with the challenge of post-industrialism and its related economic problems.

This new theoretical context is a great chance for the minorities, the marginals and the people from the periphery, such as women, who had been historically deprived of the right to self-determination: for them, the crisis of the old schemes of subjectivity can be useful. Feminist analyses of the 'crisis', therefore, stress its positivity, that is to say the extent to which feminists allow for alternative values to be postulated. Post-modernism in this case means the systematic loosening up of scientific discourse, working towards displacing reason from its central position, so as to reduce its status to that of simply another kind of discourse among a plurality of possible discourses. Post-modernism is a sort of radical scepticism without relativism. It takes as its starting point the historical decline of the modernist project that equated industrial modernization with progress, and progress with scientific rationality and technological development. The environmental crisis more than any other exemplifies the dangers implicit in the modernist project and reveals the paradox of a scientific-minded system that lays the conditions for its own self-destruction. In such a context, a post-modernist position is the only defensible one in terms of environmental ethics and political agency.

Harding, in a recent revision of her own work on feminist theory, asks, what sort of epistemology is possible and desirable 'after the fall of universal woman'? (Harding 1992: 91). She emphasizes the originality of the contribution of post-colonial and Black feminist theorists and advises all feminists to redirect their theoretical agendas towards a more comprehensive approach, learning from the practice of economically disadvantaged non-European women. Harding suggests that the most effective way to accomplish this is for white feminists to reinvent themselves as 'others', becoming less entrenched in their own cultures. Concretely and as far as the issue of women, the environment and sustainable development is concerned, this entails: learning more about non-European cultures in order to be able to assess the impact upon them of Western science and technology; boycotting the consumerism induced by Western culture, which rests on the economic exploitation of the South. In this respect, she supports the appeal made by DAWN.[2]

Strongly influenced by Haraway's 'situated knowledges' approach, Harding criticizes the fantasy of parthenogenesis that characterizes Western accounts of the history of knowledge. Links between the classical cultures of Antiquity and Mediterranean, African and Middle Eastern cultures are systematically underplayed, creating a self-inflating view of the West. As opposed to this tendency, Harding calls for a practice of situated politics: instead of developing all-inclusive epistemologies, feminists should learn to think starting from the perspective of subjugated others, especially Black, poor and gay women. We shall return to this point.

The new feminist epistemologies

Analysing female oppression in terms of simultaneous symbolic disqualification by patriarchal theoretical representations and concrete exploitation and humiliation in their daily social lives, post-modernist feminists — especially Black feminist theorists and post-colonial critics — focus both on the in-depth structures of subjectivity and the simultaneity of different levels of oppression. This results in the definition of feminism as an epistemological as well as a political struggle. Epistemology here means the political process of comprehending and redefining women as subjects of alternative forms of knowledge and of inscribing these changes into a new social and historical reality for women.

It is quite clear that the aims of feminists who have grasped the historical opportunity of radically questioning the disciplinary foundations of scientific thinking differ from those of male thinkers about the 'crisis' of Western reason. The essential point of divergence is feminists' concern to give their struggles a sexual-specific character, aimed at redefining and empowering the becoming-subjects of women in a cross-cultural perspective.

The central tenet of the post-modern radical epistemology is that the self-legitimation of the One (the male) rests on and is nourished by the exclusion of the Other. Although this takes different historical forms and various manifestations from one culture to another, it remains a constant factor in the organization of society. In this framework, the internal logic of domination by symbolic disqualification cannot be remedied by a straight reversal of the balance of power. Such reversal would in fact leave the dialectical opposition intact; it is the very structures of the framework, not its propositional contents, that must be tackled in order to overcome the power relations that sustain it. In short, it is not enough simply to let women into positions previously occupied by men, be it places of consequence, such as the parliament, the church, the university, development and planning agencies. What matters is that women as newcomers into these places be allowed to redefine the structures in such a way as to make them less discriminatory not only for women but ultimately for all people.

This analysis results in a methodology as well as in a political strategy: it calls for a different reading of women's 'otherness', for a radical redefinition away from domination and subordination. Can difference be disentangled from this hierarchy of values? Can it be made to express new, positive, alternative values? Will women be allowed to *make a difference*? Starting from their experience of sexual difference as depreciation and oppression, can they reshape it into something positive?

More specifically, we think that over the last ten years the central question in feminist theory has become: how to reassemble a vision of female subjectivity after the certainties of gender-dualism have collapsed, privileging notions of the self as process (Scott 1990), complexity (Braidotti 1991), interrelatedness (Haraway 1990), post-colonial simultaneities of oppression (Spivak 1989; Mohanty 1987 and others) and the multilayered technology of the self? In other words, the social and symbolic fate of gendered dualism is at stake here.

> The overall impact of post-modernism is that many other groups now share with Black folks a sense of deep alienation, despair, uncertainty, loss of a sense of grounding even if it is not informed by shared circumstances. Radical post-modernism calls attention to these shared sensibilities which cross the boundaries of class, gender, race, etc. That could be fertile ground for the construction of empathy-ties that would promote recognition of common commitments and serve as a base for solidarity and coalition (bell hooks 1990:27).

The theorists emerging in the 1990s are consequently working along the lines of a multiplicity of variables of definition of female subjectivity: race, class, age, sexual preference and lifestyles count as major axes of identity. They therefore innovate on the classical notion of materialism, in that they are bent on redefining female subjectivity in terms of a network of simultaneous power formations. We shall argue next that a trend seems to be emerging that emphasizes the situated, specific, embodied nature of the feminist subject, while rejecting biological or psychic essentialism. This is a new kind of female embodied materialism.

When speaking of subjectivity, one must begin with the idea of embodiment, that is: of real-life women as bicultural, empirical subjects. It is essential to note the extent to which feminist post-modernist positions have assimilated the insights of psychoanalysis and post-structuralist theory, namely, that bodily experience can neither be reduced to the biological, nor confined to social conditioning. In a new form of 'corporeal materialism', the body is seen not as a natural given or a biological essence, but rather as an area of intersection of the natural with the cultural, where multiple codes of power and knowledge are at work. The body is not an essence, and therefore not an anatomical destiny: it is an individual's primary location in the world, one's primary situation in reality. Consequently, in the radical feminist philosophies of sexual difference, the strategy of repossessing the body aims at elaborating alternative forms of knowledge and representation of the subject. The embodied nature of subjectivity is posited so as to allow for the radical subversion of culture.

This leads to a radical rereading of materialism, away from its strictly Marxist definition. We have seen that for most theorists of difference, the theoretical and political importance of the idea of the embodiment of the subject is that it allows for a critique of dualism as a form of violence. Dualism is a mode of thinking that conceptualizes boundaries as fixed barriers, in a confrontational mode, as for the dividing lines that separate sexuality from society, that is, the private from the public. To uphold the rigid differentiation of the two poles of the dichotomous opposition is to perpetuate an ancient form of violence, an oppositional vision of thought that associates the work of reason to a sort of psychic warfare.

Central to this new feminist materialism, which rests upon the post-structuralists' redefinition of the body and of the relation of knowledge to power, is the work of de Lauretis and Mohanty (de Lauretis 1984, 1988; Mohanty 1987, 1988). Relying on Foucault's notion of the 'materiality' of discourse, de Lauretis approaches the construction of female identity as both a material and a symbolic process. Gender is a complex mechanism — a 'technology' — which defines the subject as male or female in a process of normativity and regulation of what the human being is expected to become.

The key notion in de Lauretis' idea of the regulative function of gender is that this notion produces the very categories it purports to explain. Gender as a process of constructing the subject produces such categories as: men, women, heterosexual, homosexual, pervert and so on. De Lauretis' idea, that gender constructs certain sexed identities, benefits from and builds on Black feminist theorists' idea that the process of gender intersects with other normative variables, such as race and class, to produce a formidable power system. De Lauretis sees gender as a process which organizes differences on the basis of race and other crucial variables, for the purpose of constructing socially 'normal' subjects. She therefore calls for feminists to destabilize the normativity of the dominant forms of sexed identity, and to find new definitions for the female feminist subject.

This position can be summed up as follows: what if the patriarchal mode of representation, which can be named the 'gender system', produced the very categories it purports to deconstruct? Taking gender as a process, de Lauretis emphasizes a point that Foucault had already brought to our attention, namely that the process of power and knowledge also produces the subject as a term in that particular process. Basing her analysis of subjectivity on the co-extensivity of power and the process of becoming-subject, de Lauretis borrows the Foucauldian notion of 'technology of the self' to express the material foundations of this vision of the subject and, more importantly, of the ways in which gender functions.

In other words, what lies at the heart of this materialist redefinition of gender as the technology of the self is the notion of the politics of subjectivity, in the twofold sense of both the constitution of identities and the acquisition of subjectivity meant as forms of empowerment, or entitlement to certain practices. The French term *assujettissement* renders both levels of this process of subjectification; it is both a material and a semiotic process that defines the subject through a number of regulative variables — sex, race, age etc. The acquisition of subjectivity is therefore a process of material (institutional) and discursive (symbolic) practices, the aim of which is both positive — because they allow for forms of empowerment — and regulative — because the forms of empowerment are the site of limitations and disciplining.

On a more theoretical plane, what we see as the central issue here is identity as a site of differences; feminist analyses of the gender system show that the subject occupies a variety of possible positions at different times, across a multiplicity of variables (sex, race, class and so on). The challenge for feminist theory today is how to invent new images of thought which can help us think about change and changing constructions of the self: not by way of the static formulated truths or ready available counter-identities, but the living process of transformation of self and other (Cornell 1991). Whereas previous gender-based perspectives emphasized differences between the sexes, what comes into focus here is differences among women, which prompt the need to find new common grounds for political coalition. We shall return to this point.

Haraway, a primatologist, can be described as one example of a feminist post-modernist whose proposals for alternative methodologies for knowledge production are particularly innovative. She contests the white, male knower and his claim for objectivity first and foremost, on the grounds of his invisibility, the ability to see without being seen, hence avoiding responsibility for what he sees (Haraway 1991). She calls this the 'god-trick'. The disembodied knower is to be replaced by an embodied subject that discloses the position from which she/he is seeing and speaking. Thus, we shift from disembodied to situated knowledges.

A central feature of Haraway's proposal is the conception of the object of research as agent, as active participant of the research project. The embodied subject, in recognition of his/her own split and multiple identities, can reach the object of research by placing him/herself into the position of the object (Haraway calls this mobile positioning). This allows the subject to strike up power-sensitive conversations with the object.

Thus, subject and object of research engage in 'conversations' on a more equal footing. Fox Keller's analysis of the work of Barbara Maclintock had already brought out this point about the affinity between the scientist and the object of research, but Haraway develops this insight into a radical epistemology. The researcher, by positioning her/himself as closely as possible to the object/agent learns to see from the latter's point of view compassionately, but without pretending to be the other. Being in a certain position does not necessarily facilitate a critical vision. The subject, split into multiple positions and multiple identities, is able to see from one of these positions within him/herself rather than pretending to 'be' the object; this is the image of the feminist subject engaged in research. To be completely the other, in all his/her/its full positionality, is impossible.

Unless this sort of approach to research (on women's conditions in the South for example) is adopted, non-Western women as the objects of research will, in this case, be confined to a position of 'otherness': either neglected and excluded, or, at the other extreme, iconized as total victims. Non-Western women researchers of the DAWN network have proposed to develop an alternative vision of development from the point of view of the 'poor Third World woman'. But the image of the 'poor Third World woman' as the conjunction of all types of subordination, the ultimate other, may simply become a fetish. As Haraway points out, subjugation in itself is no ground for any privileged access to superior vision. Subjugation might provide some clues, because visions from below the platforms of power are less prone to distortion, but subjugation in itself holds no key to better or more objective vision.

The limits of expansion have led to the global integration of all peoples and nature, understood as human and natural resources, into the project of progress (Haraway 1991). Western capital associated with the Western patriarchal project of science and technology at the nexus of power have created a monolithic order. First through colonialism and now via the development process, the Western powers have turned everything into resources for appropriation in which, finally, the object of knowledge itself is only matter for the seminal power, the act of the knower (Haraway 1991:197). What can feminists do about it?

Haraway's answer rests on three notions, all of which have to do with political agency in the sense of transformations in both an ethical and an epistemological sense. Firstly, the notion of feminist theory becomes redefined in terms of non-taxonomical figurations; secondly, feminist subjectivity is reconceptualized as 'cyborg' — that is, a multiple, complex and highly technical form of consciousness; and thirdly, scientific objectivity is redefined as 'situated knowledges'.

Taking as her main point of reference the impact of the new technologies (micro-electronics, telecommunication and video-games including video-wars) on the condition of women in society, Haraway stresses the importance of the global village in accommodating a new wave of offshore and electronic cottage industries, most of which employ women. Reflecting on the changes that this new system of production imposes on society at large, Haraway challenges feminists to recognize the political and conceptual complexity of their times. Like Spivak (1989) she is aware of the new forms of domination and exclusion implicit in the contemporary high-tech world order.

In Haraway's analysis, biotechnology is the radically new factor in the 1990s; that is, the degree of autonomy, mastery and sophistication, attained by devices that take 'life' and 'the living organisms' as object. Much of this technology is optical; it has to do with increased powers of vision. Nowadays, the biotechnological gaze has penetrated into the very intimate structure of living matter, seeing the invisible.

An integral part of these technological developments is the new weaponry developed for war. Need we remind ourselves that the human technological subject is an eminent war-monger? Given the contemporary technological co-extensivity of war and the bio-sciences, feminists are directly implicated in the confrontation with technology and, consequently, are intimately concerned by modern warfare techniques.

A political coalition is thus both possible and necessary today between feminists in peace movements and post-modernist epistemologists working on technology. In other words, women fighting for peace, far from upholding an essentialized vision of nature as nurturing and therefore as analogically female (this is the theory of women as 'naturally' pacifists, because of their reproductive capacity), can be seen as unveiling the belligerent function of technology, that is to say as proposing a critique of technocratic culture. Haraway's work has the merit of reminding us that women's political activities need to be recoded in a denaturalized and non-essentialistic manner. By the same token, she urges feminists to make a greater effort to find imaginative and innovative forms of representation for their political positions.

Firmly implanted in the tradition of materialism, Haraway reminds us that rethinking the subject amounts to rethinking his/her bodily roots. Following Foucault, Haraway draws our attention to the construction and manipulation of individuals, so as to make them function as docile, knowable bodies in our present social system. She invites us to think of what new kinds of bodies are being constructed right now, that is: what kind of gender system is being constructed under our very noses.

Here, Haraway's main interlocutor is Foucault. In his analysis of the constitution of modern bodies, Foucault develops the idea of 'bio-power' as a simultaneously political and epistemological device. The political regime of bio-power aims at drawing both an anatomical cartography of the human body, and at elaborating a discourse about human subjectivity. This results in legitimating, on the one hand, an empirical kind of knowledge about the bodily mechanism and, on the other, the transcendental structure of subjectivity.

This point about the simultaneity of scientific, political and imaginary or cultural factors in the production of systems of power is important.[3] It results in technology not being seen *a priori* as opposed and inimical to humanity, or the human and social sciences. It is rather that a primitive sort of anthropomorphism pervades the technical universe: all tools are therefore products of the creative human imagination, they mimic and multiply the potencies of the body. Technology fulfils the human's biological destiny in such an intimate way that the organic and the technical complement become adapted to each other. For Haraway as well as for Foucault, this mutual receptivity of the organ to its technical extension, of biology to technology, is the reason why the distinction nature-culture is discarded in favour of the discourse on bio-power: the political reflection on the subject as an embodied organism, a bio-cultural entity *par excellence*.

While sharing a great deal of these premises with the French epistemologists, however, Haraway also challenges Foucault's redefinition of power. Strong of the feminists' critiques of the gender-undifferentiated notion of 'power' in Foucault's work, Haraway also supports Jameson's idea (Jameson 1984) that a post-modernist politics is made necessary by the historical collapse of the traditional left and that it represents the left's chance to reinvent itself from within. Haraway notes that contemporary power no longer works by normalized heterogeneity, but rather by networking, communication redesigns and multiple interconnections. She concludes that Foucault 'names a form of power at its moment of implosion. The discourse of bio-politics gives way to technobabble' (Haraway, in Nicholson 1990:194).

Whereas Foucault's analysis rests on a nineteenth century view of the production system, Haraway inscribes her analysis of the condition of women into a contemporary analysis of the post-industrial system of production. Arguing that white capitalist patriarchy has turned into the 'informatics of domination' (ibid: 203), Haraway argues that women have been 'cannibalized' by the new technologies; the process of assimilation of women into industrial or post-industrial societies is such that they have disappeared as sex-specific social agents. In other words: the post-industrial system makes oppositional politics utterly redundant; in a context of dissolution of political identities based on sex or class — which is the negative aspect of the post-modern condition — a new politics must be invented, on the basis of a more adequate understanding of how the contemporary subject functions.

Feminists in the 1990s must replace naive beliefs in global sisterhood or more strategic alliances based on common interests, with a new kind of politics, based on temporary and mobile coalitions and therefore on affinity. Arguing that 'innocence and the corollary insistence on victimhood as the only ground for insight has done enough damage' (Haraway 1991:157), Haraway calls for a kind of feminist politics that could embrace 'partial, contradictory, permanently unclosed constructions of personal and collective selves'.

The central question here is the extent to which sexual difference meant as the difference that women can make to society, — that is, not as a naturally or historically given difference, but as an open-ended project to be constructed and acted out politically — also allows women to think of all their other differences. Foremost among them: differences of race, class and sexual lifestyles. But how can all these differences avoid resulting in fragmentation? Can women be represented and act as a collective political and epistemological subject? If the universal standpoint necessitates neutrality, the question then becomes not only how to think sexual difference as positivity, but rather how to avoid essentialism in the sense of biological or psychic determinism in the feminist project to redefine female subjectivity.

Related to this redefinition of identity is the question of how to rethink differences and otherness. How to restore inter-subjectivity so as to allow differences to create a bond, that is a political contract among women, so as to affect lasting political changes? In terms of other humans, the question becomes: is there a space for the unappropriate/d others? (Trinh Minh Ha 1989) How can feminists build a new kind of collectivity in differences?

Donna Haraway's aim is to think of an anti-relativistic, specific community of historically-located semiotic-material subjects, seeking for connections and articulations in a non-ethno/gender-centred manner. In this respect, her main interlocutor is Harding, who defends instead a view of feminist theory based on the positivity of female experience and its potential to redefine values of common interest. Haraway invites us to think of the community as being built on the foundations of a commonly shared basis of collective figures of speech, or foundational myths, which are also turned to purposeful political use as tools for action. These foundational myths, which are tools for intervention in reality, in that they have impact on our imagination, are also situated knowledges because they make feminism accountable. In other words, feminism is about grounding, it is about foundations. It is also about story-telling: the collective sharing of certain myths and belief-systems. Again, the role played by women writers and artists in the making of commonly shared myths and beliefs must be emphasized.

Haraway suggests eliminating the image of 'Mother Nature' altogether because in the current situation it implies women's collective status as victim. Instead, she suggest a new image — that of nature as a coding trickster (Haraway 1991). She proposes the image of the 'cyborg' as a suitable metaphor or political myth, by which to represent the feminist knowing subject. The cyborg is a creature in a non-dualistic and therefore a post-gender world, outside the symbolic system centred on the phallus; it is also the post-nuclear and the post-industrial representation of a subject that is no longer universalistic: it does not claim to represent the generic human viewpoint, but rather recognizes and even embodies the specificity of spatio-temporal locations. The recognition of specificity, however, is not mere relativism: being situated somewhere is rather the prerequisite for avoiding normative, regulative, hegemonic and exclusionary forms of thought.

To emphasize the fact that 'situatedness' is other than relativism, Haraway stresses the connection-making quality, the need for inter-relationality, receptivity and communication. The cyborg as a working image is a figure of a combination between the human and the technological; it answers the difficult question: how do we figure a collective non-generic feminist humanity? How do we reconcile the radical historical specificity of women with the insistence on constructing new figurations of humanity as a whole?

The post-modernist epistemological project thus defined is not specifically feminist - though feminism fits into it, having contributed historically to creating the *a priori* conditions for a critique of the universal, rationalist paradigm. The specificity of the feminist standpoint is in terms of gender differences and gender-specific analyses, but everything in feminist theory and practice makes it capable of elaborating general theoretical frameworks. In an attempt to translate Haraway's flamboyant language into a more sedate style, Sandra Harding makes some concrete suggestions for how the cyborg-theory of a situated subject could lead to a revalorization of 'rainbow politics'(Harding 1992b). Following are the concrete applications that Harding sees:

1) The deconstruction of false universalism of Western knowledge systems. Harding describes the blind faith in the powers of rationality as the central myth of 'indigenous' Westerners. She argues that 'from an anthropological perspective, faith in scientific rationality is at least partly responsible for many of the Western beliefs and behaviours that appear most irrational to people whose life patterns and projects do not easily fit with those of the modern West' (Harding 1991:3).

In this respect, Harding suggests that it would be a major step forward if Westerners made an effort to learn more about people of Third World descent, their lives, histories, thoughts and writings.

2) Revalorizing the term 'feminism'. This term is widely used as a critical epithet in the Second and Third Worlds and in some Western sub-cultures, by women as well as by men, 'to prevent women from organizing across class, race and national borders and even just to "keep women in their place".' (Harding 1991: 6-7). An equally pernicious tendency, according to Harding, consists in rejecting the term 'feminism' but then advance the very same intellectual and political programmes as those defended by the feminists. The negative charge of the term 'feminism' is particularly strong in the work of Third World women, who see it as synonymous with Eurocentric and class oppressive agendas.

3) Decentring the whiteness of feminism. In light of the above, we need to decentre the dominant position occupied by white, middle-class, heterosexual Western women, while still generating feminist analyses from the perspective of women's oppression. In other words, how to be situated without being ethnocentric. Harding connects this to the project of 'reinventing ourselves as others', which is a sociological version of deconstructivism. Once people of European descent learn to see themselves as bearers of race, and their race is perceived as a structural relationship, whiteness will no longer be an invisible feature and the identification of whiteness with a universalistic stand will cease. This is a form of 'disloyalty to civilization' which will encourage cross-cultural coalitions among women.

4) Broaden the scope of feminist struggle. Harding stresses how important it is to conduct scientific and political arguments in the places where scientific and political decisions are being made. This means that efforts must be made to reach as wide a field of forces affecting women in society as possible. This also opens the door to coalitions with men on issues of common concerns.

5) Taking the challenge of Black/post-colonial/non-Western epistemology seriously. It is not easy to 'add' women of colour to discussions about science and technology, because of the dearth of books and other material written by them, a fact that is significant and should be examined. Their scarcity is one of the effects of racism and it makes it all the harder for Western and non-Western women to interact. The starting point for meaningful interaction, however, must be the recognition that there is no typical 'Third World woman' that can be the object of study of Western science and technology. There is no universal image of the oppressed woman, but only different kinds of feminism, generated from different conditions in women's lives. One important consequence of this is that feminist scholars must learn to claim the perspectives of 'despised' identities of minority or marginal women.

In conclusion, post-modernist politics requires rainbow politics, in the sense of situated coalitions for replacing well-intentioned but ineffectual concerns for emancipation with programmes for supporting them at the scientific and epistemological levels, as well as through political organization. As we have tried to argue throughout this chapter, this emphasis on the politics of coalition requires as its precondition the acceptance of differences among women as a positive factor. In the words of Kum-Kum Bhavani:

> I am not simply a woman, nor Black, nor a university professor, not Indian, nor someone who teaches social psychology and feminist studies, nor an aunt, nor heterosexual, nor a socialist. Each of these categories is both circumscribed and limited by the other categories, and each of them can always change. Indeed they have!. . .And I would always claim, when asked why I went to women's groups, trade union meetings and to anti-racist demonstrations that it was necessary to organise autonomously, at that moment, according to our identities, in order to usher in the day when our differences would not be barriers to communication and fulfilling relationships, but, rather would be causes of celebration of the diversity of humanity. While my optimism has become rather daunted in the era of this current New World Order, I still know that this is the aim for all of us who try to make the world a better place (Kum-Kum Bhavani 1992: 17-18).

Notes

1. See Chapter 6 on Alternatives with Women for a New Era, DAWN.
2. See Chapter 6.
3. This theoretical approach seems to characterize the French epistemological school from Bachelard down to Foucault. It is an interesting point of cross-cultural exchanges that an American thinker like Haraway is so close to the French tradition that consists in not regarding technology as an anti-humanistic device.

4. The Relationship between Women and Nature: Debates within Feminism

It must be stressed that in this chapter discussions about images of women as Eve, femme fatale, sinner and whore which are important in feminist discourse are left aside as having no direct relevance for the purpose of this book. An important development within feminism is the emergence of ecofeminism which has been highly influential within the WED debate. In order to better grasp the feminist roots of ecofeminism[1] we shall discuss some aspects of feminist thought in the context of the history of the women's movement.

Feminism has been one of the most inspiring and subversive critical analyses and practices of this century. Its opposition to the dominant modes of production and politics, its re-evaluation of accepted ways of thinking and behaving, its critique of culture and everyday life is derived from a wide variety of positions which sometimes intersect and at others are contradictory. Together they form a complex chorus of voices in which certain themes, dominant at times, then temporarily dormant, return with different accents and emphases. A recurrent topic of debate within the feminist movement has been the relation between women and nature. Feminist thinkers have been fascinated by the eternal conundrum of how to denounce male dominance and to fight for women's special concerns, while denying that women are 'naturally' subordinated and thus 'special'.

Because the women's movement, as the political expression of feminist concerns, has never spoken with a single voice, it has been very difficult to characterize. As a definition we find the following description most useful. We understand a women's movement as the whole spectrum of conscious and unconscious individual or collective activities, groups or organizations which are concerned with diminishing various aspects of gender subordination.[2] Today, the demand for women's education is routinely made by wide sectors of society and can hardly be called subversive any more. Less than a century ago this same demand triggered violent reactions.

The women's movement is striving towards the transformation of society. There is no consensus on what this transformed world should look like and it is even impossible to conceive of such a consensus. Transformation should be seen not as a product, but rather as a process. Most women's movements seem to agree that a minimum package is one that ends subordination on the basis of gender, race, ethnicity and class, and stops degradation of the environment.

Streams within feminism

Several attempts have been made to categorize the various streams within the women's movement, most of them dating from the mid-1980s when apparently the need for labelling was strong. Focusing on present day, white, American feminism, Eisenstein (1984) distinguishes three phases with their corresponding theoretical perspectives: 1) visionary and utopian feminist writers called for equality and sisterhood; 2) characterized by an insistence on difference, which in Eisenstein's view led to essentialism and the metaphysics of Mary Daly; and 3) that feminism should recognize diversity, put more emphasis on socio-economic issues (which in the US were neglected) and reclaim its radicalism.

Young (1985) takes a different approach and distinguishes between humanist and gynocentric feminism. In her view humanist feminism 'defines gender as accidental to humanity' and urges both women and men to 'pursue self-development in those creative and intellectual activities that distinguish human beings from the rest of nature' (Young 1985: 174). Gynocentric feminism is based on recognition of the superiority of values embodied in traditionally female experience, and rejects the values (violence and individualism) embodied in traditionally male-dominated institutions.

According to Fraser (1992) Kristeva identifies three types of feminism. Her first two categories overlap with Young's typology, an egalitarian, reform-oriented humanist feminism, versus a culturally-oriented gynocentric version of feminism. Under this last category she subsumes the *écriture féminine* of such French writers as Cixous and Irigaray who aim to foster the expression of a feminine sexual and symbolic specificity. The third category Kristeva distinguishes consists of those feminists who claim that the category 'woman' does not exist, and that collective identities are dangerous fictions.

Jaggar (1983) distributes four nametags among various feminist streams: liberal, marxist, socialist and radical. As already pointed out in the introduction to this book, we are wary of the labelling exercise in which we are involved in the case of the feminist movement for the following reasons. First, because we are struck by the complexity of views expressed by authors commonly classified in one of the above-mentioned categories. Second, because we fear that such a neat exercise might lead to distorted and simplified views of the movement, and to fragmentation and divisiveness. As the previous chapter indicated, we would like to stress that for us the transformational power of the women's movement lies in its varied approaches to women's subordination and in the recognition that this diversity is a source of its strength, as it enables women to challenge patterns of domination from various perspectives and several levels simultaneously. For us, feminism is not a canonized body of theories, but rather a widely divergent, sometimes contradictory amalgam of positions.

The first wave of feminism

A popular misconception concerning the first wave of the feminist movement arises from the idea that their major concern was its obsession with equal rights for women, and women's equality with men. Women in Europe, Latin America and the United States, as a 'legally inferior caste' (Oakley, 1981), were severely hampered by their lack of any rights, therefore, naturally the attainment of equal rights was a serious concern. But the early women's movements were much richer in their ideas and debates, much more radical and subtle than we nowadays give them credit for. Thus, today's dichotomy of equality versus difference is not completely novel. Looking back into that history might enlighten present day political struggles.

A central concern of the present 'post-modern' phase of feminism is the conviction that women's subordination is a construction. But this is not novel; the debate on 'equality versus difference' was introduced in the earlier phase of the movement (see previous chapter), even though the accents were put differently. As Oakley (following Walters) writes about Wollstonecraft's *Vindication*:[3] 'the most radical aspect of the *Vindication* is its central idea that femininity is an artificial construct, an imposition of patriarchal culture, yet is regarded as an immutably natural state' (Oakley 1981:4). This conviction in different wordings and with different emphases would be echoed by feminists well into the twentieth century.

There were also certain streams and writers in the women's movement who departed from a view which emphasized women's difference from men. This idea was most pronounced in discussions on prostitution and traffic in women and children. Women were seen as morally superior, and in that capacity had a special responsibility to defend humanity's level of morality against human (read male) vices. Female virtue was set against male vice.

As Jansz (1990) and Scott (1988) point out, the issue of 'difference' figured in the women's movement in two other ways. First, women made use of their own separate, homo-social spheres to organize their activities, including those centring on equal rights. Second, when they argued for equal political rights they did so on the grounds that being different from men should not deny them the rights men had.

A similar argument was heard in the debate on women's education. Virginia Woolf, in *Three Guineas* argued that women should be allowed the same education as men, on the grounds that access to knowledge was coveted by all. On the other hand, many earlier male and female protagonists for women's education defended the issue with an appeal to women's special status as mothers: better educated women would be better mothers.

Echoes of this debate are still heard. As di Leonardo writes, both 'presentday essentialists and conservative anti-feminists have continued to draw on the nineteenth-century storehouse of moral motherhood symbolism, stressing women's innate identity with and nurturance of children and nature' (di Leonardo 1991: 26). Although di Leonardo fails to mention the critical ways in which present-day essentialism departs from the 'female virtue' perspective, she does point to the inherent danger of such essentialist positions. The way the first wave of the women's movement faded away does give rise to serious concern. The conservative swing taken by the women's movement in the 1920s and 1930s is one of the major causes of its downfall. When 'female virtue' was primarily located in the revaluation of motherhood, the women's movement was swamped in campaigns to improve women's position in the home, for instance by setting up domestic science institutes.

In the US, this right-wing backlash, in which the first wave of the women's movement was submerged, was nourished both by fear of the Bolshevist revolution and by the increase in wealth and consumerism (Rapp and Ross, 1986), as well as by what they call the heterosexual revolution. This movement, building on ideas of what were supposedly women's and men's 'natural' sex drives, promoted companionate marriages between heterosexual partners. Havelock Ellis and other sexologists discredited the homo-social sphere of feminism and female friendships. Posing as feminists they claimed to provide women with the right to a vaginal orgasm. This sudden concern for women's sexuality stemmed from an insistence on women's 'natural' passivity. The spinster was out, long live the yielding wife.[4]

Nazi Germany

The most disturbing example of the potential implications of an appeal to traditional womanhood as a 'natural' identity were to be found in Nazi Germany. Many German women supported an ideology and practice that effectively expelled them from public influence, while embracing a role geared towards the 'increase and preservation of the species of the race' (Koonz 1987). Women had been granted suffrage in 1918 and fundamental legal equality between the sexes had been ensured by the constitution in 1919. Hitler's promise to end 'the war between the sexes' by rescinding these reforms attracted men who were concerned about what they perceived as this incursion on their natural rights. According to Hitler: 'The wonderful thing about nature and providence is that no conflict between the sexes can occur as long as each party performs the functions prescribed for it by nature' (cited after Koonz, 1986:270).

But Hitler's speeches on a 'natural' womanhood also attracted large numbers of women. His appeal to nature was close to the discourse of German, middle-class women's organizations in the late 1920s, as Koonz (1986) convincingly demonstrates. For, as she suggests, leaders of this movement had for decades based their claims to equality on the proposition that women, if emancipated, could offer invaluable services to the community, based on their special characteristics. 'In the face of anti-feminists' hysterical anxieties about "masculinized" women, proponents of emancipation. . . vowed: "We want our special nature to be especially esteemed." . . . Women in politics . . .emphasized Romantic notions of women's special nature' (Koonz 1986: 272). Thus women claimed their own 'Lebensraum' within public life beyond the reach of male hegemony (conceived as the realms of finance and formal politics), for only then could they bring 'social peace' to the nation.

The Nazis were the first to set up a Women's Bureau, in 1934, focusing on marriage counselling, mother-care centres and mother's education. Women were seen to have a special ethical responsibility as 'bearers of culture'. Even within Nazi ideology, however, the location of women's special concerns might differ. Conservative women promoted home economics, while more 'progressive' Nazi women attempted to rescue women from prostitution rings, attacked pornography and opposed divorce reforms and abortion. Some Nazi women leaders even had their spiritual sides, claiming that their work was truly 'missionary'. Koonz quotes one Nazi woman who claimed that she fought ' . . . to save culture and virtue in a world possessed by materialism' (Koonz 1986: 278).

The troubled example of women in European Fascism illustrates the complexity and longevity of the association between women and nature. The woman/nature or equality versus difference debate meandered through various streams of the women's movement throughout the first wave, with differing political consequences. It is noteworthy that the meaning ascribed to nature carried different connotations, and that the sex considered to be more 'natural' also differed. As Strathern (1980) has demonstrated, no single meaning can be ascribed to nature or culture in Western thought. There is no consistent dichotomy, only a 'matrix of contrasts'. As indicated, sometimes men were seen as closer to nature (male vice), and women were called upon to 'civilize' them. More often, however, women's supposedly closer connection to nature justified male domination. Only the dichotomy itself is constant, as is women's subordination, hence the emphasis feminist theorists have placed on the critique of dualism (see previous chapter). If women were seen as more virtuous and as members of a superior moral order this provided an excuse to exclude them from the more profane bastions of male power in politics and the economy. Conversely, if they were depicted as less rational than men, as childlike and capricious, these attributes were considered sufficient reason to keep them under male supervision.[5] Feminists reacted to this either by denying their special association with nature (equal rights), or by claiming a superior morality (female virtue, bearer of social peace). This last option could be deployed for totally opposite political practices. In the first decades of the women's movement it served as an important rallying point, the basis of women's separate, homo-social associations. But in Nazi Germany the location of women's moral superiority lay outside the bastions of male power; they could reign supreme only in the home and in their organizations. Women therefore became powerless to resist their ultimate degradation and the glorification of racism and virility with all its tragic consequences.

The second wave

At the end of the 1960s and the beginning of the 1970s the second wave of feminism hit the press in many countries in Western and Northern Europe and in the US. A radical, aggressive movement of young women startled society with brazen actions, daring analyses and bold tactics. These women, who had grown up in a political environment of hierarchical, conservative and racist tendencies which were challenged by a no less hierarchical leftist movement, decided to do away with hierarchy. In the US, the Black civil rights movement provided a political momentum and inspiration. In Europe the women's movement arose in the wake of student unrest (Paris 1968) and mass protest against the Vietnam war. There the origins of the second wave of the women's movement were located in a workers' and students' movement which was rooted in a discourse with stongly Marxian and Freudian overtones. Despite its aversion to authoritarian power and hierarchy, European feminism has always maintained close ties with socialism. The emphasis on consciousness-raising was inspired by the Black consciousness movement in the US.

The search for identity which started in these homo-social consciousness-raising groups initially led to an investigation of the roots of women's common oppression. Factors such as race and class were downplayed. The realization that gender identity is not universal, but multiple and often contradictory, came later, and only after the intervention of Black women and women from the South, who protested against the homogenizing trend adopted by white Western feminism. Feminist identity politics grew out of a passionate search for a new praxis of feminism, coupled with a rejection of the knowledge systems which had produced an identity of women as passive and 'naturally' subservient. As de Lauretis writes, the '. . . feminist concept of identity is not at all the statement of an essential nature of Woman, whether defined biologically or philosophically, but rather a political-personal strategy of survival and resistance that is also, at the same time, a critique and a mode of knowledge' (de Lauretis 1986: 9).

The present wave of the women's movement was largely nourished on women's resentment of the fact that the mere acquisition of legal rights has failed to incorporate effectively their issues on the agenda of parliaments, political parties, trade unions and other political bodies. Apparently, the successful outcome of the first wave of the women's movement's insistence on equality and reforms (for which the first wave is remembered) had not effectively challenged women's subordination. The critique of male domination had to be stronger. Three different and sometimes overlapping strategies were employed: a search for the roots of women's power; attacks on male sexism, especially in science in general;[6] and, in particular, biological determinism.

In the feminist culture of the 1970s the search for matriarchies became popular (see Gould Davis, 1971 and Morgan, 1972). A return to goddess worship was also seen in some sections of the women's movement as a move which might ultimately lead to the coming of a new women's era characterized by nurturance and non-violence. (We shall return to consider this position later in this chapter.)

The feminist critique of male science started by attempting to make women's activities and experiences socially recognized and analytically visible. Various intellectual traditions were attacked for their sexist biases and, as in the case of Marxism, concepts (such as labour, production and reproduction) were redefined. As we argued in the previous chapter, the limitations of these efforts became clear when feminist scientists began to realize that women could not simply be written in without distorting the very basis upon which the construct of science was built. Science began to be seen not as the vessel of an eternal, objective truth, but, as Hubbard put it, as:

> [A] human construct that came about under a particular set of historical conditions when men's domination of nature seemed a positive and worthy goal. The conditions have changed and we know now that the path we are travelling is more likely to destroy nature than to explain and improve it. Women have recognized more often than men that we are part of nature and that its fate is in human hands that have not cared for it well (Hubbard, 1982:80).

When science was unmasked as an edifice erected in the interest of male domination over nature and women, essential, universal, rational man himself was deconstructed (see Chapter 3). This critique, again, led to the realization that 'woman' was not a universal category either. 'Once essential and universal man dissolves, so does his hidden companion, woman' (Harding 1989: 17).

Socio-biology was the main target of the feminist critique of science. Socio-biology is a branch of science that attempts to link social behaviour with biological drives. Male promiscuity, for example, is justified by reference to a man's drive to propagate his genes through as many offspring as possible. Rape, too, is explained by men's uncontrollable sexual drive. Similarly, socio-biologists claim that women's domesticity and sexual passivity have a biological basis and, therefore, are 'natural' (Birke 1986). Haraway quotes Barash, one of the founding fathers of socio-biology, who claims that 'socio-biology . . . may help us discover our own nature and allow us to eavesdrop on the whispers of biology within us all' (Haraway 1991: 73-4). This exercise of eavesdropping has laid the foundation for 'scientific' proofs of an innate male aggression and female passivity. Bleier points out the sloppy science behind it all. She demonstrates that socio-biology's claims which justify racial discrimination and women's subordination are based on 'inferences drawn from fallacious analogies, speculations, subjective belief and illogical thought processes' (Bleier 1991: 250). Haraway goes one step further and attacks the basis of socio-biology itself. Based on her own reading of the interpretation of primatological research, she concludes that 'the patriarchal voice of socio-biology is less the effusive sexism that ripples over the whole plane of the text than it is the logic of domination embedded in fashioning the tool of the word' (Haraway 1991:74).

Even before this debate reached its heyday in circles of feminist academics, Shulamith Firestone dealt with it in *The Dialectic of Sex* in 1970. This book became immensely popular in the women's movement of the 1970s and was widely discussed. Drawing on Utopian socialists such as Fourier and Owen and the socialist thinkers Engels and Bebel she makes the case for 'the deepest revolution of all', that of cybernetic socialism. To facilitate this revolution, she writes, women must fight for the elimination of sexual classes and to seize the control over reproduction. Only then, with technological child-bearing, would women be freed 'from the tyranny of their biology' (Firestone 1970:238), would all women and children be integrated in the wider society, would economic exploitation be abolished and sexual freedom prevail. Thus, Firestone not only demonstrated that women's association with nature was a man-made construction, she wanted to control nature completely by the removal from women's bodies of biological reproduction.

Écriture féminine

If Firestone's solution to the biological determinist underpinnings of women's subordination is to do away with the biological aspect thanks to advanced technologies, feminist writers such as Cixous and Irigaray in France and Daly in the US, opted for a revalorization of the feminine. Again, others writers agree with Haraway who strongly advises against this course: 'I believe it is . . . less responsible in present historical conditions to pursue anti-scientific tales about nature that idealize women, nurturing or some other entity argued to be free of male war-tainted pollution' (Haraway 1991: 107). Is this debate for or against female biology then a replay of that in the first wave of the women's movement? As we shall argue, the issue at stake is similar, but the debate itself has become both more complex and more urgent with the realization that nature itself is in danger and the ecofeminists' insistence on women's responsibilities for the environment. Paradoxically, it is the emergence of concerns for the environment that redistributes the terms of the debate on women and nature. Also, the various agents within this debate present more complex and subtle analyses.

The turn French deconstructivist feminists such as Cixous and Irigaray have taken in the debate on sexual difference is a move beyond the empirical body. Not biology, but discourse becomes the terrain on which sexual difference expresses itself. What these feminists are concerned with is the repression of 'the feminine, the bodily, the unconscious' as the outcome of the workings of male-dominated science, with its insistence on certain standards of objectivity, rationality and universality, as Dallery writes. 'It is the phallocratic discourse which silences women's voices' (Dallery 1989:53).

Deconstructivist feminism has been accused of being essentialist and biological reductionist, for instance by de Beauvoir. She has insisted that this kind of post-modern feminism is based on the ontological differences between women and men and is essentially concerned with the 'construction of a counter-penis' (Dallery 1989:54, quoting Simons and Benjamin). But, writes Dallery, this is not what this kind of feminism is actually about. Deconstructive feminists are not concerned with bodies, as you cannot 'know' bodies without referring to the discourse by which they are constituted. In the view of Cixous and Irigaray human bodies are always mediated by language, and must always be read as signs. So, according to Dallery,

> French feminism, *écriture féminine*, essentially deconstructs the phallic organization of sexuality and its code, which positions woman's sexuality and signified body as a mirror or complement to male sexual identity. And, correspondingly, this discourse constructs the genuine multiple otherness of woman's libidinal economy — her eroticism — which has been symbolically repressed in language and denied by patriarchal culture (ibid).

For these authors there is no 'real' body which can be empirically deconstructed in its relation to nature. The task they set themselves is that of 'constructing a non-phallomorphic sexuality' (Dallery 1989:60). The praxis of these feminists is thus not so much located in socio-economic and political struggles as in the deconstruction of symbolic speech. Their major contribution to the women's movement is in the realm of the symbolic rather than in that of the political and ideological, and in their insistence on women's erotic pleasure. It remains doubtful, however, whether this 'praxis' appeals to feminists in the South, whose praxis is much more related to socio-economic and political issues and who resist uses of the homogenizing term 'woman'. Also, the move away from empirical nature has made the link with the physical environment, in which women live, problematic. Their deconstruction of the (phallo)logocentrism of Western knowledge on the other hand is directly relevant to the efforts of ecofeminists to attack male-dominated structures of knowledge.

Cultural feminism

The revalorization of the feminine which American feminists such as Daly, Griffin, Morgan and Rich propose is more culturally and spiritually oriented. Women's greater humanism, pacifism, nurturance and spiritual development are celebrated. And all this, because women are closer to nature. Griffin, in *Reclaim the Earth* (1983) maintains that women, being less severely alienated from nature than are most men, must and will liberate the earth.

Rich (1977) locates women's closest relation to nature in motherhood. This is linked up with what she calls the 'cosmic essence of womanhood' which connects women with the essentially creative and nurturing aspects of nature. But motherhood is not only analysed as a 'reality'. Rich also points out that, as an institution for reproduction, it has become the site of women's subordination:

> The ancient, continuing envy, awe, and dread of the male for the female capacity to create life has repeatedly taken the form of hatred for every other female aspect of creativity. Not only have women been told to stick to motherhood, but we have been told that our intellectual or aesthetic creations were inappropriate, inconsequential, or scandalous, an attempt to become 'like men' (Rich 1976: 39).

It is because of the process of women being pushed into this 'body-trap', that they have reacted by denying their association with nature altogether. Understandably, Rich argues, in doing so women have thrown away the baby with the bathwater:

> The body has been made so problematic for women that it has often seemed easier to shrug it off and travel as a disembodied spirit. But this reaction against the body is now coming into synthesis with new enquiries into the actual — as opposed to the culturally warped —

power inherent in female biology, however we choose to use it, and by no means limited to the maternal function (ibid:40).

If Rich is mainly concerned with women's actual biological power which, according to Braidotti (1991), might eventually lead to a new feminist ethic, Daly is focusing on women's spiritual essence. In Gyn/Ecology (Daly 1978) she sets out to produce a list of male crimes against women, ranging from Chinese footbinding to European witch-hunting. In her next book, *Pure Lust* (1984) Daly speaks of the 'polluting, poisoning, contaminating evil of men's rule of phallocracy, . . .which is the root of rapism, racism, gynocide, genocide and ultimately biocide' (Daly 1984:379), and proposes that women go on an individual psychic voyage to overcome male domination. As women are 'rooted, as are animals, trees, wind and seas in the Earth', whereas men are 'radically separate from the natural harmony of the universe', only women can take this route. This path towards a 'hagocentric psychic space' will eventually lead us to rediscover our affinity with nature and it will of necessity in Daly's view subvert male language, creating the 'radiant words' which will liberate 'lusty women.' (Segal 1987:18,19).

Daly also points to the necessity of overcoming dualistic male-dominated science.

> The inexhaustible Other encountered by a Be-Witching woman is, first of all, her Self, Who flows in underground connectedness with all Elemental be-ing. This Self is Virgin — uncaptured and untamed — transcending the labels of man. . .The famous "subject-object" split of patriarchal science and philosophy is challenged by the fact/act of her realizing her Self as Other (Daly 1984:394).

Close to the post-structuralist praxis of deconstructing male-dominated discourse, Daly concludes:

> Decoding the myths and unsnapping the traps that have kept us from bonding, we weave with the Grace of Be-Friending...Weaving new Wonders, we intend to be Fore-Crones of Gnostic Nag-Nations (ibid:411).

Daly has been immensely influential in the American women's movement. Following her appeal to 'weave' our own forms of knowing, feminist pacifists in their peace camps, for instance, have elevated the spider to a symbol of women's spiritual power, warning visitors not to destroy the webs in the toilets. In ecofeminist discourse the term 'weaving' is also widely used, as for instance in *Reweaving the World* (Diamond and Orenstein 1990).

It is a small step from Daly to the celebration of strong and creative female power by adherents to the worship of the goddess, such as Carol

P. Christ. She writes about the 'legitimacy and beauty of female power' which is the 'affirmation of the female body and the life cycle expressed in it' (Christ 1991). To her the relationship between women and nature is quite straightforward:

> Because of women's unique position as menstruants, birthgivers and those who have traditionally cared for the young and the dying, women's connection to the body, nature and the world has been obvious. Women were denigrated because they seemed more carnal, fleshy and earthly than the culture-creating males...as symbolized in the myth of Eve, who is traditionally viewed as sexual temptress, the epitome of women's carnal nature...The denigration of the female body is expressed in cultural and religious taboos surrounding menstruation, childbirth, and menopause in women... The symbol of Goddess aids the process of naming and reclaiming the female body and its cycles and processes. The life-giving powers of the Goddess in her creative aspect are not limited to physical birth, for the Goddess is also seen as the creator of all arts of civilization, including healing, writing and the giving of just law (Christ 1991:294-8).

Christ's women are not embodied signs, but fleshly empirical beings who are conscious of the perils of today's nature. The link with the ecological movement is obvious in her work, as it is with Daly, who calls herself an ecofeminist. The feminist spiritualist movement based upon these and other writers has become very strong in the last decade. With its emphasis on the ultimate unity of all living beings (but with women having a special responsibility) it has been one of the feminist streams which has most inspired ecofeminism. But, as King (1989) points out, this alliance is not without its problems, for much as they stress unity with nature, they do so on an essentially dualistic basis.

Feminist spirituality has been criticized from other sides as well. In common with King, the social ecologist Bookchin (1990) as well as Biehl (1991) criticized this feminist stream for its reversal of hierarchies and perpetuation of dualism. Another point of criticism is the absence of recognition of women's multiple forms of oppression. The Black American feminist writer Audre Lorde wrote 'An Open Letter to Mary Daly' (Lorde 1984), in which she points out that 'there is still racism beyond sisterhood': 'To deal with one without even alluding to the other is to distort our commonality as well as our difference' (ibid:97). Daly did not react to this attempt to stimulate a debate between black and white feminists.

Some feminists from the South have levelled similar forms of criticism, pointing out that universalizing women's oppression, these 'cultural feminists', as they are commonly called, ignore specific ethnic, class and economical factors of oppression. Promoting universal earth-centred pro-woman spirituality, they ignore the struggles of women of colour to assert their ethnic identities against the imperialism of Western rationalism (Warren 1987:14-7).

Not all Southern feminists share this critical view. To some extent the position of cultural feminists (or nature feminists) is shared by the Indian feminist Vandana Shiva who idealizes women as natural saviours of nature while severely criticizing Western-imposed forms of development. Some Latin American feminist groups want to revive the witches' tradition or celebrate moon festivals.

Differences among women

Stressing women's identity with nature, the goddess or each other (Rich), the weak point of these authors is the neglect of the intersection of race, ethnic, gender and class relations. Women are homogenized as a category and there is a tendency to romanticize their special powers. As de Lauretis (1986) points out, this notion of a female 'true self' has as an underlying factor '...a male-imposed false consciousness [which] is evident in the work of cultural feminists such as Mary Daly' (de Lauretis 1986:12).

Other feminists such as Segal deplore the fact that

> Daly's voyage of the mind, possible only for the few (affluent, highly educated, white, Western, free of needy dependents), could hardly be further removed from the grassroots, anti-elitist activism flourishing in the early days of the women's liberation movement in the US and Britain (Segal 1987:121).

As indicated above, the US feminism grew out of the Black consciousness movement, while in Europe the echoes of that movement (the Black Panthers were popular in Holland too in the 1960s) and the demonstrations against the war in Vietnam, with its emphasis on anti-imperialism and respect of the Third World's right to define its own interests, inspired many women who would later found the women's movement. Yet these 'Black' roots were quickly forgotten by the white middle-class feminists who formed the core of the women's movement in the West. We suggest two factors were responsible for this development. First, the insistence on the political dimensions of what had hitherto been regarded as women's individual problems. The focus on the personal led to a disregard of the concerns of women who did not directly belong to the movement. And second, the relationship with the left. Many feminists of the 1960s and early 1970s had a leftist background. Some women remained there, trying to 'reform' Marxism by 'filling in the holes'. This led to a reconsideration of central Marxist concepts, such as labour and reproduction. But, even though the central categories of

Marxism were reformed, the Marxist focus on labour and class relations was not undermined, ignoring both racism and the subjugation of nature. As a consequence, many turned their back to Marxism and in doing so became reluctant to discuss such issues as imperialism or the exploitation of working or Black women.

It took Black women like Angela Davis and the writer Toni Morrison to explode and expose the whiteness of the women's movement. Both Black and poor women began to complain that the 'sisterhood' which the women's movement of the 1970s was trying to create had a decidedly white, Western, bourgeois character. As Huggins expressed it: 'Black women, who have worked for necessity, are apt to view women's lib as a white middle class battle irrelevant to their own, often bitter, struggle for survival' (Huggins 1991:8). The male chauvinism of Black leaders such as Cleaver and Fanon obviously did not escape the notice of Black women either, as Giddings (1984) has documented.

With the post-modernist insistence on fragmentation and flux in the 1980s, the debate on differences largely dominated the thinking of the women's movement. Nowadays many women realize that solidarity between women is not a given, but has to be constructed on the basis of a careful realization of differences among women, and the various political consequences these may have. Hooks sees this as a vital process: 'Unless we can show that barriers separating women can be eliminated, that solidarity can exist, we cannot hope to transform society as a whole' (bell hooks 1991: 29). Besides, as hooks suggests, we should bond not on the basis of shared victimization, but rather on the basis of 'our political commitment to a feminist movement that aims to end sexist oppression' (ibid:31). Bunch points out that it is '...patriarchy [which has] utilized diversity as a tool of domination. We should not fall into this patriarchal trap but instead celebrate diversity as variety, creativity, options in life styles and world views' (Bunch 1990: 50).

Women in the South have added their voices to this debate.[7] Theirs is a struggle against both poverty and subordination, for survival and respect. Such feminists as Afshar and Agarwal (1989) point out that women in the South criticize the women's movement where it is generalizing about women, but also see that women worldwide have certain things in common.

> [A]lthough in their biological reproductive role women experience a communality of functions and responsibilities, they are less cohesive in their experiences of domesticity and the extent to which the double burden of nurturing and productivity come into daily conflict (ibid:3).

Another group of women who have forcefully demanded attention to the politically cohesive effects of highlighting the issue of differences among women, are those writing and working from a lesbian perspective. Again, this group of women is not homogeneous, nor have they adhered to similar ideas and practices throughout the history of the women's movement. The tensions between lesbian and heterosexual women in the West had led to a call for political separatism, such as Johnston made in *Lesbian Nation* in the 1970s (Johnston 1973). Following this line, some saw heterosexuality as the root cause of all women's oppression. Among many others, Wittig (1975) pointed out the beauty of women bonding, socially and sexually. Many lesbians nowadays see compulsory sexual object choice as one of the factors contributing to women's oppression. Both aspects of the woman/nature debate — women as closer to nature and women's identity as a social construct — are incorporated in lesbian theorizing. All lesbian authors support a view of women as embodied sexual subjects, while lesbian identity has generally been theorized as socially constructed.

The insistence on difference and the realization that women's identities are socially mediated by various, sometimes contradictory processes, is particularly strong in the work of those feminists who adopt a constructivist perspective. Segal, who is a self-proclaimed constructivist and socialist-feminist, deplores the essentialism linked with theories which depict men as innately violent, and women as maternal and nurturant. She warns against the dangers of thus reinforcing sexual polarities (which in her view women set out to challenge in the first place). This type of feminism, she writes, 'encourages a defensive, even reactionary politics because it places women outside all mainstream political struggle'. To her this is a 'politics of despair and retreat' (Segal 1987:37). She maintains that the lives of both women and men can be as much determined by class, ethnic, regional and national issues as by their sex. Women therefore need to engage in collective community struggles (ibid:231). In this perspective then, women's special relation with nature disappears. Not surprisingly Segal ignores the whole issue of women's concern with the struggle against environmental degradation.

The disappearance of nature from socialist-feminist discourse is in line with the critique made by ecofeminists, such as King, who points out that socialists share the anti-naturalism and basic dualism of capitalism which is inherently anthropocentric, based as it is on human domination of nature (King 1989:117).

Feminist post-structuralist analysis is mainly constructivist as well. But in contest with socialist-feminist analysis the emphasis has shifted from the one of social processes to discourse analysis, from 'power itself to the politics of its representation'(di Leonardo 1991:16, quoting Seyla Benhabib). The topic of discussion is no longer the female body, but the 'female subject [as] engendered across multiple representations of class, race, language and social relations', as de Lauretis formulates it (1986:14). And if the female body is discussed, it is not seen in its empirical reality, but in its metaphorical dimension, as the 'docile body', constituted by and constituting a network of social power relations (Bordo 1986).

Essentialism versus constructivism

The major dilemma in this regard lies in how far the opposition believed to exist between essentialism and constructivism is itself a consequence of dualistic thinking, a point which we already raised in Chapter 3. Fuss claims that there is no essence to essentialism and that 'constructionism really operates as a more sophisticated form of essentialism' (Fuss 1989:xii). In her view the divide between essentialism and constructivism is less relevant than the question why this opposition was constructed. She convincingly demonstrates that essence operates even within such strict constructivist texts as produced by Wittig (1991).

In a similar vein King wonders why essentialism has always been associated with biological determinism and the idea of a fixed female nature. She warns against an 'absolute social constructionism' such as that on which socialist-feminism relies, as 'disembodied' (King 1989:131). She reclaims history as an element important to essentialism and asserts that '...the embodied woman as social historical agent, rather than product of natural law' is the subject of ecofeminism (ibid).

With the Moral Majority in the US and neo-fascist groups in Europe, feminism has come under stronger attack in the 1990s than it did in the 1970s and 1980s. Central to these attacks is a nostalgic appeal to woman's natural role as nurturer and her accordingly subordinated social position. As we have seen above, appeals to women's special links with nature have always formed part of reactionary ideological currents. Our excursion through the woman/nature debate, however, has not only identified these potentially negative and dangerous implications; we want to emphasize that appeals to women's close association with nature have also been a strong mobilizing force. We shall return to this point in Chapter 5. And, as is the case with the French *écriture féminine*, it is the basis of a scathing critique of male-dominated discourse.

The answer to the question of the link between women and nature needs to be open-ended. Women's bodies have been theorized at the same time as an empirical reality, a socio-historical construct, the site of subordination, and the symbolic representation of the other. Likewise, women's association with nature has been seen as a source of power, a call for mobilization, and as an appeal alternatively to passivity, sexual purity, or forced sexual labour serving male needs.

On a more conceptual note, we propose to move beyond the essentialism-constructivism split. Women's reality is both embodied and engendered, and historically constituted, culturally specific and informed by class and race/ethnic relations. Women's political commitment is shaped by these intersecting and shifting realities and should not be viewed one-dimensionally. Essentialist claims can have a critical mobilizing potential but can also function in a reactionary way. Constructivist analyses can be politically very powerful but if they lead to a disembodied perspective on women's lives, may lose touch with women's reality.

A fruitful position in our mind is the recognition that women and nature are simultaneously subjugated, and that this subjugation takes historically and culturally specific forms. If women take themselves seriously as social agents and as constitutive factors in this process, their praxis to end this double subjugation can be rooted not so much in women's equation with nature, but in taking responsibility for their own lives and environment. Key concepts in this regard, as already noted in the Chapter 3, are connection and affinity. These two words indicate that the process of women's bonding, with each other and against the destruction of the environment, will never be easy or automatic, but the result of conscious action of individual women committed to fight against the subordination of nature, their sisters and themselves.

Notes

1. See Chapter 8 for a discussion of ecofeminism.
2. This definition was arrived at while working on 'The Triangle of Empowerment; Policies and Strategies related to Women's Issues', Geertje Lycklama (ed), Armida Testino, Virginia Vargas, and Saskia Wieringa (eds), (forthcoming). Further work on defining women's movements was done in the introduction to 'Sub-versive Women; Women's Movements in Africa, Asia, the Caribbean and Latin America', Saskia Wieringa (ed), (forthcoming).
3. Mary Wollstonecraft originally published her *A Vindication of the Rights of Woman* in 1792.
4. See Jeffreys (1985) and Smith-Rosenberg (1985) for an analysis of this period.
5. Motherhood and domesticity of women was also emphasized by the colonial powers in their overseas dominions. Both women and Third World people in general were seen as childlike, emotional, irrational and instinctive and in general as closer to nature, a viewpoint that provided justification for white, male, European superiority. Such arrogance was bolstered by depicting Asian and African societies as backward, stagnant, chaotic and primitive (de Groot 1991). The 'mission' of white men thus was to bring 'culture' where nature reigned and especially to improve women's degraded status. In a perfidious mixture of appeals to a 'natural' Victorian morality and a desire for 'social reforms', measures were propagated which in some instances benefited women (such as

the right to education and an end to widow burning) but which in others eroded their political, economic and sexual rights (as in the case of the erosion of matrilinear customs).

6. The first wave did not completely ignore this issue, witness the scathing critique on male bias in the medical science by Aimée Duc in a novel originally published in 1901 and recently rediscovered (Duc 1984).

7. See Chapter 6 pp. 116ff.

5. Women, the Environment and Sustainable Development: Emergence of the Theme and Different Views

Women, environment and development (WED) as a theme within the development debate has increasingly attracted international attention during the last two decades and has been taking shape in a number of different streams of thinking. This chapter broadly sketches out how the WED debate has evolved, who are some of the major actors and how the particular concepts, positions and ideas interact. The historical evolution of WED is treated at some length because this has not yet been recorded elsewhere.

The theme of WED originated in the context of economic development of the countries of the South, that is, discussions on Women in Development (WID) and Environment and Development as well as from within social movements in the South, such as the Chipko and Greenbelt movements. In order to trace WED's origins, and document it's evolution within the development debate, it is important to keep in mind the history of the last three UN development decades and the global economic situation as it evolved within these. The second part of this chapter, in view of the two global conferences on women and environment in Miami (November 1991) and the UNCED process (1992) outlines how the topic of WED has gained a new international momentum. This is due to the fact that a larger circle of actors including development critics, political activists, feminists, women environmentalists, and ecofeminists from the North, South and also the ex-Eastern bloc have entered the environmental debate, particularly the WED debate.

In the North, women and environment as a theme evolved within the women's movements in the mid-1970s (Spretnak 1990) with the emergence of ecofeminism, mainly in the US. Implicitly, the relation of women to the environment also emerged as an issue for many women who took part in the peace and anti-nuclear movements at the time. Only recently in the preparatory processes to the Miami Conferences and UNCED have these streams intersected in a more systematic way.

As a result of the fundamental questioning of developmentalism the WED theme opens up, women and men working within the field of development assistance started to question the sustainability of development in the South. In this context they began to understand the topic of WED not solely as observers from the North who assist the South in its economic development but they began to question the sustainability of the dominant model of development in their own countries as well.

It should be noted here that from the start WED, as a theme within the development debate, encompassed a variety of professional fields such as forestry, agriculture, irrigation and water systems. It includes all women's interrelations with the environment in the context of economic development as well as all the effects that environmental degradation has had upon women's lives. Examples of these are an increased work burden to provide household necessities (fuel, water, fodder for animals and so on) mostly in rural areas, as well as the effects of air and water pollution, and increased exposure to chemicals in the workplace in urban settings. Local circumstances vary considerably in respect to the ecological zone (tropical forests or arid zones) as well as cultural, social, class, race, ethnic and age of people living in them.

Women in Development (WID) in a historical perspective

During the 1950s and 1960s the development organizations perceived the economic role of women in reproduction only: as home makers, bearers and rearers of children, and housewives. This was reflected in the approach to women's development: programmes in family planning and population control, mother and child health care, nutrition, home economics and so on. For women, development was seen as an enhancement of their role as home makers, wives and mothers; Caroline Moser (1989) has termed this the 'welfare approach'. Women were seen as mere beneficiaries of development within their reproductive role in the economy, while their productive roles, for example in agriculture, were disregarded. This approach is still widely used today; small, women's programmes in 'female domains' (handicraft production, knitting, sewing, mother and child health care for example) can easily be attached to ongoing development projects without challenging existing gender relations and patriarchal structures in society.

Ester Boserup in her influential book *Women's Role in Economic Development* (1970) was one of the first researchers to document the considerable contribution of women in the productive sectors of the developing countries' economies, particularly in agriculture. She showed not only that women do not automatically benefit from development programmes, but on the contrary, that the development process had often led to the relative and even absolute deterioration of women's role and status *vis-à-vis* men. Men were increasingly drawn into the modernizing agriculture sectors while women stayed in subsistence agriculture with no access to credits, training and technology. Economists and development planners ignored women's major, often predominant, contribution of labour in agriculture and other productive activities within the household and the community. Boserup concluded that the introduction of new agricultural methods had a negative effect on women in the South by changing patterns in the sexual division of labour and displacing them from their traditional areas of work. Herbicides, for example, overtook women's role in weeding; newly introduced high yield varieties of crops pushed women from their traditional role in seed selection for traditional crops. With the use of modern technology, men not only became increasingly engaged in commodity production for export but also took over women's traditional tasks. Women continued to produce food for household subsistence by traditional methods of cultivation on marginal land unsuitable for cash crop production.

With declining terms of trade internationally, commodity prices fell as did remuneration of men's labour, while women had to compensate for and supply the means of subsistence for the family. Boserup's theme was equity, an equal share for men and women within the rural household. She documented the importance of intra-household dynamics: due to traditional patterns of control over capital and land, men benefited from modern agriculture, while women did not necessarily benefit equally.

Boserup's work has been an important contribution to WID thinking because it brought out clearly the dimension and importance of gender within the process of development. Her contribution was instrumental in establishing WID as an accepted area of study. She also challenged the myth that a family income would be equally available to all members of the household. But as Whitehead (1990), one of Boserup's many critics has pointed out, she used her findings to popularize the idea that sub-Saharan Africa had initially been a predominantly female farming area, and that modernization had mostly benefited men often at the expense of women. In the light of more recent research, however, Whitehead showed this to be an oversimplification of reality. Production data show that export (largely employing men's labour) and subsistence (women's labour) crop production rise and fall together. Both are produced by a variety of techniques, and subsistence crops are also grown as cash crops. Boserup also underestimated women's involvement in the 'modern' sector of the economy. Whitehead, therefore, contested the notion of a separate subsistence sector with a 'feminine nature'. She highlighted the connections between women's role in food production and the changing nature of African agriculture within complex historical processes of commoditization, locating women's gender specific situation within these processes. She warned that to emphasize the crisis solely in the form of gender conflicts could result in masking a more general crisis of the peasantry (Whitehead 1990:54-68).

Boserup and other women who pioneered in researching and conceptualizing women's role in economic development contributed to the formulation of policies to translate their findings into development practice. The term Women in Development (WID) was coined in the early 1970s. WID became institutionalized first in the form of separate sections, departments, project components and so on within the donor countries' development bureaucracy. After the Women's Decade and the 1985 Nairobi Conference on Women and Development women's bureaus and ministries were also established in the countries of the South.

By the mid-1970s WID started to become a more or less respected area of study; the number of publications on women and development topics has steadily increased ever since. Women and men sociologists and anthropologists, as well as a slowly increasing number of women development professionals in technical fields such as agriculture, forestry, and engineering for example, from both North and South, moved into the field of development work. The understanding of rural communities in the South and women's role in the local economy, as well as cultural specificities which determine women's lives, increased considerably.

Lobbying activities by WID specialists resulted in a wider concern about and interest in women's role in the development process and the need to adequately account for their contribution. The first UN conference on Women and Development in 1975 was held in Mexico City under the rubric 'Equality, Development and Peace'; subsequently, the years 1976-1985 were declared the Women's Decade. The major outcome of the Decade was the formulation of the Forward Looking Strategies (FLS) at the 1985 Women and Development Conference in Nairobi that marked the end of the Decade. The FLS outline aims to fulfil the demand for equality between the sexes and women's full integration into the mainstream of economic development. Women were to be given equal access to education, training, and such resources as land and capital.

WID had originally addressed the demand for equity (Moser, 1989, the 'Equity Approach'). But, in the wake of the Mexico Conference, governments and development agencies reformulated the need for targeting women in the context of poverty eradication only because the demand for equity was associated with Western feminist ideas. The demand for equity was later linked to the argument of economic efficiency (Moser, 1989, the 'Anti-Poverty Approach'). Women came to be seen as a valuable 'resource' to be 'harnessed' for economic development.

In the 1980s the international economic situation and the debt crisis led to increasing poverty of populations in the South and to what was termed the 'feminization' of poverty. An increasing number of women became the providers of family subsistence, while men often migrated in search of employment. Women suffered disproportionately from cuts in government spending for health care and social services, in so far as these cuts were compensated by women's increasing workloads. Development was seen to become more efficient and effective through women's increased contribution (workload), their participation and equity were seen as the same thing. Caroline Moser called this the 'Efficiency Approach' to women's development.

The 1980s were the period of a considerable growth in the women's movements in the South. In 1984 the first Development with Women for a New Era (DAWN) meeting took place in India. A group of women researchers from the South had joined forces to criticize the Western development model as well as the WID approach itself.[1] These women from the South began to formulate their own ideas regarding women's development within the framework of an alternative development model. During the 1985 NGO Forum, held parallel to the UN Conference on Women and Development in Nairobi, the DAWN women presented their ideas. Important exchanges between Northern and Southern women's movements and NGOs took place during the two events. The motto of the UN as well as the NGO Conferences was 'Equality, Development and Peace', as a decade earlier.

As Lycklama à Nijeholt (1987) has pointed out, the quest for integration of women into the mainstream of development left no opportunity for them to choose the kind of development they wanted. It was assumed that women wanted to be integrated into a patriarchal Western mode of development. DAWN members were playing an important role in stimulating Northern women also to think about alternative visions of development from a feminist perspective. At the Forum in 1985 the idea of transformations of patriarchal societies at large as well as development according to feminist ideals was stressed. The need for women's autonomy, as a means for them to gain control over their lives, bodies and sexuality *vis-à-vis* men and social institutions, was seen as a prerequisite for such larger social transformations to take place (Lycklama à Nijeholt 1987:33). Autonomous women's organizations were seen as important institutions for women to formulate their own demands. A few years later the Dutch development minister Pronk, for example, took up DAWN's line of argument and formulated the Dutch approach to WID as empowering women to transform gender as well as all other relations, including North/South relations (Dutch Ministry of Foreign Affairs 1991). Such progressive thinking however, remained confined to the policy approach to WID and did not extend to policies on other areas of Dutch development co-operation.

DAWN's and other, mainly Southern groups' concept for women's development has been termed 'Empowerment Approach' by Caroline Moser. It has not been very popular with many governments and aid agencies because of its potential for challenging both local and global patriarchal power structures.

The shift from women in development to gender and development

A recent development from within aid agencies since the late 1980s is the transition from WID to Gender and Development (GAD). The WID approach is associated with a concern to increase women's participation and benefits, thereby making development more effective. Gender and Development represents a transition to 'not only integrate women into development, but look for the potential in development initiatives to transform unequal social/gender relations and to empower women' (Canadian Council for International Cooperation 1991:5).

Gender training – with its tools of gender analysis and gender planning – has recently been institutionalized in most development agencies. This approach is a shift in theory away from WID's sole preoccupation with women towards a:

> gender and development trend . . . [that] . . . analyzes the nature of women's contribution inside and outside the household . . . sees women as agents of change rather than as passive recipients of development assistance . . . question[s] the underlying assumptions of current social, economic and political structures . . . [and] leads not only to the design of interventions and affirmative action strategies which will ensure that women are better integrated into on-going development efforts . . . [but] . . . to a fundamental reexamination of social structures and institutions. (Rathgeber 1988, cited after Feldenstein and Poats 1989: 3)

The GAD approach aims for full equality of women within the framework of economic development. Women experts within the World Bank and the UN Food and Agriculture Organization (FAO) and many other development organizations have begun training development experts in 'gender literacy', that is, accounting for women's concerns on all levels and in all fields of the organizations' work. This encompasses screening policy documents, employment policies, planning of projects, sex segregated data collection, monitoring and evaluation procedures, and so on. All development agency staff pass through compulsory training in gender analysis and gender planning.

GAD, an important element in bringing about equity for women, is the most recent and progressive product of thinking about women and their role in the development process. If fully implemented, it will necessitate important changes within development institutions. In GAD as well as in WID, however, the original feminist concerns are diluted and appear in an instrumental garb: women are 'added' on all levels and in all spheres. GAD, as an approach, does not fundamentally question the assumptions of the dominant development paradigm itself, which is firmly rooted within the logic of modernization and the economic growth model. Also, women's projects in development programmes address women's problems only partially, by, for example, introducing income generation activities. Such programmes imply that women have time to do more work. Women in the South have very few margins for changing – for instance, work patterns – because they are already heavily overburdened. The feminist concern for changes in the sexual division of labour is evaded; rarely do development programmes lead to increasing men's work burdens. Women's lives and problems are rarely seen in their full complexity. If they are, it would be obvious that they cannot be addressed effectively within the confines of development projects; to so address them would imply more radical changes in society at large.

Approaches to women's development must go beyond the level of improving administrative procedures in development practice, and maintain the broader perspective for the 'transformation of development into a process which leads to a society where people, women and men, are no longer oppressed and exploited' (Lycklama à Nijeholt 1987:34). Apart from giving women the democratic right to participate, it is quite possible that if women were represented on all levels of decision-making they would bring different views into the development process and debate different views. Perhaps, also, different values would contribute to change development from within the institutions. In this respect, WID and GAD are important facets in the variety of positions contributing to transformations of development from within mainstream institutions.

The effectiveness of WID and GAD is limited in so far as, operating as they do in the institutional framework of development agencies and projects, they cannot solve the development crisis alone. Women's quest for equity does not address the roots of the crisis and its epistemological foundation which affect both women and men, as Chapter 3 showed. It is not within the means of development agencies to influence global economic processes and patriarchal structures that have led to women's subordination and their disproportional pauperization relative to men. Within the development context, WID's and GAD's effectiveness will depend entirely on the goodwill of governments in the South, mostly represented by men, and their willingness to allow for far-reaching improvements of women's status in their own countries.

Women, Environment, and Sustainable Development (WED) in historical perspective

In the early 1970s a growing interest in women's relations with the environment in the countries of the South emerged within the development discourse. The following pages briefly review some events that fuelled the emerging WED debate.

The oil 'crisis', initiated by the oil producing countries in 1973, as well as the large-scale effects of drought in the Sahel, sharply jolted the North into a realization that natural resources were not infinitely exploitable. Development planners began to give serious attention to the need for a more systematic global energy planning for the future.

For development planners it was clear that in the coming decades the majority of the South's peoples would depend for their energy needs on wood fuel and that oil or other energy sources would be simply too costly for them. Women, in their role as users of wood, were to become the target group for a twofold strategy to grapple with the future trends of diminishing resources of wood energy: a) reduce wood fuel consumption by introducting wood-saving stoves; and b) initiate large-scale afforestation to increase wood supply.

This twofold strategy was implemented within the larger framework of replacing wood fuel with other sources of energy in the long run. Energy development was based on urban-oriented and integrated grid systems, that is, national electrification in line with energy plans for modern urban sectors and their economies.

It was soon realized that women not only used but were also responsible for collecting wood fuel (Ki-Zerbo 1981; FAO 1984; Cecelski 1985; Agarwal 1986). Development projects (often forestry projects) and national forestry and energy departments established extensive fuel-saving stove programmes, in which educated, mostly urban women were involved as experts and promoters and thus entered the newly emerging field of 'women and the environment'.

The proposal to maximize wood-fuel production in the South was imbued with a number of generalizations rooted in the large-scale national and regional energy planning procedures and a commercial forestry framework of thinking. The shortage of wood-fuel was identified as a problem to be solved by national planners; hence, energy planners advocated large-scale forestry plantations, regardless of local circumstances and needs. Later, recognition that forestry projects implemented without local people's involvement were doomed to failure led to the emergence of the concept of Community Forestry.[2]

Another misconception of development planners was their assumption that firewood consumption for domestic energy use by households was the cause of large-scale deforestation and environmental degradation in the South. A powerful image emerged of poor people in the South, with too many children, using too much fuel; the poor were seen to have no choice but to destroy their own environment. Whereas this may be true for some areas in the South, it cannot be generalized. As Madhu Sarin, an experienced stove-promoter working in the Himalayas pointed out, deforestation in this area was due much more to commercial tree felling and the extension of agriculture into forest land than to domestic fuel consumption (Sarin 1991).

By the mid-1970s, due to Boserup's work, an interest in women's role in agriculture as well as in rural development at large had emerged. In light of global economic problems, increasing environmental degradation and the feminization of poverty in the South the debate on the specific effects of these processes on women gained momentum. It is important to note that the WED debate started from within environment-related disciplines such as forestry (fuelwood energy) and agriculture in the context of development. It became increasingly recognized that women had to spend more time and energy to obtain fuel, water and fodder for household use. Women were subsequently seen as the major victims of the crisis, emerging as the poorest of the poor. In fact, women and the poor were often one and the same group and those two terms came to be understood almost interchangeably.

At the NGO conference held parallel to the 1972 UN Conference on the Human Environment in Stockholm, the initiatives of local people in India to protect their forests -- the now widely-known Chipko Movement -- were reported by Sundarlal Bahuguna, the movement's leader. The success of the Chipko women's activities later inspired other local initiatives in the South, and also those wishing to stimulate bottom-up, people-oriented development work.

The first Western women forestry experts then working in Community Forestry projects were also influenced by the Chipko women. Community, or Social Forestry, is defind by the FAO[3] as 'any situation which intimately involves local people in a forestry activity. It embraces a spectrum of situations ranging from woodlots in areas which are short of wood and other forest products for local needs, through the growing of trees at the farm level to provide cash crops and the processing of forest products at the household, artisan or small industry level to generate income to the activities of forest dwelling communities. It excludes large-scale industrial forestry which contributes to community development solely through employment and wages, but it does include activities of forest industry enterprises and public forest services which encourage and assist forestry activities at the community level.'

Because women had emerged as the main actors in this movement it was concluded that rural women understood that it was in their own interest to protect the environment. It was during the 1972 UN conference that the South's problems of environmental degradation and the growing scarcity of natural resources *vis-à-vis* a growing population were placed firmly on the UN agenda. A parallel concern of development agencies was to take into account the need to address environmental issues within the process of economic development.

The United Nations Environmental Programme (UNEP), which was to act as a catalyst and co-ordinator on environmental issues within the UN, was established after the Stockholm conference. The task of the Environmental Liaison Centre International (ELCI), founded at the same time, was to integrate NGO input into UNEP. The headquarters of both organizations are in Nairobi. Both agencies became active in the field of WED around the mid-1980s.

In 1984, UNEP initiated a programme to enhance women's participation in environmental management and consequently established the Senior Women's Advisory Group on Sustainable Development (SWAGSD), comprising a group of senior women specialists interested in environmental issues working in different development organizations. This group structured the input of women on environment and sustainable development within the 1985 UN Conference on Women and Development and were instrumental in the adoption of key paragraphs in the final Conference document: the Nairobi Forward Looking Strategies. As a result the topic of women and environment entered the UN's agenda.

At the Nairobi Forum 1985, held parallel to the UN Women and Development Conference, ELCI organized a workshop on 'Women and the Environmental Crisis'. Women's actions and special role in environmental management were presented in case studies that documented women's involvement in forestry, agriculture, energy and so on, based on the experiences of women living in the South. Women were portrayed in these case studies as environmental managers whose involvement was crucial to the achievement of sustainable development. These studies were powerful tools to further the WED debate and stimulate international recognition of women's problems in relation to natural resource management. Active at the Forum were women such as the Kenyan Wangari Maathai, leader of the Green Belt Movement[4] and Vandana Shiva from India, much of whose thinking and writing has been inspired by the Chipko movement. These two and many more women from the South present at the workshop later gained international prominence in the WED debate and became spokespersons on behalf of the South's poor women.

The ELCI workshop participants drew up a Plan of Action for Women, Environment and Development setting out how different organizations can contribute to awareness-raising and advocacy; strengthening women's leadership in environmental action; providing information to and educating the public; networking and training.

In the years following the Nairobi Conference, of five programmes[5] set up by ELCI, one was a WED programme initiated to form a network of African women researchers, called WEDNET, to work on WED related issues in the region. WEDNET's activities include workshops and exchanges within Africa on forestry, environmental security and sustainable development linking up development workers, community groups, NGOs, researchers, and so on. Their most recent work is a compilation of the indigenous environmental knowledge of women in several African countries.

In 1992, the Asian and Pacific Women's Resource Network published a number of case studies of local communities' environmental action, collected by women in the Asian and Pacific region in the follow up of the Forum 85 Nairobi Conference. This collection, in its candid reflection of the perspectives of the local groups themselves in their own words, is unique.

By the mid-1980s the media were increasingly presenting images of poor women from the South, burdened by heavy loads of fuel, fodder and water, against a backdrop of barren landscapes. These images served to alert the public and development agencies in the North to the problems of women in the South brought about by environmental degradation.

In 1986 the UN Secretariat for the Advancement of Women appointed UNEP as the leading agency on women and environment. The UN's Drinking Water and Sanitation Decade (1981-1990) highlighted women's role in these areas. The task of the UN International Research and Training Institute for the Advancement of Women (INSTRAW), was to devise training manuals, specifically for women, in view of their primary role in the supply of drinking water and responsibility for their families' sanitation standards. There was a significant increase in the literature on issues such as women's roles in forestry, agriculture, and animal health, that documented the gender specific tasks women performed, as well as case study material illustrating the effects of environmental degradation on women, and their responses.

The Brundtland Report, *Our Common Future*, published in 1987, promoted long-term strategies for achieving sustainable development (defined as development that meets the needs of the present without compromising future generations' ability to meet theirs) (WCED 1987:45)[6] and highlighted the importance of environmental issues in the development process. In the years following publication of the Brundtland Report, the WED debate – conducted mainly by women working on environmental and women-related issues in UNEP, FAO, UNIFEM, INSTRAW and many other bilateral aid agencies and NGOs – focused on the imperative for women's involvement in strategies and programmes aimed at 'sustainable' development. Gradually, 'women, environment and development' became 'women, environment and sustainable development'.

In the late 1980s national and international events organized on the WED theme gained increased momentum. The images of poor women in the South as victims became transformed into images of strength and resourcefulness. In the wider debate on sustainable development women were increasingly promoted as 'privileged environmental managers' and depicted as possessing specific skills and knowledge in environmental care. Development agencies, advised to address women much more widely in their environmental projects, responded by sending out more women experts from the North to implement such projects, as well as promoting the training of women extension workers in the South. WED slowly became a professional field for women development experts.

More often than not, however, these women experts, trained as technicians, have little awareness of gender issues, and this leads to the implementation of environmental projects in which women are just 'added on'. Often, such projects, geared at recovering the environment, are inappropriate to serve women's needs. For example, involving women in tree planting may mean increasing already overburdened rural women's workload. Unless women are given control over the land on which the trees are growing, and wider social changes are promoted to give them decision-making power over the sale of forest products (traditionally male domains), in the long run they will not be interested in such projects.

As standard procedure in recent years, most development agencies introduced separate environmental and women's impact assessments as part of their project procedures with little success up to date. These impact assessments are often simply tacked on to project planning and evaluation procedures without significantly altering the nature of the particular project. Levy (1992) points out that both gender and environment cut across established development policies and planning procedures; she proposes a dialogue between the two separate planning sectors, which would ultimately lead away from a checklist approach towards an alternative approach to development.

In 1987 a group of women experts from different organizations met to discuss how women's concerns could be brought into the World Conservation Strategy, an important international document written jointly by the World Conservation Union (IUCN), the World Wide Fund for Nature (WWF) and UNEP in 1980. In 1991, the Second World Conservation Strategy, was published; gender issues are included in the document as a result of these women experts' comments.

In 1987, too, *Women and Environment in the Third World,* by Irene Dankelman and Joan Davidson, was one of the first books on the topic to be published. It presented case studies of women's environmental activities in the South. The views expressed in the book were decisively shaped by women from the South, albeit in their capacity as researchers or development personnel. The emphasis of the book is on the close and special connection between women and the environment.

In 1989, at a seminar in Paris, organized by the Expert Group of

Women in Development of the Organization for Economic Cooperation and Development (OECD), women from the World Bank, IUCN, the International Planned Parenthood Federation (IPPF), OECD, UNEP, and others met to discuss the nature of the connections between women and the environment and then translated the outcome into policy guidelines for WED projects. An important outcome of this policy meeting was the imperative for poor Third World women's empowerment: if women must work more in order to improve the environment they must also be the beneficiaries. Women's status must therefore be raised, they must have control over their own bodies in order to control fertility, and they must be granted access to appropriate technology in order to attain social, cultural and environmentally sustainable development (OECD/ DAC 1989). It is important to note this group's holistic conceptualization of sustainable development (see Chapter 7 for a discussion of the concept of sustainable development).

In 1989 UNFPA published a report, *Investing in Women: The Focus of the Nineties*, prepared by Nafis Sadik, UNFPA's Director, in which she drew attention to the link between population and the environment. Brandt (1989) and many others of the development establishment also saw that in coming decades, solving the problems arising from environmental degradation and population growth would present the greatest challenges. Women are recognized as central in both areas.

With accelerating environmental degradation an increasing number of Northern groups engaged in the environmental debate, as well as environmental movements, now identify population growth as the root cause of global environmental degradation. This assumption is seen as sufficient justification for stringent population control measures directed mainly at women in the South. This assignment of responsibility for environmental degradation to population growth has become a matter of fierce disagreement between women's groups and environmentalists within the UNCED process.

In 1989 the Women's Environmental Network (WEN), a group working mainly on consumer issues in the UK, together with War on Want organized a workshop on Women, Environment and Development in London. Particicpants included activists, researchers, staff of development agencies and NGOs from Great Britain, Europe and the South. The relation between women and the environment was seen by particpants as one of mutual caring and nurturing as well as the basis for a critique of the dominant development model. The Workshop's recommendations included an appeal to non-governmental, bilateral and multilateral agencies to reconceptualize the notion of development based on export-led growth, and for the integration of women and environment issues into the mainstream of their work. Women's empowerment through access to education and appropriate local, regional, and national organizational structures were deemed necessary to enable them to take part in all levels of project planning. WEN has gained international prominence in the field of WED because of successful mobilization of UK women around consumer actions to press their government to introduce more environmentally friendly production processes (Women's Environmental Network 1988, Vallely 1991). They have inspired other Northern women's groups to engage in similar consumer actions and thus promoted the cause of WED in the North.

Another important event in 1989 was the publication of Vandana Shiva's book *Staying Alive*, in which she develops her ideas of an alternative development model based on traditional subsistence agriculture. She introduces the notion of the 'feminine principle', a term originating in Hindu cosmology denoting the life-giving force she associates with women. In Shiva's view the feminine principle needs to be recovered as the basis for a truly sustainable development model. Comments on the essentialist bias of this position, as well as on its potentially empowering effect, have already appeared in Chapter 4. It will be considered further later in this chapter.

Women organize for the Earth Summit

Within the UNCED preparatory process a symposium, organized by UNCED/UNICEF/UNFPA in Geneva (May 1991) entitled 'Women and Children First', examined the impact of poverty and environmental degradation on children and women in view of their potential to contribute towards sustainable development. Participants from the UN, NGOs, and governmental organizations defined poverty as:

> ... that process which deprives people, particularly women and children, of the basic means for sustainable livelihoods, and that undermines their physical, cultural and spiritual wellbeing. (UNCED 1991:1)

The term 'sustainable livelihood', though not explicitly defined in the report, is seen as distinct from sustainable development as defined by the Brundtland Commission. It contains a participatory dimension which refers to 'increasing the capacity that people have to use resources to determine the shape of their own lives' (UNCED 1991:15).

The term 'sustainable livelihood' was proposed to replace that of 'sustainable development', which was understood to denote sustaining the dominant mode of development. Women engaged in the UNCED preparatory process subsequently adopted the former term.

Until mid-1991 women had not been an explicit concern within the governmental preparations for UNCED. Only in the NGO preparatory process women from development and environment groups as well as women's groups had been active in the national and regional consultations. Through lobbying, networking and organizing women won over some UNCED delegates with the result that decision 3/5 at the Third Preparatory Committee meeting in Geneva (August 1991), became the basis for the women's mandate in UNCED.[7]

Women's participation in UNCED was furthered by global women's conferences held successively in Miami, in November 1991. The first was the Global Assembly 'Women and Environment – Partners in Life' organized by SWAGSD/UNEP and WorldWIDE, a US-based international network of women concerned with the management and protection of the environment.[8] Five hundred invited guests from development organizations heard women from all over the world present 218 accounts documenting how they were successfully addressing environmental problems in their own communities. The second conference, 'World Women's Congress for a Healthy Planet' was organized by the women's International Policy Action Committee (IPAC), a body originating in the US Women's Foreign Policy Council and founded specifically to ensure women's input into UNCED. This second conference, organized in the form of a tribunal, was attended by about 1,500 women from 83 countries. It aimed to formulate recommendations and an action plan for a healthy planet for the next century from the point of view of women. The Women's Action Agenda was an outcome of an unprecedented process in which women from diverse backgrounds, positions and geographical regions came to a united position which criticized the dominant model of development.

From 17-21 December 1991 the global NGO Conference 'Roots of the Future' organized by ELCI, which took place in Paris, was the major preparatory meeting of the NGO community before the NGO Global Forum held parallel to UNCED. At this Conference participating groups, worldwide, synthesized their previously prepared regional statements into the Citizen's Action Plan for the 1990s: Agenda Ya Wananchi. It is noteworthy that Agenda Ya Wananchi fully endorsed the Women's Action Agenda 21, drafted in Miami a month earlier and later presented at UNCED.[9]

From 3-13 June 1992 the Brazilian Women's Coalition, together with the Women's Environment and Development Organization (WEDO), organized and hosted Planeta Femea, the women's conference held within the NGO Global Forum in Rio de Janeiro. Planeta Femea was a concentrated programme of presentations in daily workshops structured around the themes of the Women's Action Agenda 21. Within the NGO process of ratifying treaties parallel to the UN treaties to serve as guidelines for the post-UNCED process involving NGOs globally, women attending Planeta Femea attempted to spread their participation throughout the NGO treaty working groups in order to bring into them a women's perspective, but with only mixed success. Women took over drafting a Population Treaty and a separate Women's Treaty; the latter was essentially a summary of the Women's Action Agenda 21 drafted in Miami, but in a diluted version. To address this problem, a Women's Declaration initiated by members of the DAWN network emerged from the women's meeting. In terms stronger than those used in the Women's Treaty this Declaration criticized the UNCED agenda for the exclusion of such crucial factors leading to environmental degradation of the environment such as economic and military systems. In a call for action this Declaration urged world leaders present at UNCED to ensure the full implementation of the Women's Action Agenda 21 as drafted in Miami.

A women's caucus at the governmental UNCED conference itself also lobbied the official member country delegates. This conference adopted the document, Global Action for Women Towards Sustainable and Equitable Development within the UNCED Agenda 21 as Chapter 24. Chapter 24 also stresses that any successful implementation of the UNCED Agenda 21 will depend on the active involvement of women in economic and political decision-making and implementation of the following conventions and plans of action adopted by the UN earlier: Nairobi Forward Looking Strategies; the Convention on the Elimination of All Forms of Discrimination Against Women; the ILO and UNESCO conventions to end gender-based discimination and ensure women's access to land and other reources, education and equal employment; and the 1990 World Declaration on the Survival, Protection and Development of Children and its Plan of Action. Women clearly stressed the need for women's empowerment as a prerequisite for sustainable livelihoods for all people.

Ideas of Women, Environment and Sustainable Development

The WED debate encompasses several main streams of thought. One stream stresses the managerial aspects of minimizing negative effects of the process of economic development by targeting women as recipients of development assistance and simultaneously considering the effects of development on the environment. This approach is propagated by development agencies. Other approaches tend toward anti-development or transformational stances and assert that the model of Western development is fundamentally flawed, as its effect on women, the environment and the South's peoples makes evident. This line of thought calls for transformations towards alternative development (see also Chapter 6). Crucial in the different lines of argumentation is the respective conception of the woman/nature relation (see the constructivism versus essentialism debate in Chapter 4).

An economistic line of thinking conceptualizes WED from the viewpoint of women's work: the sexual division of labour that has led to women's particular role in managing natural resources. This role is seen as a product of the historical evolution of patriarchy which has assigned men roles in economic production and women the lower valued roles connected with economic reproduction.

A more 'cultural' stream of thought sees women's position as essentially closer to nature because within the sexual division of labour their work has always entailed a close relationship with nature. Women are depicted as 'naturally' privileged environmental managers who over generations have accumulated specific knowledge about natural processes that is different and more appropriate than that of men in general. This approach perceives the woman/nature relation as one of reciprocity, symbiosis, harmony, mutuality and interrelatedness due to women's close dependence on nature for subsistence needs. Women have successfully used both lines of argument as the basis for political struggles, in accordance with different strategies.

Different conceptualizations of WED in the literature

In reconceptualizing women's work, Maria Mies (1988), coming from a Marxist background, developed her argument by defining women's role in childbearing and rearing as work, and within a Marxist/feminist perspective this was an important contribution. Furthermore, for Mies, reproduction, that is, providing the basic necessities for family survival, constitutes women's closer relation to nature. Through this double role women's understanding of nature is superior to men's. Women not only work closer to nature, women 'are' nature because they give birth and nurture their children, hence they are doubly exploited within patriarchal society globally.

Vandana Shiva has become a prominent speaker on WED since the Nairobi Forum 1985. Her thinking locates her within the South's ecological and alternative development perspective rather than within WED but her work is discussed here because of her influential role in WED. Shiva (1989), as already indicated, draws on Hindu religion and philosophy which describes the 'feminine principle', *prakriti*, as the source of all life. She equates the feminine principle with women in real life and constructs the practical relation that women have with nature in Indian rural reality as the embodiment of the feminine principle. This relation needs to be recovered as a base for a sustainable mode of development. In India, according to Shiva, this mode existed before the era of colonialism. Under colonialism, and later the influence of the development process, a capitalist mode of development and green revolution technology has penetrated India's rural economies, a process that destroyed the economic base of small-scale local survival agriculture. Shiva condemns the change to large-scale, mechanized and ultimately unsustainable market-oriented agriculture. This process facilitated the marginalization of the majority of the South's small-scale farmers, particularly poor women.

Shiva sees the dominant mode of development as Western, patriarchal and based on a reductionist model of science and technology that serves the global market and is effectively destructive for women, nature and all 'others' — non-Western peoples. Shiva sets up a model of opposition between the destructive Western, white, male, patriarchal development model and the traditional Indian agricultural system that works in harmony with nature. The Western model propagates monocultural plantation techniques in both forestry and agriculture in service of the market and capital accumulation. The traditional Indian economic model is described as having preserved a mutual relationship with nature through the cultivation of multicultural plantations meant for local subsistence production, using only what nature produces within the traditional farming system.

In common with Mies, Shiva's thinking stems from a search for an alternative development model. Both conclude that to recover the systems of subsistence agriculture globally is the solution. The Western development model's commoditization of nature, as well as women's and non-Western people's labour, has resulted in capital accumulation in the affluent 'developed' countries and poverty in the 'developing' countries.

For Mies, Northern women's major role lies in denouncing, and abstaining from, unnecessary consumption with the ultimate aim of undermining capitalism. Shiva cites women's prominent role within the Indian Chipko movement as evidence that the life-creating and preserving 'feminine principle' embodied by these women must be reclaimed as the source for an alternative global development model. 'Recovering the feminine principle as respect for life in nature and society appears to be the only way forward, for men as well as women, in the North as well as in the South' (Shiva 1989:223).

Staying Alive (1989), in which Shiva developed her argument, has been very influential in shaping WED, as well as environmental and alternative development thinking especially in Northern NGOs and social movements, and in development agencies. She has been much less influential in her own Indian context. The problem with her approach is the essentialism she has constructed in the concrete relation of women with nature in subsistence agriculture as a theoretical category – the feminine principle as the life-giving force. She propagates the idea that only poor, rural women, bearing the brunt of the environmental and developmental crisis in their daily struggle for survival, know, and have known, how to survive since time immemorial and therefore have the solutions to the crisis.

Shiva idealizes Indian subsistence agriculture and recreates a past where people lived in perfect harmony with nature, and women were highly respected in society. But this romantic past may never have existed. Subsistence agriculture in India replaced tribal people's cultures, often by violent means. Indian history shows that the agricultural system was introduced on the sub-continent only with Arian invasion. In India, there is a large number of tribal peoples outside the caste system who, even today, are not integrated into society. Shiva's model of traditional society fails to account for highly exploitative structures along the axes of race, class and caste within Indian society today; she also ignores patriarchal structures within Indian society. Instead, she lays blame for the environmental crisis wholly on 'the state' and the global economy. Shiva's total neglect of class in Indian society has brought her much criticism, especially from Indian Marxist scholars.

As already indicated, both Mies and Shiva propagate a global model of subsistence agriculture. The question is, however, would the subsistence model alone, even though attractive in certain aspects, be a viable option in the present situation, especially if we think, for example, of the densely populated countries of Europe as well as India?

Yet, what Shiva (and many other scholars too) has brought out in her argument is a fundamental questioning of the Western model of development as the only possible model. Instead, she outlines the validity of subjugated and marginal people's knowledges in the search for sustainable models for development and environmental protection. She illustrates that such knowledge is sophisticated rather than 'primitive', being based on generations of close observation of natural processes, albeit often relevant in a specific local setting only. She also introduces the question of different values and perceptions: what is real material poverty and what is only culturally perceived as poverty? Are rural people living off local resources 'backward' *vis-à-vis* urban people in the North who are overconsuming global energy and natural resources at unsustainable levels? In this respect she contributes to a challenge of the epistemological assumptions underlying the dominant development model and highlights its violence to people and nature and destructive effects on local cultures and lifestyles[10].

The positions taken by many Northern (and Southern) NGOs on WED have been strongly influenced by Shiva. Within the wider search for an alternative development paradigm, many of them wholeheartedly embrace the idea of women's privileged position in environmental management and their closer connection to nature. Often they take ecofeminist thought (see Chapter 8) as a source of inspiration for their perspective on WED. It is noteworthy here that the work of Vandana Shiva has had an important impact on the Northern environmental movement.[11] Many social movement-oriented NGOs subscribe to the notion of an intrinsically closer woman/nature connection, situated in the imperative for alternative development models based on changed North/South relations and different value systems. NGOs oriented strictly towards development work subscribe more to aid agency views.

Development agencies' conceptualization of WED

Mainstream development organizations' line of argumentation on WED is cast within the frame of an improvement of present development practice. Usually the neglect of women and destruction of the environment within the development process are compared. This argument basically stresses the institutional nature of the problem. If only women and the environment were considered in development practice the environmental crisis could be solved. Consideration of both 'poor Third World women' and the environment is seen as crucial for the attainment of sustainable development. The conceptualization of the woman/nature connection in this type of argument is often not explicit, but rather implied as 'special', that is, inherently closer than that between men and the environment. The sexual division of labour usually forms part of the argument: women depend on nature directly for survival because they collect fuel, fodder and so on for domestic use, while men are mainly engaged in cash crop production for the market. Women's increased workload due to environmental degradation is another important element in this argument, which in practice leads to a call for the implementation of more women's development projects in fields related to the use of natural resources. Rarely is a connection made between macro-economic and political processes: overconsumption of natural resources by the few in the North and poverty of the many in the South.

In both the Mies/Shiva and many NGOs arguments and those propagated by development agencies, women's and environmental interests to a certain extent become identical: the cause of the restoration of the environment becomes the cause of (poor Third World) women. The two lines of argument differ in their proposed solution to environmental degradation: on the one hand that the basic parameters of the development model need to be radically rethought; and on the other that they simply need to be improved.

Within the UNCED process, during the second Miami Conference, these two positions merged into a united critical stand against the dominant development model by women worldwide.

Of interest for the evolution of the WED debate is the shifting image of poor Southern women as the 'Poor Third World Woman' manifested mainly in Western development media (Häusler 1990). But, whereas the image of poor Third World women in the mid to late 1980s typified them as victims of the environmental crisis, more recently the emphasis was put on their strength (see Davidson in OECD/DAC WID, 1990). Recent WED publications depict women as privileged environmental managers because of their intimate knowledge of natural processes due to their closer relationship with nature: therefore, women are seen as the answer to the crisis; women have the solutions; they are privileged knowers of natural processes.

This valorization of women's ways of knowing may seem positive to us, but the accuracy of promoting them as exclusive and privileged knowers of natural processes is doubtful. This issue is somewhat problematic because, in the rural economies of the South, men also possess such knowledge, except related more closely to their own traditional areas of work.

Within the developmentalist framework women are seen as *the most valuable resource* in the process towards achieving sustainable development. 'Current wisdom is to see women not just as victims but as major local assets to be harnessed in the interests of better environmental management' (Davidson in OECD/DAC WID, 1990:5).

The imagery of women as 'valuable resources' and 'assets' has now prompted development planners to seriously consider women's roles in environmental projects and in virtually all environment-related project documents there is at least rhetoric about women, but the instrumentalization of women for the sustainable use of the environment and environmental recovery needs to be seriously questioned.

As indicated earlier, experience derived from involving women in environmental projects such as tree plantations shows that the end result is ambiguous: while they invest their valuable time planting and weeding tree plantations, they have no legal control over the resources created. Women rarely benefit from tree planting schemes involving pine or eucalypts, for example, because these trees are unsuitable for local use; but when the trees are sold men reap the benefits and get the money. Hence, the imperative for women's involvement in environmental projects clashes with the market orientation propagated in most development projects.

In response to these difficulties Davidson (ibid) asserted that women's participation in environmental projects must be complemented by strategic policies to ensure their involvement in all stages of development projects and thus increase their access and control over resources, training, education and family planning. In this way sustainable development can be achieved. Hence, environmental projects will eventually facilitate women's empowerment in society. In this line of argument women's empowerment, understood as their increased access and control over their bodies and resources, is yet further evidence of the interlinking and common interests both of women and the environment: women care for the environment and this eventually facilitates their empowerment. Wangari Maathai, for example, uses this argument in her booklet on the Greenbelt Movement (Maathai 1988). This Movement's primary concern is to restore the environment in the rural areas of Kenya; as a welcome byproduct tree planting will facilitate women's empowerment because they can show that they have a valuable contribution to make to the economy, which in turn will give them confidence and status in their own communities and in society at large.[12]

In a specific situation women's initiatives may lead to an improvement in the environment as well as their empowerment, but to define this as a replicable and normative procedure seems questionable. It would simply reinforce the notion that if only women were involved in environmental projects the crisis could be overcome. The wider social, political and economic changes needed in order to arrive at a sustainable mode of development become secondary or are evaded.

For movements in the South, such as Chipko and Greenbelt, the asumption of an inherent women/nature connection as a basis for political action is acceptable because it accords with traditional notions of women as 'natural' carers and nurturers in the rural societies in which they originate. It must also be noted that neither movement sees itself as exclusively a women's, let alone a feminist movement. From our perspective, the problem with these movements' approaches is that women's empowerment has to take place within the confines of the traditional sexual division of labour and gender ideologies. Yet, for example, to compensate for gender-specific ways in which women suffer from environmental deterioration might necessitate a change in the sexual division of labour resulting in men taking on traditionally female tasks. Also, for women who are de facto household heads, existing gender ideologies are often an impediment to their assumption of the legal position as head of household, thus making them even more vulnerable and subject to ostracization within their own societies in absence of the male head of household.

Criticism of the WED approach expounded by Shiva (1989) and subscribed to by many NGOs, North and South, comes largely from members of Northern women's (and environmental) movements who, for some decades, have grappled with the woman/nature connection in their emancipatory struggles. These, mainly Northern, critics argue that to equate women with nature has reinforced women's continued subordination to men. While in the South's cultures the male/female relation has traditionally often been seen as complementary, in the North's perspective this relation has been one of superiority/inferiority since the middle ages. Therefore women from the South find identifying with nature less difficult and hence use this type of argument as a basis for their struggles. Neverthless, there have been important initiatives by Northern women, for example, the Greenham Common actions or the campaigns organized by the Women's Environmental Network in the United Kingdom, which take their inspiration from an inherently close woman/nature connection.

From within the development context and in a different vein, Melissa Leach (1991) takes the approach of gender and development, GAD, described above, as a point of departure for her WED argument. She argues that more appropriate development policy-making is needed and sees the woman/nature link in a differentiated way. Leach examines gender relations, not simply women, and how they interact with the responsibilities, rights and activities in natural resource management and use over time. She analyses a case study from Sierra Leone where the introduction of cocoa and coffee cash crop production altered the whole pattern of agricultural production. By demonstrating the changes effected on household rice production, time allocation of different groups, land use rights and resource use access on the one hand, and gender relations on the other, she is able to show their interdependent nature. This approach allows for an identification of differences between groups of women as well as men, which a focus on women alone would obscure.

> From the environmental angle, it is possible to see how changing gender relations – such as in control over crops or money – alter resource management practices, with tangible ecological effects. From the gender angle, looking at environmental change from a micro-political economy perspective provides the useful opportunity to analyze gender relations in a way which puts resource issues right up front (Leach 1991:15).

In conclusion she recommends participatory planning procedures for development projects and for arising social conflicts to be resolved by the different men's, women's and mixed interest groups.

As mentioned earlier, the stress on improvement of development practice advocated by this gender-focused approach neglects such dimensions of the ecological crisis as international economic processes, unfavourable exchange rate mechanisms and terms of trade that favour the affluent North. There is no room to question the epistemological assumptions underlying the dominant mode of development. The silence about the need for wider transformations in development that could facilitate a sustainable development model on a global level serves basically to preserve the status quo by slightly improving the present model. Leach's analysis, however, supports the arguments in Chapter 1, in which we point out that the interconnections between women, the environment and sustainable development are not based on the sex of the actors alone. The focus of the WED debate on the woman/nature and man/nature connections obscures the dynamic aspects of environmental degradation and how it affects different groups, women as well as men, over time. Besides the wider changes necessary to halt environmental destruction in both the South and the North, the process of environmental recovery is as much women's task as it is men's. Leach's propositions represent an important input into the improvement of development project procedures and hence, are an important element for prospective transformations from within mainstream development agencies.

Bina Agarwal (1991) develops an approach to WED that encompasses many elements of the WED debate outlined above in a holistic way. She combines the levels of material reality and ideological constructs of meanings in her analysis of the Indian experience of the environmental crisis, its causes, effects and responses to it. She argues that women are both victims of this crisis in gender-specific ways as well as important actors in resolving it. Agarwal, like Shiva, draws on experience in India, but unlike Shiva she asserts the need to contextualize the fact that poor rural women have emerged as main actors in the environmental movements in India because, due to their marginality. they have had to maintain a reciprocal link with nature. For Agarwal, the woman/nature link has been socially and culturally constructed, not biologically determined (Agarwal 1989:60).

> the link between women and the environment can be seen as structured by a given gender and class (caste/race) organization of production, reproduction and distribution. Ideological constructions such as of gender, of nature and of the relationship between the two, may be seen as (interactively) a part of this structuring, but not the whole of it. This perspective I term feminist environmentalism (Agarwal 1991:8).

From this position Agarwal calls for struggles over material as well as symbolic resources. She suggests as a two-pronged strategy the need to grapple with groups who control resources, and ways of thinking about resources, with the help of media, educational, religious and legal institutions. Feminists, she suggests, should challenge and transform notions about gender as well as struggling against the actual sexual division of labour; and environmentalists should challenge and transform the representations of the relationship between nature and people as well as the actual methods of appropriating natural resources for the benefit of the few. She concludes by stressing the need for a transformative rather than a welfarist approach to economic development.

Agarwal's argument is most in line with our own thinking on WED because she contextualizes the material situation of women within the ideological construction of the woman/nature connection, pointing out that in reality this construct caters to certain vested interests.

From yet another point of departure, the Development with Women for a New Era (DAWN) network presented another Southern women's position in their publication *Environment and Development: Grass Roots Women's Perspective* (Wiltshire 1992), which was specifically prepared for UNCED. Refraining from an explicit elaboration on their understanding of the woman/nature connection, DAWN's position is predominantly based on an analysis of global economic processes as perceived by Southern women: overconsumption in the North and by elites in the South coupled with excessive military spending, unfavourable terms of trade, the debt crisis, structural adjustment programmes and export-oriented production increasing the burden on the environment in the South.[13] Starting from an analysis of women's experiences of environmental degradation in different regions in the South, Wiltshire contests the Northern developmentalist myth that the poor are destroying their environment, that population growth is responsible for environmental degradation, and that local people in the South need to be taught by Northern 'experts' how to recover their environment. Her critique concludes with an appeal to include women in environmental policy-making, planning and programming because of their 'special' environmental knowledge. Wiltshire refrains from romanticizing the woman/nature connection, but a certain essentialism can be read into earlier DAWN statements on the 'poor Third World woman' as the intersection of all forms of domination – based on sex, nationality, race, class and caste – resulting in her privileged perspective in defining parameters for an alternative development paradigm (see Chapter 6).

The thrust of Wiltshire's argument however, is an attack on the international economic order and affluent lifestyles in the North, and of elites in the South. Wiltshire stresses the imperative for democratic, decentralized and people-centred approaches to natural resource use. This basis for 'material as well as spiritual well being, cultural integrity and human rights will yield more effective and long term results for balanced population growth and sustainable development' (Wiltshire 1992:24).

WED and the UNCED process

As indicated earlier, an increasingly transformative view on women, the environment and sustainable development entered the UN system within the UNCED preparatory process. In the proceedings of the 'Women and Children First' workshop (May 1991) the need for a new development paradigm is explicitly stated (UNCED 1991:37). Participants from the North and the South were representatives from different UN organizations, from universities, research institutions and development agencies. A vision statement in the workshop proceedings makes a number of recommendations for far-reaching changes, including an end to violence, militarization, economic growth, misdirection of science, technology and industry, oppressive economic, social and political structures, to the destruction of basic human and ethical values and to the general exclusion of women's concerns.

> We are determined to change the a-symmetric and dominant relationship of the economy with nature, of men with women, and of the North with the South. Our aim is nothing less than a revolution on behalf of women, children and the environment (ibid:35).

The draft decision for consideration of the Third Preparatory Committee to UNCED in article 281 also called for 'an end to a developmentally unsustainable world order and trend and a replacement by a new development paradigm that takes into account the rights of people, especially women and children' (UNCED 1991:37).

The process set in motion within the UNCED preparatory process by women from NGOs, aid agencies, research institutions and grassroots action groups which culminated in the Miami conferences, especially the 'World Women's Congress for a Healthy Planet' and the drafting of the Women's Action Agenda 21, represents a historical landmark. Despite their widely differing positions, political persuasion and geographical origin, women collectively agreed to challenge the dominant paradigm of development. In Miami, women asserted the centrality of people in the development process as the point of departure for their political analysis of access, use and distribution of natural resources at all levels from the household to the international level. The global developmental and environmental problems were summarized as wasteful overconsumption in the developed world, inappropriate development leading to debt and structural adjustment in the South, increased poverty and continued land and forest degradation, environmental damage, pollution, and toxic wastes, population growth, creation of ecological refugees and last but not least, excessive war and military spending associated with environmental damage. The Women's Action Agenda 21, based on the principles of global equity, resource ethics and empowerment of women, represents the basis for a paradigmatic shift in development as demanded by women globally, and provides detailed recommendations on how to deal with the problems. In Miami women demanded the right to bring their perspectives, values, skills and experiences into policy-making on all levels and to be on an equal footing with men in UNCED and beyond. They called for a 'Healthy Planet' in which participatory democracy, open access to information, accountability, ethical action, justice and full participation of women are realized. They challenged the present development model with its economistic conception of sustainability and suggested a more holistic notion of politically, socially and culturally sustainable development, that is, sustainable livelihoods for all.

The Miami Conferences represent a major breakthrough because for the first time ever women across political/geographical, class, race, professional and institutional divides came up with a critique of development and a collective position on the environmental crisis, arrived at in a participatory and democratic process. The problem was no longer seen as confined to the South but as global; the global crisis was identified in its regionally different manifestations. Separate statements in the workshop proceedings (World Women's Congress for a Healthy Planet 1992) by women from Africa, Latin America and the Caribbean, the Middle East, North America, Europe, the Pacific as well as women from the South, women of colour from North America and indigenous women outlined the different ways people and the environment suffer from the global crisis in their regions.

The Planeta Femea in Rio de Janeiro 1992 did not go beyond what was achieved in Miami. The spirit of the women's conference was clearly one of enthusiasm and solidarity and women had every reason to celebrate their success in asserting their presence at the NGO Forum. Nevertheless, the event revealed many problems that, despite the women's achievement in asserting their presence within the UNCED process, remain to be dealt with in the future. One was the overly simple assumption of the existence of a global sisterhood and the associated silence about problems related to differences between women. Possibly, this was because, while aware of the pressing need for cross-cultural alliances, the short run-up to UNCED left no time to work out the practical implications of their own beliefs. Political differences came to the fore, but were not openly addressed. The spectrum of positions ranged from demanding equality for women in all matters relating to the environment (held by Bella Abzug, chairperson of IPAC and a central figure in the forum), to rejecting the Western development model in its entirety (expressed by many DAWN women, in particular, its present chairperson Peggy Antrobus). Planeta Femea proceedings were sometimes dominated by women who had been heavily involved in the UNCED preparatory process and saw the urgent need to tactically ensure women's input into mass media and the main conference at the cost of silencing others. Some women, notably Brazilian women of colour, felt marginalized in the forum because they were not given enough space for expression. Related to these was the relegation of most problems to the other 'others': governments, some environmentalists, economic and political systems, and men.

Because of these impediments, without an equivalent degree of critical discussion, there were no positive confrontations of differences among women. Instead, there was a masked tendency to emphasize commonalities between women, resulting in an implicitly essentialist position – women as closer to nature than men – as the basis for a collective position. Some women did see themselves as better environmental managers than men, and as privileged knowers about the environment, but this position was not propagated in a naive way, rather there was a more or less tacit assumption that women see themselves as nurturers of the planet, as people who 'care'. As Bella Abzug stated repeatedly, women 'care', therefore they have the right to be heard when the future of the planet is at stake. Arguing that women have a special connection with the environment has undeniably had the effect of forcefully bringing out their right to be heard by other actors involved in the environmental debate and within the UNCED preparatory process. Yet, this position, as we have argued earlier, will have to be problematized in the future for building politically effective alliances between women globally, as well as between women's and environmental, developmental and other movements.

Planeta Femea proceedings were somewhat disappointing in so far as the participating women had done little concrete strategizing for the future. The workshop on consumerism was a notable exception because here women made some concrete proposals for future action and strategies. One of the major impediments was that the emerging WED movement lacked a strong grassroots base. Participants in the second Miami Conference, who had arrived at a common position, were mainly women from developmental, environmental, reproductive rights and feminist groups as well as women from academia.

It is imperative for women globally to increase networking and collective strategizing, despite inevitable differences, in order to maintain the momentum created in Miami. At the same time women must increasingly form coalitions with environmental and other movements on specific issues; women taking part in these movements need to address the male bias inherent in the groups they are part of. Events at the 1992 Global Forum certainly made clear that a major task ahead for women will be to push for women's perspectives and needs to be considered not only in theory, but also in practice by governments as well as NGOs.

But women involved in this process must take care to avoid reproducing hierarchies and reversing dualisms in the process of forming new coalitions. New types of politics and non-dominating epistemologies are essential in order to effectively address the continuous spread of patterns of domination. It is here that we hope to contribute to the ongoing WED debate by offering our analysis and pointing to the in-depth arguments and discussions which so far have not been articulated. Important lessons can be drawn from the experiences in collective strategizing between the women's movements, feminist politicians and feminist bureaucrats who succeeded in placing women's concerns on the UN agenda since the early 1970s (see for example Lycklama, Testino, Vargas, Wieringa, forthcoming).

These are some of the major challenges for women involved in the post-UNCED process globally. Before the 1995 Women and Development Conference in Beijing, where a common platform on women and the environment is also planned, there is time to develop the potential to mark a period of historical changes within the global women's movement.

Notes

1. Some Northern women, too, were present at the founding meeting of DAWN. See Chapter 6 for an outline and critical review of DAWN's position.

2. For a critique of Community Forestry see Häusler (1991).

3. FAO, 1978, Forestry for Local Community Development, Forestry Papers No. 7 Rome.

4. The Greenbelt Movement is based in Kenya and has gained wide publicity through its leader, Wangari Maathai after the 1985 Nairobi Conference. The goal of the organization is to establish public green belts and fuel wood plots by local people, especially women, in the spirit of self reliance. The objectives of environmental recovery go hand in hand with local women's empowerment as they actively engage in improving their own as well as environmental conditions in their area.

5. The other four were food security and forestry, energy, industrialisation and human settlements, international environment and economic relations.

6. For the full definition and a discussion of the concept of sustainable development see Chapter 7.

7. For a more detailed account of how women gained access to UNCED see Corinne Wacker's article in WIDE (1992, 1:12–15).

8. WorldWIDE publishes a global directory of women professionals working in environment-related disciplines.

9. For a report on women's input into the Paris Conference see Celine Ostyn, in WIDE (1992, 1:26-7).

10. Recently, Shiva has concentrated her critique on biotechnology approaching it from a WED perspective by pointing out that the control over biodiversity was traditionally women's domain; women for example selected seeds for the next year's crop. Patenting of seeds brings an end to reproducing seeds within the rural household, which in turn, also contributes to women's disempowerment and farmers' poverty.

11. Shiva herself pointed out in a presentation during an IPAC study day held in June of 1991 in Amsterdam that hitherto she had addressed mostly male representatives of the environmental movement in the Netherlands and that this was the first time that she spoke there before a female audience.

12. It is important to note that Maathai has tactically used her prominent position

as the leader of the now internationally renown Greenbelt movement. She was actively involved in the movement against the Kenyan one-party state. As a result she was jailed, but her international recognition as one of Kenya's most important women leaders made it difficult for state forces to silence her. Due to international pressure she was soon released.

13. See diagram by Antrobus in Wiltshire (1992:6).

6. Alternative Development

The alternative structuralist and the alternative normativist approach to alternative development

In Latin America, Africa and Asia, Marxist scholars provided an important critique of the dominant Western development and opened out alternative development perspectives by questioning its benefits for the South at large. Starting in the 1950s neo-Marxist scholars had refined the original Marxian notion of the South's unitary feudal mode of production by providing a more differentiated analysis of world capitalism and its operation in particular Third World countries. Dependency theory as developed in Latin America by scholars like André Gunder Frank and the later work of Samir Amin[1] on the centre-periphery world capitalist model are included in what Sheth (1987) termed the alternative structuralist approach. He uses this term because this approach emphasizes the role of global economic structures in its explanations for Third World countries' impoverishment. A more recent move within this line of thinking is world system theory associated with the work of Immanuel Wallerstein which conceptualizes the operation of the world economy in terms of the internationalization of capital heading towards an impending crisis of world capitalism.[2] From their various ideological backgrounds writers subsumed under the label of alternative structuralism agree upon the negative impact of the world capitalist system on the Third World. They are propagating a reordering of the global economic system in favour of Third World countries to be brought about mainly by changes in the capitalist centre, the First World countries, and on state levels. Since the problems are seen as mainly structural, Sheth (ibid:158) pointed out that changes in non-state organizations or changes in consciousness by affected people that would render impossible the perpetuation of injustice are not addressed, hence there is a degree of blindness about the need for grassroots and intermediary levels of changes.

Like the dominant development model's protagonists, alternative structuralists emphasize the primacy of state agency in bringing about changes. Thus their analysis remains within an economistic framework and the notion of primacy in the agency of the state and elites in the South to counter the process of capital accumulation in the North. The question of agency in the process of transformation is encapsulated in discussions of '"objective" forces which work inexorably towards intensifying the crisis, thereby precipitating the collapse of the world capitalist system, in whose place, it is hoped, would emerge something like a world socialist system' (Sheth ibid:159). In terms of political action the proposal for delinking the Southern economies from the global system emerged from this line of thinking, albeit often with no concrete plans for action to bring about such a process in practice on local, national and regional levels. Even though the alternative structuralists have considerably contributed to an understanding of the continued deterioration of Southern economies they do not fundamentally question the notion of progress brought about by modernization with rapid economic growth.

We now turn to what Sheth has labelled the alternative normativist approaches to alternative development. He understands these as being more heavily concerned with practice than those of the proponents of alternative structuralism. Alternative normativists propagate a more holistic understanding of human well-being than do the alternative structuralists by emphasizing the role of self-reliance, alternative lifestyles, culture and material as well as non-material human needs. The notion of economic activity and growth as the central basis for the satisfaction of human needs is seen as secondary. Structures of interdependence and co-operation are assumed to require self-reliance and autonomy rather than the existing patterns of competition between the weak and the strong, where the former are either dependent upon or subjugated to the latter in an overall structure of domination (ibid:160).

Sheth's criticism of the alternative normativist approaches to alternative development mainly revolves around the fact that they operate from the assumption of a universal validity of their alternative norms and values and thus reproduce the dangers inherent in all types of universalisms, including that of the dominant development model. As Foucault has made clear, in any type of universalism the danger of the spread of patterns of domination is inherent, even if the aspirations of universalism in question are positive. The collapse of socialism may serve as an illustration of this point.

Sheth (ibid) points out that the articulation of values and their realization must depend on a participative democratic process involving all actors, not solely the norm-setting elites. Furthermore, what alternative development means in a particular social and cultural context may vary considerably from society to society. The role of grassroots movements in this articulation process is crucial for a bottom-up process of change; the involvement of people's own visions of how to deal with their problems is imperative. This view opens up new possibilities for the reconstruction of the South, away from only one valid model of development towards polycentric and polyphonic developments (Nederveen Pieterse 1991). In this context the quest for 'an alternative development paradigm', in the singular, to replace the dominant development paradigm, as was sought by many actors in different citizen's movements North and South within the UNCED preparatory process has indeed become questionable. As we shall see later, citizens' movements no longer seek 'an alternative development paradigm', and now acknowledge the need for multiple development styles (see, especially, the new idea of bioregionalism described in Chapters 7 and 8).

Examples of recent positions along the lines of alternative normativist approaches may be found in the work of some Indian scholars, who, in common with feminist critics of science, have contributed to a critique of the dominant development model by questioning its foundation, the epistemological framework of Western science as the only valid way of arriving at knowledge and its claims for universal truth. In particular, such scholars as Ashis Nandy (1987a, 1987b, 1988), Shiv Visvanathan (1987, 1990), and Vandana Shiva (1988, 1989), see Western science as the basic model of domination in our times, as the ultimate justification for all institutionalized violence. They, as do Western feminist critics of science, perceive the Western mode of development endorsed by their own political leaders as violence and terrorism, in theory and in practice. The contradictions of the project of Western-style development come out most clearly at the grassroots level in the South, at the extremities of power.

Visvanathan (1987) writes about development as slow genocide. He identifies the modern Indian state committed to science and in the hands of national elites as the primary force for the destruction of the environment. Since independence the Indian nation state has been wholeheartedly committed to modernization. India has advanced to a regional superpower with massive government spending on militarization: Westernized elites have adopted affluent consumerist lifestyles while sizable parts of the population have been marginalized by the modernization process and subsist below poverty level. Such large-scale projects as dams, nuclear power plants and so on, have displaced people from their land with devastating effects, in the name of development. Indian society today is extremely exploitative of its own marginalized population and natural resource base. In response local people have staged impressive protest actions against development projects.

The Chipko movement in India is an often cited example of the clash between the modern Indian state integrated into the international economy on the one hand, and local people's survival interests, on the other. Diverse pressures on the natural resource base in the Indian Himalayas, where the Chipko movement is located, are high. The national economy needs water and electricity as well as timber for urban mass consumption, while the rural economy needs water, fuel, fodder and timber for local survival. To satisfy the needs of the growing urban populations, intervention by the Indian state into the Himalayan environment as a source of natural resources is hardly avoidable. The sustenance of the Himalayan forests as a base for local survival becomes increasingly difficult in view of continued pressure on the fragile mountain environment. Thus local survival and national mass consumption interests have been clashing in the struggles of the Chipko movement with conflicting views on and use of nature's resources.

As noted in Chapter 5, Vandana Shiva has used the Chipko movement as a basis for her analysis. She argues that modern science is the cognitive basis of developmentalism (Shiva 1989). According to Shiva, and in parallel to the understanding of Western feminist critics of science, it is the product of white, Western, male thinking which is essentially reductionist and serves an economic structure based on exploitation, profit maximization and capital accumulation in the North. Shiva sees 'reductionist science' serving the interests of the global market economy as the root cause for the ecological crisis. As an illustration she sets up an opposition between scientific forestry with monoculture plantations producing pulp and timber for the global market and diversified natural forests producing a multitude of products for local needs. Reductionist science establishes a monopoly on knowledge used in the interest of an economic pursuit.

> Stripped of the power the state invests in it, such a science can be seen to be cognitively weak and ineffective in responding to problems posed by nature. As a system of knowledge about nature, reductionist science is weak and inadequate; as a system of knowledge for the market, it is powerful and profitable (Shiva in Nandy 1988:239).

In an essay on the meaning of sustainability Shiva outlines a critique of the Western science of economics by distinguishing the market economy from what she calls people's survival and nature's economy.

> Development and economic growth are perceived exclusively in terms of processes of capital accumulation. However, the growth of financial resources at the level of the market economy often takes place by diverting natural resources from people's survival economy. On the one hand this generates conflicts over natural resources, on the other hand it creates an ecologically unstable constellation of nature, people and capital (Shiva n.d.).

Sustainability for Shiva involves the regeneration of nature's processes and a subservience to nature's and not the market's laws of return. Visvanathan (1990) also provides a critique of the now dominant concept of sustainable development as defined by the Brundtland Commission. He points out that at the basis of the concept lies an instrumental view of both people and nature.

Shiva describes how traditional agriculture in India has, with minimum external input, been truly sustainable by being in harmony with natural cycles and using a diversity of traditional crops. The introduction of green revolution agriculture was an act of violence against nature and people: it exacerbated differentiation amongst the peasantry; large farmers, who could afford to invest into high-tech agricultural input, benefited and pushed many small- and medium-scale farmers out of agricultural production. Its impact on nature was destructive in that it led to production of few high-yield varieties of crops only, dependent on foreign input of fertilizers and seeds. Crop production is concentrated on the requirements of the export market (Shiva 1988).

People who work their land with traditional methods are usually perceived as poor and backward but, so Shiva argues, they in fact have an acceptable standard of livelihood. She concludes that, in India, through the introduction of development most people have become materially poor because, deprived of their livelihood, they had to sell their labour on the market for cash. This critique of the dominant development model's values leads her to redefine such crucial terms as development, progress, sustainability, poverty and wealth. Redefining such terms is a salient feature of Shiva's and many others' critique of the dominant Western development model.

Shiva's critique of Western science is not essentially new because she draws on earlier European critiques. But highlighting the interconnections between science, capital and the state from a Southern perspective gives immediacy to the direct perception of science as violence in theory, acted out in practice. Shiva and others postulate the need for a 'people's science of life' in order to simultaneously overcome poverty, degradation of the environment and subjugation of marginalized peoples. Such a science would be based on observation, the recuperation of people's subjugated knowledges, the use of feeling, intuition, and experience as ways of knowing. Goonatilake (1983) discusses some of the problems in defining a non-Western science.

In similar vein, Esteva (1987) argues for a regeneration of local people's space to counter the ills that development has brought to communities at the grassroots level. Esteva understands himself as a deprofessionalized intellectual who is involved in grassroot level actions and networks in Mexico. In a lucid critique of the West and developmentalism as a dehumanizing venture he describes how local groups are recovering their own knowledge and culture as a basis for another mode of development. The recovery of old values, such as hospitality, is a crucial element in recuperating the dimension of 'being' from the imposed primacy of 'having'.

What the above-mentioned alternative normativism development critics point to is that there is no single, valid road to development, namely the Western one, and that participatory democracy and respect for nature is central to socially and ecologically sustainable development. In common with the alternative structuralists, they challenge the North as the originator of the problems. Alternative normativists, however, attack not only the global capitalist system dictated by the North, but consumerism in the North as well as by their own elites in the South. They propagate a shift in values, simple lifestyles based on local cultures, and human and nature's integrity as opposed to the perception of people and nature as resources. Such 'resourcing' is also criticized by many Western feminists, for example Donna Haraway (1991).

While this kind of argument is persuasive, its problems lie in the tendency to idealize everything local and traditional while glossing over indigenous structures of exploitation and domination that were in place before the advent of development. The caste structure in India, the role of moneylenders, class conflicts and, most notably, the subordination of women, are cases in point. Recent movements towards communalism and religious fundamentalism in India and the Arab world are associated with the recovery of traditional cultures with, amongst others, serious consequences for women's status.

It would also be too sweeping to totally negate the validity of Western science and modernity, as this could lead to a dead end; we cannot simply turn back the clock. As was argued in Chapter 5, it is not feasible to go back in history and return to subsistence agriculture globally as, for example, Shiva and Mies propose. Shiva (1989) takes an anti-modernity position and advocates the total ban of national, in favour of local resource use. But positive and negative elements exist in modernity as well as in tradition. Nandy (1987a:116) rightly points out that the choice today is not between modernity and tradition in their pure forms but between critical modernism and critical traditionalism (see Chapter 3 for a feminist post-modern position on this point).

Possibly the only solution is to find grounds for democratic negotiations between the different and sometimes conflicting interests where all parties involved will have to negotiate the satisfaction of their respective needs which will allow for the means of survival of all. Development critics agree that there must be room for choice to live according to different world views, cultures and values that manifest in different styles of development. That is not to say that they must necessarily be preserved unchanged but that people should have the choice of the direction in which they want to change. Meanings and terms for coexistence must become subject for negotiation. As Sheth (1987) has argued, the adoption of values also needs to be subject to a participative democratic process. In these negotiations the questioning of consumerist urban lifestyles both in the South and the North and the destruction of nature that they imply are crucial. Export-oriented economies in the South, with their wasteful use of natural resources, often benefiting urban elites to the detriment of local people, are also important issues to be questioned.

As solutions to the development crisis become a matter of global survival, and large-scale development programmes introduced to the South represent a formidable legacy of failure, the voices of grassroots' people have been incorporated into the development discourse enunciated by mainstream development agencies. In a movement of inner reform of development and as a response to alternative development thinking and people's movements in the South, Northern NGDOs and the development industry at large have continually adopted and operationalized the newly emerging ideas from development critics and citizen's movements. The concepts of people's participation, participatory action research, non-formal education, indigenous knowledge systems, community forestry, low-level input and organic agriculture – in existence already in the 1970s – were successively co-opted by the development industry. But as these new reformative elements move from the margins to the centres of power, new and more sophisticated structures of domination are emerging simultaneously. As for example Majid Rahnema (1990) has demonstrated, participatory action research, in its inception a tool to help local people formulate their problems as they see them, has already been used as a new tool for domination by outside researchers to manipulate local people's perceptions according to the outsiders' views. Community forestry, developed in response to the imperative for people- as opposed to industry-oriented forestry has turned out to follow the same logic as conventional forestry, only on a smaller scale. It uses the rhetoric of people's participation without differentiating between the often conflicting interests of the peasantry along the axes of class, caste and gender. Local elites, in collusion with forestry department staff, have already learned to use Community Forestry rhetoric in their own favour with the effect that under the guise of people's participation local leaders became included in the group of benefactors of foreign aid flows (Häusler 1991).

The empowerment of local people to become agents in their own development, as called for by development critics, has become institutionalized by many NGDOs and is often stripped of its critical potential in the process. As Rahnema (in Sachs 1992:122) points out, institutionalization of empowerment by progressively minded NGDOs has in fact had the result of consolidating state power. When the development worker considers it essential to empower local farmers, for example, he assumes that they, in fact, have no power or at least not the right one. He sees it his mission to 'give' them the power they need. 'In the current participatory ideology. this formula is, in fact, nothing but a revised version of state power..' (ibid). Local and dispersed forms of resistance, disobedience, non-co-operation, boycotts and ridicule of 'powerful' people, as forms of exercising power, are indirectly dismissed and devalued as irrelevant. Rahnema argues that state power has thus been reified as the 'real' power to which everyone had access, provided they were ready to participate in the predetermined development design. Ultimately, this vision of power proves useful to the development establishment.

Yet, we would argue, these internal reforms of the development industry should not be entirely dismissed. As emancipatory ideas emerge, become popular, and are co-opted, new ideas and strategies are emerging. This process should be seen as part of ongoing and continuous struggles between 'empire and emancipation' (Nederveen Pieterse 1990), where humanization happens in the border zones.

The Amazon Development Fund, an initiative taken by the UK-based Gaia Foundation, indicates a new trend in alternative development (Gaia Foundation 1991); the following brief description of this project provides an example. In preparation for UNCED, the 500 years anniversary of European colonialism in the region and the international focus on the Amazon forests, a multitude of organizations started to build up a network. Forest peoples, NGDO and NGO workers, lawyers, development experts and individual government officials who have been working for many years towards the cultural and ecological integrity of the region are starting to work together towards the implementation of sustainable development strategies for the region, also taking into account indigenous people's priorities. Committees representing all the different interests decide what kind of development projects will be funded. Issues such as land rights, preservation of indigenous cultures and languages with the help of appropriate education systems, and means of livelihood for all inhabitants of the Amazon forests, are being negotiated with all parties involved. Due to the high publicity for the problems of the Amazon forests, large funds for development from many different groups and agencies in the North are made available to the region. These can be channelled into the implementation of the negotiated proposals on the grassroots level directly. Complicated logistics for isolated development projects with specific Amazon Indian groups can thus be avoided. At government level in Brazil, Bolivia, Colombia and Ecuador there have been a number of motivated individuals – for example, the former Brazilian minister for the environment, José Lutzenberger – in a political position to take action in this direction and contribute to transforming the governmental apparatus from within.[3]

This seems to be a promising example of how to bring about the required changes in development practice which will involve negotiations and the right to self-determination by the affected people. It is, however, also prone to the spread of new patterns of domination, because funding mechanisms leave considerable scope for control over Indian affairs by outsiders. Also, in the case of the Amazon region, there are politically powerful groups of loggers, ranchers and politicians ready to defend their vested interests with violent means. The story of the rubber tappers union in Brazil and the murder of its leader, Chico Mendes, documents the nature of these conflicts. The alliances between rubber tappers, indigenous people and international environmental groups, aimed at preserving the Amazon forests and the livelihoods of their inhabitants, has brought about new types of politics of alternative development (see Hecht and Cockburn 1989).

The cause of indigenous people in the context of visions for alternative development is important. There are many other examples of indigenous people's struggles, such as those of the Penan people of Malaysia, the Mohawks in Canada and other tribal societies. These peoples see themselves not as owners of resources but as part of nature, and hence use their environment in a sustainable way. They developed lifestyles, accumulated intimate knowledge and developed techniques over centuries, to live in harmony with nature. Their knowledge could at some point become crucial to the survival of the ecosystems in which they have been living. But as the developmental nation states, representing the vested interests of their Westernized elites, are increasingly using national natural resources, these peoples have become obstacles to development; many of them refuse to be integrated into mainstream development. Indigenous as well as other marginalized communities organize themselves and strike alliances with each other, and internationally with Northern citizen's movements in their fight to reappropriate and reclaim their own local spaces.

What is becoming increasingly clear is that people marginalized by the development process are carving out their own paths in solving their problems. In the fight against growing poverty not only indigenous people, but also many other marginalized communities in the South, are reviving their old methods of farming, recovering their subjugated knowledges and forms of local organization. They again grow their indigenous crops to become independent of expensive Western seeds and fertilizers and claim control over their local forests and other commons. With the collapse of the developmental nation states in Africa for example, a return to these methods is increasingly becoming a matter of survival.

Along with the struggles in the South are people's efforts in the West, and in the East, aimed at devolving centralized bodies' control over local spaces to local communities, for example, the farm co-operative movements in North America and Europe, and the growing activities of the Japanese women's Seikatsu Club. People in a particular area link with farmers who produce (often organically grown) food for local consumption. Costs for producing food are divided between shareholders and thus risks are not shouldered by the farmer alone, but spread over a larger group. Production and consumption are directly linked without involving excessive transport costs and profits for middle men. Owners of small- and medium-sized farms opt out of centrally determined agricultural production quotas and prices and thereby secure their own survival. The biological and bio-dynamic farming movement in Europe has been growing steadily in the last decades and is now subsidized by funds from the European Commission; the German government, too, provided support for farmers who practise biological farming (see also Chapter 8, on bioregionalism).

New types of political processes have been evolving as coalitions, increased networking and communications between groups interested in alternative modes of development, regionally and globally, have been emerging in recent years. The UNCED and NGO Global Forum preparatory process was an impressive illustration (see also Chapter 7).

In the debates on alternative development women's concerns often figure only marginally, even though within the non-governmental sector's process leading up to the Global Forum, and even the governmental UNCED process itself, women have received much more attention than in the past.

Feminist critique of development by DAWN (Development with Women for a New Era)

The DAWN network links women researchers living and working in the South and provides a powerful critique of the dominant mode of development (including WID approaches) as seen by women in the South. DAWN's aim is to develop a global women's network, able to provide guidelines for action based on research carried out by them with the goal to develop an alternative development paradigm, a programme for 'society from women's perspective' (Sen and Grown 1988),[4] based on Southern women's experience, perceptions and analysis.

Since the UN Women's Decade, independent networks, movements, alliances and organizations have developed globally, many of which share DAWN's commitment to women's empowerment. The DAWN group opposes the contention that feminism in the South has been imposed by white, Western, urban middle-class women, pointing out that feminism in the South has had an independent history since the 19th century, albeit not always in the form of independent and autonomous movements. Having been an important force for political change, feminism in the South has grown within struggles for national liberation from colonialism, as well as in peasants' and workers' struggles.[5]

Since its foundation in 1984 the position advocated by DAWN has developed further. It must be stressed that in common with other positions we have explored, DAWN's statements include a variety of views from women researchers in the South. DAWN women have, however, presented their position in exceptionally unitary statements, despite their inevitable differences along the axes of region, race and class.

Peggy Antrobus, from Barbados, DAWN's current co-ordinator, outlined the basis for an alternative type of analysis of development by women from the South (Antrobus 1989). For her, this analysis should be grounded in theories of development and social change which recognize the differences between those that aim at maintaining the status quo and those that seek to promote social change. The latter should recognize the limitations of a focus on economistic, materialist and positivist approaches to social science. DAWN's research methodology is bottom-up, that is, starting out from an analysis of micro-level experiences of poor, rural and urban women living in the South and linking these to the macro-economic level, on the assumption that experience at the micro-level and its analysis should inform macro-economic analysis and vice versa. Their analysis is holistic, integrating social, cultural, and political dimensions into economic analysis. DAWN members recognize the political nature of the process of development as well as the fact that concepts and causes of 'development' and 'underdevelopment' reflect imbalances of power within and between nations, rather than the presence or absence of resources. DAWN women base their alternative analysis on feminism, rejecting the separation of private and public domains: household from economy, personal and political reality, feeling/intuition and rationality. Above all they advocate that all women's work should be validated and accounted for in national accounting systems. They further promote a new practice of science, a science of empathy that uses intuition and reason simultaneously.

DAWN members question the present development model based on economic growth, and advocate a 'people-centred' approach, and equitable development based on the values of co-operation, resistance to hierarchies, sharing, accountability and commitment to peace, values also endorsed by the international women's movement.

As we have argued earlier, one great strength of Southern feminists has been to identify the multiple nature of subordination of women living in the South – simultaneously on the bases of sex, race and class, as well as their position in the international economic order. Consequently, DAWN promotes women's empowerment within the context of wider international and societal changes. As Antrobus points out, women's empowerment can come about only by examining all internal contradictions of race, class and nationality. The empowerment of women must, therefore, address oppressive structures on different levels simultaneously.

The DAWN group's empowerment approach challenges the dominant mode of development on a more fundamental level than did WID in its original assumptions (see Moser in Wallace and March 1991). Empowerment of women in the South has to be part of the empowerment of their countries *vis-à-vis* the North. The empowerment approach focuses on a reading of power that differs from that stipulated by WID: instead of defining power as domination over others – implying that a gain of power for women would mean a loss of power for men – the stress is on women's increased self-reliance and internal strength. Women shall have the right to make their own choices through acquiring control over material and non-material resources. The WID assumption that development is basically benevolent is also questioned by DAWN whose approach thus takes into account the international economy's influence on the increase in poverty of both men and women in the South. DAWN also criticizes WID thinking by asking whether women in the South want to be integrated into mainstream Western-designed development at all. Within the WID framework these women have no say in determining in what kind of society they want to live and, implicitly, have to adapt to an imposed model from the North. Government agencies and the development establishment are only reluctantly supporting the radical changes within their own organizational framework that this empowerment approach calls for. The wider social and political changes advocated by DAWN are, however, reflected in Gender and Development (GAD) thinking (see Chapter 5). DAWN sees political mobilization, consciousness-raising and popular education as crucial to effect women's empowerment.

WID, as advocated by Northern development agencies, was, according to DAWN, flawed in the very beginning by assuming that women in the South were outside the economic mainstream and needed only access to resources and services in order to contribute to the growth of their national economies. Research during the UN Women's Decade showed clearly that women's contribution was central to development; in fact it was the very base on which development was constructed, albeit in a way that was deeply exploitative of women's time, labour, paid (in the workplace) and unpaid (in the household), and their sexuality (Antrobus 1989). The main critique of WID is that women's programmes lead to the super-exploitation of women's time in the face of the economic crisis. Ultimately, WID is meant to preserve the primacy of the economic growth model, a model that is capitalizing on gender roles of women in the reproductive sector to meet the basic needs of the poorest sectors of society. Under Structural Adjustment Programmes it is women who have to compensate for cuts in government spending for social services, and it is women who work as cheap labour in free trade zones to increase export-oriented production.

For the coming years DAWN has identified three key issues on which research and policy development should focus: alternative economics, reproductive rights and women and environment. These topics will contribute towards setting up a framework for the formulation of an alternative development paradigm for the future. Case studies have revealed regional differences in the economic situation with varying effects on women's positions, and these variations will have to be taken into account when developing alternative policies.

The issue of the environment, new to DAWN's agenda, has been taken up in response to the emergence of environmental movements in the South in which women have assumed a central role. DAWN members intend to put on the agenda a politicized perspective on the use of natural resources. This position provides yet another angle from which to criticize the economic growth model. DAWN women have already challenged the spread of the North's consumerist lifestyle in connection with their critique of Structural Adjustment Programmes and their effects on women in the South. Consumerist lifestyles, adopted also by Third World elites, are seen as the root cause of the debt crisis that affects both women's increasing workload and environmental deterioration. The value system underlying the present growth model of economic development, in that it puts profits before people, is seen as a key problem. In response, Antrobus proposes to create a counter-culture to consumerism.

The DAWN analysis of the environmental crisis thus makes a strong link between economy and ecology.[6] DAWN women see that an analysis of the ecological crisis demands an holistic approach. The issues of health, technology, distribution, power and social organization are all seen in connection with the environment. As Peggy Antrobus recently pointed out[7] a poor, Third World woman's first environment is her body. If her child is dying, it is useless to talk to her about trees. The real issues are seen as maldevelopment and economic injustices within the global economic system as they are manifesting in the South: invariably, cash crop production oriented towards quick returns has a devastating effect on soils. Militarism, the export of nuclear and other hazardous wastes to the South, nuclear testing, especially in the Pacific, and the General Agreements on Tariffs and Trade (GATT) negotiations, if adopted, will all have a negative impact on the environment and people. Within the GATT framework, for example, the provision of environmental conservation will be left up to general market mechanisms.

Like other development critics from the South[8] the DAWN women see the environmental debate as a Northern discourse mainly initiated by Northern environmentalists. DAWN refutes the argument of population growth, identified by many environmentalists as the major reason for environmental degradation in the South. For DAWN this argument helps to evade the responsibility of macro-economic processes for the overuse of natural resources and large-scale inequalities that drive the South's poor to environmentally vulnerable land. In this context the increasingly coercive application of population control measures in the South are condemned by the DAWN women.

Reproductive rights are a major concern for women in the South. The increased interest in the correlation between population growth and environmental degradation has created a new sense of urgency for DAWN to work on this issue as one of their priority research areas. DAWN members stress that ultimately a successful reduction of birthrates will depend on individual women's desire to have fewer children, and this in turn largely depends on their social and economic situation. Women have the right to make decisions about their own bodies and must not be forced to accept contraceptive devices that they know nothing about, nor want, and which may be harmful to their health. DAWN researchers are challenging the patriarchal and capitalist nature of prevailing population policies which instrumentalize women in the South to reduce their birthrates at the North's quest to safeguard the global environment (Wiltshire 1992; see also Chapter 7, pp. 142ff.).

Women, especially poor women from the South, are seen as central in the balance between population and land, reproduction and production, sustainable development and ecological disaster. Poor, Third World women are seen by DAWN women as the source of the new alternative because their situation is typified by the conjuncture of all types of oppression based on race, class, and gender.

As mentioned in the opening of this chapter, DAWN presents a powerful challenge to mainstream WID, and to development theory and practice in general. Perceiving women's problems in terms of multiple subordinations that need to be addressed simultaneously avoids the pitfall of WID that explains women's deteriorating situation solely in terms of the male/female opposition. But as Chapter 2 noted, the imagery of the 'poor Third World woman' as the ultimate other, conjuncture of all forms of domination, and hence as offering the only position that can inform the search for future alternatives, is problematic. In line with the argument throughout this book, we cannot accept this part of the DAWN analysis, because in our understanding, this image fails to account for differences between women in the South. As Haraway (1991) has pointed out, this image may backfire, as it confines Southern women to otherness. Visions from below the platforms of power are less prone to distortion, but subjugation does not necessarily result in superior vision.

However important may be consideration of poor, Southern women's perspective in bringing about transformations of the dominant mode of development, this assumption could lead to another totalizing vision of development from one particular perspective only, that is, that of poor women in the South. This move could result in a mere reversal of hierarchies, not to their transcendence. Another related problem is rooted in the DAWN women's claim to speak from the perspective of poor women, while they themselves are often from urban, middle-class backgrounds, notwithstanding their personal commitment to poor women's empowerment.

Devaki Jain, also member of DAWN, proposed that women collectively develop a feminist perspective on global development to present at the 1995 International UN Conference on Women and Development in Beijing (Jain 1990). For the first time in the network's history DAWN women have invited Northern women to join them in a critique of the global economic model. Together with three Northern women's networks: Women in Development Europe, (WIDE), the Canadian Institute for Research and Advancement of Women, (CREO), and the US-based Alt-WID network, DAWN founded a Coalition for Alternative Development during the women's conference, Planeta Femea, at the Global Forum 1992 in Brazil. The first step is to develop an alternative economic framework from women's perspective. Northern women's networks are asked to develop critiques of their own countries' economic and social development based on the analysis developed by DAWN and then endeavour to influence their own governments accordingly. The women participating in this coalition aim to come up with an alternative economic framework as the basis for a new development paradigm and action-oriented programmes from women's perspective globally.

This alliance between Northern and Southern women is very encouraging and, if it is built on mutual respect for each other's positions and political struggles, could prove to be very fruitful. Connection and affinity between women globally and a recognition of their multiple positionality are key issues in such an alliance in order to arrive at a qualitatively different collective basis for struggle. The North's knowledge about the South, enshrined in Northern academic institutions and development agencies, has enjoyed a privileged degree of credibility over the South's knowledge of itself. A major challenge for women will be to ensure that this aspect is addressed in both Northern and Southern academic institutions. DAWN, and many other Southern critics of development, have provided important elements for an analysis of the North as the originator of the present development model and its crisis. But merely to reverse the old hierarchies of North over South, implicit in DAWN's proposal for Northern women to apply their theoretical framework to their own societies, may backfire. It is imperative that together, women from both North and South, must attack unequal North/South relations from their respective positions. The dominant development paradigm as well as the epistemological assumptions upon which it is based must be challenged from various sides simultaneously, from within the centres of its dispersion and from the so-called margins. The resulting 'rainbow' politics (Harding 1992), based on situatedness and specificities of struggles, are potentially much more powerful if they are based on strategic alliances between women (and others) from both North and South, as is argued in Chapter 3.

Notes

1. See André Gunder, Frank, 1967, *Capitalism and Underdevelopment in Latin America*, New York: Monthly Review Press; for a Marxist reformulation of dependency theory see Samir Amin, 1974, *Accumulation on a World Scale: A Critique of the Theory of Underdevelopment*, New York: Monthly Review Press.
2. For a discussion on the differing positions in world system theory see Amin, Samir, Giovanni Arighi, André Gunder Frank and Immanuel Wallerstein, 1982, *Dynamics of Global Crisis*, New York: Monthly Review Press.
3. Since the beginning of the Gaia Foundation's initiative, clashes within the Brazilian state have led to Lutzenberger's dismissal as environment minister.
4. This book is based on a report originally written for the Nairobi Women and Development Conference in 1985.
5. See also Jayarwardena (1982) and Wieringa (forthcoming).
6. See also DAWN's most recent statement on the environment, prepared for the Global Forum at Rio de Janeiro 1992 by Wiltshire (1992); this is briefly outlined in Chapter 5.
7. In a presentation at the Annual Women in Development Europe (WIDE) meeting, Dublin, 27 February to 2 March 1992.
8. See for example Rajni Kothari (1981-82).

7. Environmental Reforms and the Debates on Sustainable Development

In response to growing public awareness of environmental degradation and pressures from environmental movements, academics, professionals and so on, few countries now lack an institutional and legal framework for the protection of the environment and regulation of the use of natural resources; in fact the number of international environmental regimes is on the increase. Since the UN Conference on the Human Environment in Stockholm in 1972 and the subsequent establishment of the UN Environmental Programme (UNEP), environmental issues have figured with increasing prominence on the international and, in particular, the UN agenda. The process of public hearings initiated by the Brundtlandt Commission in preparation for the report *Our Common Future* (WCED 1987) set a model for the work of UN institutions, which involved different citizens' groups, business and industry, and so on, in consultations within the preparatory process leading to the UN Conference on Environment and Development (UNCED) — the 1992 Earth Summit. Environmental reforms within the global economic system accelerated rapidly with the preparatory process towards UNCED.

An illustration of environmental reforms is the expansion of the environmental industry: companies which deal with technologies, research, and know-how in cleaning up the environment. Paradoxically, the continued environmental damage is the reason for their existence. The export of 'environmentally friendly' technology to the South and to Eastern Europe is an industry with much potential for growth to benefit industrialized countries in the future. Ironically, as already noted in Chapter 2, the West is engaged in transferring its own redundant and environmentally destructive technology to the South and East due to pressures within the industrialized countries for cleaner technology.

Another symptom of transformations is the emergence of new interdisciplinary areas of scientific investigations, new disciplines, for example: environmental and ecological economics; environmental sociology; or new professional fields, such as environmental accounting or international environmental law. A new type of technology geared towards redressing and monitoring environmental destruction and contamination is being developed as a prospective growth industry. New 'green' symbols are increasingly in evidence in the North, and such new symbols are rapidlly becoming an integral part of common knowledge and awareness. The image of spaceship Earth with its limited resources and complex interrelationships between all animate and inanimate life forms has become common. Popular and political discourse has now incorporated ecological terminology; everybody is becoming an environmentalist.

Environmental concerns also play an increasing role in the development industry. The UN's Food and Agriculture Organization (FAO) which promoted green revolution projects in the South (dependent upon chemical fertilizers, imported high-yield seeds, pesticides, and mechanization of production) now also supports low external input agriculture, and recognizes the need to take into account people's knowledge, hence the development industry's growing interest in indigenous knowledge systems. In most development organizations environmental impact assessments (and assessments of the impact on women) are becoming routine at project level. For example, in line with other organizations, the World Bank has set up a Central Environmental Department and four regional technical environmental divisions to deal with the environmental screening of World Bank projects. Yet, the number of staff members in the environmental department of the World Bank is too small to effectively screen all projects. Activities of the department's staff are not popular with their colleagues in other departments who often see environmental screening as disruptive to the smooth operation of project procedures; and recommendations are frequently modified or manipulated in order to ensure that a particular project is acceptable for implementation. Much, however, remains to be done to integrate the policies on environment into overall development aid and credit policies. Such integration would require fundamental changes in development practice, which, as some critics argue, would have to break with the economistic logic of development itself, namely, its main principle that more economic growth is needed to pay for environmental repair. The South's criticism of Western 'ecological imperialism' (for example Kothari 1981/82) points out that Northern environmentalism is geared mainly to protecting the Northern environment and mode of development. The greening of the development industry from within serves to perpetuate its own existence by co-opting ideas from people's movements and NGOs in the South (see Chapter 6).

Common to all the above proposals is their aim to improve the system while failing to fundamentally question the basis of the present mode of development. The motor driving current reforms is the emergence of a broad movement towards pro-environmental changes encompassing all sections and divisions of society and geographical regions, and comprising different formal and informal, governmental and non-governmental, local and regional organizations and groups of concerned citizens, experts, and professionals, which have developed and consolidated strong international networks. Addressing environmental problems from their perspectives, experiences and knowledge each, in a specific way, contributes to the process of greening the industrial growth model of development on different levels and to differing degrees. But it has become increasingly clear, especially within the UNCED process, that interests differ considerably between those who want simply to 'green' the system within prevailing global political and economic power structures and those who want to radically change it. The latter, mainly citizens' groups and social movements, see substantial changes in power relations as the prerequisite for sustainability. Those holding to these opposing positions, however, do not operate in isolation from each other; as Chapter 6 made clear, ideas from the margins travel into the centres of power and can thereby contribute to changing the system from within.

We turn now to the beginnings of environmental thinking. Environmentalist thinking in the West is not new, but dates from the end of the 19th century (MacCormack 1989) when the predecessors of today's environmental movements were active in the nature conservation organizations in North America and Europe. Some of these early conservationists have advocated the protection of species, landscapes and selected areas for almost a century. With some exceptions[1] the environmental movements in the South gained momentum largely in the 1970s. During the last decade, nature conservation organizations have undergone an evolution in their approach as they began to include social, economic and political issues. For instance, the International Union for the Conservation of Nature (IUCN), founded in 1948, was one of the first conservation organizations to link the environmental crisis with development, and to promote sustainable development. Conservation organizations' original aim – the 'selective' protection of nature – has been reformulated into the maintenance of biodiversity. Previously guided largely by ethical and aesthetic concerns, conservation organizations now stress the intrinsic value of nature, and the imperative to preserve the integrity of the mutiplicity of ecosystems. Once limited to the margins, this approach has been taken up by many governmental bodies.

Fuelled by the problems related to the accelerated destruction of the environment these changes also reflect a general shift in attitudes towards nature. Protection of nature in select sites or of specific species advocated by some conservationists is no longer a central concept. Realizing that the use of natural resources within the present economic growth model of development must be limited, there has been a re-evaluation of the human/nature relationship itself in some quarters. The assumptions and attitudes which have legitimized human domination over nature are being challenged. Anthropocentrism (or androcentrism), which promulgates the utilitarian value of nature for ensuring the survival of humankind, is increasingly subject to criticism in light of the need to understand the complexity of ecosystems, interdependence between humans and nature, and symbiotic relationships and promote a holistic perception of the planet.[2]

This shift in perception of the human/nature relationship accords with different responses to the environmental crisis, one of which is to see environmental destruction as an unforeseen and unintended side-effect of development, of the complexity and scale of production which necessitate environmental reforms of the system. The notion of environmental reform is based on the assumption that the system can be remedied by improving the tools (better science, appropriate technologies, the introduction of environmental accounting into the operational system of enterprises/national economies, and better management of resources). This move calls for increased and more sensitive environmental awareness and transformations in ethical attitudes towards an acceptance and implementation of enlightened stewardship of nature by human beings, which is advocated by mainstream institutions.

The processes of transformation within this position are typified by diminishing faith in science and technology as a panacea for environmental ills. Recognition of the irreversibility of damage to the environment should lead not only to reducing its extent but to preventing further destruction in the immediate future. Reforms alone, though important, are not enough, it is the root for causes of the widespread environmental destruction that must be addressed.

Adherents of deep ecology, social ecology and of ecofeminism, for example, challenge the dominant mode of development as inherently wrong. They point to the deep cultural roots of the crisis and call for a reconceptualization of development based on equitable relationships between humans and humans, men and women, and humans and nature (see Chapter 8).

UNCED and the NGO Global Forum in 1992

UNCED was instrumental in setting up the necessary legal framework for implementing sustainable development on a global level. The three years' preparation for UNCED were decisive in accelerating the processes of pro-environmental reforms and changes. Within the preparatory process the non-governmental sectors (business, youth, environmental, women's and many other groups) were involved in lobbying their government representatives. Governments, often in consultation with citizens' representatives, drafted national reports on the state of the environment to be presented at UNCED. Alternative reports, drafted by NGOs, fed into an alternative process culminating in the organization of the Global Forum held parallel to UNCED in Rio de Janeiro (see Chapter 6 for a brief description of this process).

The plan of the governmental UNCED process was to ratify several documents, primarily Agenda 21, the programme for action for the 21st century. This long-term plan for environment and development addresses:

1) Social and economic issues, for example development assistance, population control and the alleviation of poverty.
2) The protection of nature and the management of natural resources
3) The role of NGOs and other social groups (for example, youth, women, trade unions, the business sector, local government) in sustainable development.
4) The financial means for implementation; technology transfer, science for sustainable development; environmental education, information and decision-making and new institutions.

Also planned were: ratification of binding conventions on climate change, which contained limitations for emissions of greenhouse gases by individual countries; the biodiversity convention, which aimed at the preservation of plant and animal species and limitations to patenting of biologically engineered organisms; and a forestry convention.

The Earth Charter, intended to lay out the ethical principle for human/human and human/environment relations as the basis for sustainable development, was replaced by a less far-reaching document: the Rio Declaration.

Much less than originally planned was achieved during the preparatory process and at UNCED, due to clashes of interests. The United States played a key role in watering-down of the formulations of prepared texts for ratification at UNCED. The proposed biodiversity convention, in particular, suffered from President Bush's tough stand of not sacrificing any national interests. In effect, the large number of species endemic in the South are still open to unregulated use by the biotechnology industry. Also, the proposed climate convention was blocked by the US delegation which refused to commit the US to cuts in greenhouse gas emissions which other industrialized countries were quite willing to accept.

Pledges for finance to implement the proposed changes made in Rio amounted to some US$ 2.5 billion, a fraction of the UN-estimated US$ 70 billion needed. Many rich nations resisted raising their aid levels to 0.7 per cent of GNP, a goal set already two decades ago. But all the industrialized countries committed themselves to increase financial assistance specifically for environmental development projects. The Global Environmental Facility (GEF), as implemented by the World Bank, the UN Development Programme (UNDP), and the UN Environmental Programme (UNEP), are all committed to channelling increased assistance to the South for environmental programmes.

The World Bank's record for undemocratic proceedings and lack of transparency plus its domination by Northern countries' interests, are causes for questioning the benevolent impact of future projects to be devised and funded through GEF, with only token representation of Southern and NGO voices in the decision-making concerning the distribution of funds.

Within the official UNCED process, environmental recovery was predominantly seen in terms of channelling more money into environmental programmes; a fundamental rethinking of the Western development model and the global economic system as such did not take place. Even though it was in the interest of Southern political leaders participating in the Earth Summit to employ this line of thinking in order to bargain for more development funds to be channelled to the South, NGOs have criticized the fact that in the UNCED proceedings most issues responsible for the crisis were omitted. The impact of unfair trade mechanisms (via GATT negotiations, for example), the problems posed by debt repayment, which exacerbate environmental problems by necessitating increased exports of natural resources, were not taken into account at UNCED. Ironically, even a substantial increase in fund flows for environmental recovery to the South may amount to just a fraction of the environmental destruction created in the South through continual export of natural resources to the North.

A non-binding declaration of forest management principles and preservation of forests was signed at UNCED. But the text of the declaration promotes conversion of forests to plantations and other commercial uses, largely ignoring the rights and survival needs of indigenous forest-dwellers. Conservation of existing forests was not addressed.

Action Agenda 21, too, is non-binding, even though it will serve as a yardstick to measure governments' performances in the future. Already during the fourth Preparatory Committee Meeting (PrepCom IV), references to transnational corporations' (TNCs) activities had been deleted from Agenda 21.There is no doubt that the TNC lobby is highly influential at national government levels. In fact, TNCs have succeeded to date in remaining free to pursue their activities without accountability either to any government or international body. Additionally, regulations regarding the export of nuclear wastes from the North to the South found no place in the Rio Declaration; neither is there any reference to a ban on testing nuclear weapons.

The climate and the biodiversity treaties were signed only in watered-down versions and, as already noted, the latter was not signed by the US, but President Clinton seems set to rectify this. Also, in the absence of any commitment to regulate the use of the South's (or North's) natural organisms – plant and animal – the biodiversity convention leaves the biotechnology industry free to continue exploiting them.

Agenda 21 also incorporates institutional changes. The Commission on Sustainable Development (CSD) is a body specifically set up to monitor the follow-up of UNCED and the implementation of Agenda 21.

At the 47th session of the UN General Assembly in New York on 22 December 1992 member country delegates decided to set up the CSD as a functional Commission of the UN Economic and Social Council (ECOSOC). The CSD comprises 53 seats for member states with a representative number from the five UN regions: 13 from Africa, 11 from Asia, 10 from Latin America and the Caribbean, 6 from Eastern Europe, and 13 from Western Europe. CSD will report annually to ECOSOC.

In a move to restructure and streamline the economic, social and sustainable development activities within the UN system, the UN Secretary-General initiated the creation of three new departments, which will be based in New York: the Department for Policy Coordination and Sustainable Development (of which the CSD secretariat will be part); an Interagency Committee on Sustainable Development, which will report to the Administrative Committee on Coordination (ACC) (headed by the Secretary-General); and a high-level Advisory Board of eminent persons as foreseen in Agenda 21.

NGOs with a Consultative status in ECOSOC are said to be able to participate in the CSD; in addition, Agenda 21 and the UN general Assembly provided the mandate to accredit other NGOs who had participated in UNCED.

The CSD secretariat, as part of the Department of Policy Coordination and Sustainable Development, will have three offices: in New York, in Geneva, and a liasion office in Nairobi. It will be the task of the CSD secretariat to liaise with NGOs and the major groups represented in Agenda 21 (such as women, youth and indigenous people).

Effective lobbying of country delegates by many Northern and Southern NGOs which had participated in the UNCED process and their close monitoring of the proceedings at the working group sessions preceding the UN General Assembly meeting in New York, resulted in the issues of NGO participation and the need for gender balance on all levels in the follow up of UNCED and within the CSD being taken-up in the proceedings at the General Assembly meeting.

Directly after UNCED, there was a strong feeling that an alternative and independant organization should be set up to complement CSD's activities. The Earth Council, chaired by Maurice Strong, UNCED's former Secretary-General, was therefore set up with headquarters at San José, Costa Rica, in March 1993. This council consists of eminent personalities from science, business and other sectors of civil society and aims at liaising with the CSD and the NGOs active in the UNCED process. It sees itself as an 'ombudsman' on sustainable development matters from a moral rather than a political perspective and aims to draw up an Earth Charter consisting of a 'set of principles and values to guide the transition towards a more equitable and sustainable future' (The Network, Centre for Our Common Future, March 1993, p.5).

In 1991 at the global NGO Conference Paris, as has been noted earlier in this book, groups from the different regions synthesized their visions for the future in the documents 'Roots for the Future' and 'Agenda Ya Wananchi', a citizens' Action Plan for the 1990s. At the International NGO and Social Movement Global Forum in Rio these NGOs representing social movements drafted and ratified alternative treaties which included all the issues omitted from the official UNCED agenda, for example: the role of global economic and political power structures, the need for social equity, participative democracy, an end to militarization, a moratorium on nuclear testing, the plight of indigenous people, and many more. So far 46 treaties have been prepared for signing; even now, after UNCED, the signing process remains open.

At the NGO Global Forum, representatives of citizens' movements decided against setting up a central body to monitor the implementation of the alternative treaties and instead to keep the follow-up process decentralized and responsive to regional diversities and needs. Creative and flexible use of the Alternative Treaties in the follow-up process to UNCED by NGOs and citizens' groups world-wide was encouraged.

The political landscape for the non-governmental sector globally has changed after UNCED and the Global Forum in Rio. As Martin Khor (1992b) points out, there are now stronger links between Northern and Southern groups and between development and environment activists, and, therefore an increased potential for collective struggles. It will be difficult for conservative environmentalists to identify conservation of specific wildlife species and population issues as of primary relevance to the crisis, without simultaneously addressing such issues as international global equity and global power structures. Major Northern-based environmental groups such as Greenpeace, WWF and Friends of the Earth are involved in criticizing such economic issues as aid, debt, patenting of organisms, terms of trade, GATT, the World Bank, TNCs, and the IMF. Some Northern citizens' movements are now advocating, much more vigorously, for changes in lifestyles in the North.

The outcome of UNCED falls short of the original aspirations, but it had important consequences. NGO activists, professionals and academics are developing new, alternative economic frameworks for the future, an important element in the period of transition towards sustainable modes of development. Public pressure on governments, development agencies and industry to step-up their efforts to minimize environmental destruction is increasing further.

The language of sustainable development and of interdependency has been widely adopted by mainstream political, economic and development organizations. But the newly arising eco-cratic rationality, as propagated by mainstream organizations before and after UNCED, is flawed in two ways. First, its proponents propose to implement sustainable development within the present political and economic power structures. Secondly, the new eco-cratic model of the interdependence and interrelatedness of the biosphere is rooted in systems theory and continues to subscribe to the notion that it can be understood only by experts/scientists. Under the guise of a claim to scientific neutrality the old experts claim the right to prescribe measures to redress the global process of environmental destruction from an epistemologically superior position. The visions for sustainable development coming from such other epistemological positions as deep ecology, ecofeminism, social ecology and many others interested in alternative modes of development, point to the cultural, political and economic roots of the environmental crisis. Sustainable development will hardly be a realistic goal without the contributions of all of these groups' positions, which together make up a broad movement towards pro-environmental change, whether reformist or radical. Conversely, the UNCED process has also revealed growing polarizations with the emerging trend characterized by a rise of conflicting strategies for sustainable development.

The sustainable development debate

There are now largely differing definitions and perceptions of the concept of sustainable development and what kind of changes are actually implied if it is to be made operational. This concept, a central element in environmental change, originally emerged from within the economic growth model which, in its logical consequence, has led to environmental degradation and resource depletion. Belief in the linearity of progress, irrespective of natural limits to growth, is being questioned.

Thomas Malthus, in the 18th century, based his theory on the connection between population growth and diminishing natural resources. He concluded that population growth cannot exceed available natural resources without causing famine and disease, which, in turn, would provide a natural check to population growth. This relationship, between available natural resources and population growth, is a recurring theme in recent literature on sustainable development.

Sustainable development as a policy goal has been on the UN agenda since the 1972 UN Conference on the Human Environment, in Stockholm. The importance of sustainable development has been stressed by IUCN, UNEP and the World Wide Fund for Nature (WWF) in their World Conservation Strategy, adopted in 1980. This Strategy sought to achieve three main objectives: to maintain essential ecological processes, to preserve genetic diversity; and to secure sustainable utilization of species and ecosystems. Redclift (1987) criticizes the Strategy on the grounds of an insufficient analysis of the political and economic reasons behind the deterioration of natural resources. The Second World Conservation Strategy, *Caring for the Earth: A Strategy for Sustainable Development* published in 1991, sought to address this criticism by building in social and economic concerns. It also includes a section on women's role in natural resource management.

The Brundtland Report, *Our Common Future*, has to be seen as a landmark document as it generated international interest in the notion of sustainable development. For many scholars, the Report's definition of the term has become a point of departure (see below).

The desirability of sustainable development has also been addressed by many international bodies, including: the Brandt Commission (1990); The South Commission (1990); and the Stockholm Initiative on Global Security and Governance (1991). UNICEF has postulated it as a means to off-set the deterioration in children's living conditions. Within the UNCED process the debate on sustainable development has intensified and sustainable development has moved to the centre of the international political agenda, with most governments adopting at least the rhetoric.

Despite a broad consensus among mainstream political and development institutions on the need for sustainable development, the understanding of what it means, in theory as well as in practice, differs considerably. Within the UNCED process non-governmental and citizens' movements objected to the term, which, in their view, implied more of the same, with only slight improvements. Many of these non-governmental actors, including Planeta Femea participants, no longer use the term.

John Pezzey (1989), quoted 27 sources for definitions of sustainability. In a recent article, Diana Mitlin (1992) overviews the range of definitions and broad recommendations, how sustainable development criteria can be integrated into economic decision-making, how scholars position themselves in the sustainability versus economic growth debate, and specific issues on sustainable development in the context of development assistance to the South.

The definition of the term most often referred to is that in the Brundtland Commission Report:

> Sustainable development is development which meets the needs of the present without compromising the ability of future generations to meet their own needs... Sustainable development requires meeting the basic needs of all and extending to all the opportunity to satisfy their aspirations for a better life (WCED 1987:43-4).

The Commission argues the necessity for increased economic growth, not only to pay for cleaning up the environment but also for improving the South's living conditions.

If large parts of the developing world are to avert economic, social and environmental catastrophes, it is essential that global economic growth be revitalised. In practical terms it means more rapid economic growth in both industrial and developing countries' (WCED 1987:89).

But:

... sustainable development must not endanger the natural systems that support life on Earth: the atmosphere, the waters and soils, and the living beings (WCED 1987:45).

To this end the Brundtland Commission proposed a variety of means ranging from changes in technology to legal and institutional measures.

The Brundtland Report has been much criticized on the grounds that continued economic growth is irreconcilable with sustainable development; growth for environmental recovery itself leads to further environmental degradation. Conversely, the Report's arguement in favour of continued economic growth has resulted in the concept of sustainable development being widely accepted within mainstream economic, development and political institutions, because it does not fundamentally threaten the status quo, for which the imperative for continued economic growth is a crucial element.

Michael Redclift (1987) criticizes the absence of analytical stringency in the concept itself. Any definition of *sustainable* development depends, of course, upon the definition of development, and what it is that is to be sustained, that is, the continued high levels of consumption or the fulfilment of basic needs. Definitions of wealth, poverty, well-being, needs, scarcity and so on, vary according to culture (see, for example, Shiva 1989). Moreover, as Michael Redclift points out, different perceptions of the environment are in themselves socially constructed and 'supported by social groups with different degrees of power and with conflicting economic interests' (Redclift 1987:202). Redclift's critique points out how politically contested is the notion of sustainable development. The Brundtland definition obfuscates this point by alluding to a 'common interest' in sustainable development of both the North and the South in a mode of 'partnership', without addressing the role of power relations.

In line with Redclift, Adams (1992) maintains that the concept of sustainable development has no coherent analytical core: '...sustainable development is intensely synthetic, [its] second characteristic is the apparent ease with which different ideas about development are grafted on' (Adams 1990, cited after Mitlin 1992:113). Adams points out that the British government has readily adopted the concept because it does not necessitate any major policy changes. Like Redclift, he stresses the need to place environmental issues within a wider economic, social and political context.

To address the problem of the sometimes conflicting uses of the term sustainable development, the United Nations Information Service in Geneva has recently commissioned a study to clarify what the different UN organizations mean by it (Grossmann, 1992).

Esteva and Prakash (1992), in a case study of the struggle about the Narmada Dam in India provide an illuminating example of conflicting applications of the term 'sustainable development'. The pro-dam lobby maintains that sustainable development means large-scale, centralized schemes capable of meeting the rapidly increasing food, water and energy needs of the modern Indian economy, with the state as the main arbiter. The anti-dam lobby sees the state as a puppet in the hands of national and transnational capital, and such mega projects as the Narmada Dam as benefiting mainly the urban middle class and catering to their Western-oriented, high energy consumption lifestyles. They argue that the effect on local people – loss of land, culture and livelihood, migration, uprootedness and further social and economic problems – are seen as tolerable and necessary sacrifices for the national good.

Both sides have applied cost-benefit analyses, providing different figures of the dam's environmental and social costs to prove their respective points. Each side has mobilized local peasants and villagers in support of their struggles.

> [B]oth lobbies seem equally sincere in their commitment to the same goals. Both speak the same economic language of sustainable development and the same moral language of social justice and equality. Both employ the same strategies and marches and sit-down protests for demonstrating their solidarity with the underprivileged. Most people cannot follow and understand the technical arguments which apparently divide the experts. Most cannot discern that this technical discourse may mask a genuine clash of cultures (Esteva and Prakash 1992:48).[3]

Robert Chambers (1987) attempted to provide a bottom-up, people-oriented approach to the concept of sustainability by using the term 'sustainable livelihood', which emphasizes the relation between the South's environment and poverty at the local level, fulfilment of basic needs, low risk and security. This term has been adopted in a number of NGO documents within the UNCED process, notably the Women's Action Agenda 21. Women at the Global Forum in Rio de Janeiro repeatedly stressed that their aim was sustainable livelihoods for all people rather than sustainable profits for the rich.

A recent approach to operationalize sustainable development within the development context has been Primary Environmental Care (PEC), (see Pretty and Guijt 1992), promoted by NGDOs, for example OXFAM.

Proposals such as PEC, however, deal only with environmental problems at local project or regional levels in the South and do not address such poverty-inducing macro-economic processes as structural adjustment policies and austerity measures, which impose added stress on local environments in so far as they necessitate people's increased reliance on local resources for their survival needs.

Some environmental movements in both North and South propose bioregionalism, with decentralized modes of production and decision-making. Bioregionalists propose local production and consumption at locally sustainable levels which would reduce transport costs and minimize trade. This proposal poses a different set of questions *vis-à-vis* sustainable development, a concept conceived within the present nation-state framework and the global economic system (see also Chapter 8 on bioregionalism).

Concepts of economic growth and equity in the sustainable development debate

This section highlights two recurring themes throughout the range of concepts and within the debate on sustainable development. These are: economic growth and equity, intergenerational (between generations) as well as intragenerational (within generations) (Dixon and Fallon, 1989).

One of the scholars disputing compatibility between continued economic growth and sustainable development is Herman Daly (1989). He differentiated between sustainable growth and sustainable development and stressed that development, understood as the maintenance of high levels of consumption as practised in the North, cannot be introduced globally without destroying the environment.

Hilkka Pietilä (1989, 1991), one of the few writers who contribute to reconceptualizing economics from the point of view of both women and nature, argues that economic growth is the cause of the environmental crisis and is therefore incompatible with sustainable development. She points out that a recommendation for continued economic growth is based on an insufficient analysis of the environmental crisis. Proper analysis would reveal a choice of more adequate measures to deal with the problems at hand. She criticizes the Brundtland Report's lack of analysis of the philosophical and ethical roots of the environmental crisis which led to an instrumental treatment of nature as the property of humankind. 'Also missing is all the history of development, and analyses: how and why we arrived at where we are now. The roots of maldevelopment remain untouched' (Pietilä, 1991). In recommending more economic growth, Pietilä points out, the Brundtland Commission's mistake was failing to differentiate between developed and developing countries; more growth in the West will exacerbate environmental destruction.

Brazilian sociologist Selene Herculano dos Santos (1990) argues that the Brundtland Report treats the South in an instrumental way. The concerns with poverty and aims to contain it within minimal levels of consumption are defined by the North's interests which perceive the poor in the South as main contributors to the global environmental crisis. She warns of the environmentalism expressed in the Brundtland Report as the latest form of Western imperialism.

The economic growth and sustainable development debate has raised the important question of whether economic growth, as so far understood, should continue. Other options are to redirect it to poorer regions or to change the content of the concept altogether. Roefie Hueting (1990), an adherent of the latter position, identifies growth that stands for the increase in national income as occuring in those areas of economic activities that contribute most to the destruction of the environment, such as oil and petrochemical industries, commercial agriculture, mining or transport. Growth of national product, as defined by current accounting systems, and safeguarding the environment are therefore two conflicting issues. (Hueting's ideas on changes in economic accounting will be briefly presented later in this chapter.)

Equity is another theme recurring throughout different conceptualizations of sustainable development. Its intergenerational aspect posits the need for a sustainable use of the environment, so that both present and future generations have an equitable access to resources. This view is accepted in most definitions of sustainable development, from the reformist, as outlined in the Brundtland Report, to the radical, such as that of deep ecologists who extend the concept to include equity between different species as integral to their position.

The issue of intragenerational equity is both more complex and controversial. It not only includes equal access to resources now, for instance between the North and the South; at stake is also the connection between the degradation of the environment and exploitative social systems with different groups' unequal access to economic resources within societies. The search for sustainable and socially equitable modes of development may lead towards negotiations for a new development paradigm.[4]

Stress on equity is fundamental in the debate on women, the environment and sustainable development. Women demand equal voice, equal access to and control over resources. There are, however, substantial contradictions between women's interests and environmental politics. For example, as already noted, the instrumentalization of women for environmental recovery within development projects which leads to their workload increasing and population control and family planning programmes, which in practice have mainly targeted women, often in a coercive fashion, impinge upon their right to self-determination.

In many proposals, sustainable development is linked with participatory democracy[5] and devolution of state powers to local communities. These links are explicit in the postulates of Green parties and social movements in the North as well as in the South. Participatory democracy plays a vital role in searches for social equity.

The demand is made for equity of cultures, in the context of ensuring the survival of 'indigenous' cultures which, in the past, have developed sustainable modes of living (Bunyard 1989). Sustaining cultural differentiation and equity of cultures has been perceived as essential for the survival of humankind and the maintenance of biodiversity.

The pluralization of epistemological positions and the interaction of different views are seen as important conditions for the transformation of economics, and development towards sustainability (Soderbaum 1991). Implicitly, this is also an argument for the significance of women's voices in this debate.

Environmental reforms in economics

The concept of sustainable development will not be made operational without substantial economic reform. To encapsulate here the entire range of recent changes within economics is not possible, therefore the following is only a brief discussion of environmental and ecological economics.

While much has been done in the field of economics to include the environmental dimension, much less theorizing has taken place on the position of women. The project of the Alliance for Alternative Development, initiated by the DAWN group together with three Northern women's networks, to develop an alternative economic framework (mentioned in Chapter 6), is one of the first systematic attempts to address this issue.

An important aspect of economics is the management and allocation of resources. The discipline of economics as it is practised now is the backbone of the growth model of development. The point of departure for new conceptualizations within economics is the critique of neo-classical and Marxist economics. Labelled by Boulding (in Colby, 1990) 'frontier economics', both are based on the same assumptions of unlimited growth, infinite use of resources, reductionist definitions of economic values and maximization of profits, at the cost of, among others, environmental degradation. Feminist critics of economics, for example Marilyn Waring, add to this list the undervalued and underpaid work of women.

While their point of departure is to some extent shared, there are, however, substantial differences between the two proposals that emerge from this critique, that is, the conceptualizations of environmental and ecological economics.

Environmental economics, which emerged in the 1970s, seeks to improve the neo-classical tradition initiated by Adam Smith (*The Wealth of Nations*, 1776). Addressed to the micro level of economics it leaves the macro level unchanged. Environmental economists attempt to give monetary valuation to the environment and then include it in economic cost/benefit analysis using an appropriate discount rate. David Pearce (1987, 1990) is among the scholars who developed techniques for monetary valuation of the environment and supports the idea of the compatibility of economic growth with sustainable development. This position which seeks to improve economics by 'adding environment' as an externality, has been criticized as one-dimensional and reductionist, since it fails to consider values which cannot be translated into the monetary language of prices. Furthermore, since it approaches economic activities in terms of a closed system and assumes that ecological issues are measurable, it cannot address uncertainty. Neither does it perceive the problem of irreversible environmental damage. In view of the long-term impacts of environmental degradation, the short-term horizon of economic analysis is another problem.[6]

Though criticized, the neo-classical tradition of economics can also inspire attempts to redefine such basic concepts in economics as income or capital. Seeking an economic definition of sustainability, Goodland (1989) refers to the concepts of John Hicks (the 1972 Nobel prize winner in economics), who follows the neo-classical tradition. Hicks stated that: 'income is the maximum amount that a person or community could consume over some time period and still be as well off at the end of that period as at the beginning' (Goodland 1989:11). Known in the literature as Hicksian income it implies that any production that is not sustainable should not be counted as income. It departs radically from the dominant definitions which connect income with market values.

Contrary to environmental economics, ecological economics seeks to address also the macro level of economics. Ecological economics can in fact be traced back to the 19th century. Adherents of ecological economics seek to place the economic system within the context of an 'economy of nature' (Martinez-Alier 1990, Worster 1977).

Ecological economists perceive economic processes as extensions of biological processes. Hence, they are opposed to a continuation of economic growth as it currently exists. The major tenet of this position is a redefinition of economic concepts and the values on which these are based. Whereas in attempts to improve economics new measures are devised to make polluters pay for environmental degradation, here the aim is to transform economics so that prevention is seen to be profitable. Furthermore, ecological economics transcends the dominant view that environmental conditions are predictable and resources manageable in terms of closed systems. Assumptions of open system dynamics, the principle of uncertainty, and a recognition of catastrophic, unpredictable outcomes radically depart from the frameworks of meaning of neo-classical and Marxist economics.

Extending the concept of ecological into holistic economics, Soderbaum (1991) maintains that in order to transform economics it is important to make its ethics and ideology less opaque. He questions the concept of economic man who pursues his self-interest which is the basis of the neo-classical tradition in economics. Soderbaum argues that the motivation of individual behaviour is more complex than the neo-classical followers of Adam Smith would assume and that human beings are capable not only of following self-centred 'I' strategies but also define self-interest in terms of mutuality with others. This in turn calls for the redefinition of the role of the market's operatives and its function.

Though ecological transformations of economics seems a utopian goal, it is noteworthy that the views expressed by, for example, Nicholas Georgescu Roegen in *The Entropy Law and the Economic Process*, or Herman Daly, with Herman Constanza the co-editor of the journal *Ecological Economics*, once marginalized, now receive substantial attention in the debate on sustainable development.

Strategies towards sustainable development: some proposals

Changes in economic accounting systems

Marilyn Waring's book, *If Women Counted* (1988) is the outcome of her extensive research undertaken to challenge the economic system which undervalues both women's work and natural resources. Her critique is aimed at the UN System of National Accounting (UNSNA), which serves as a set of standards for economic measurements and is used as a tool for the appraisal of economic performances at global and country levels. Consequently, the view of an economy that the system provides determines future policy guidelines. National account statistics as well as annual reports of IMF, World Bank, and UN agencies follow the UNSNA standards. The conceptual premises of the Material Product System which was used in socialist states did not differ substantially from the UNSNA.

Adopted in 1953 and conceptually intact since then, the UNSNA is rooted in economic conceptualizations which emerged in response to the need to gear British and US economies to the military effort in the wake of the Second World War. As Waring points out, the conceptual boundaries of this scientific method excluded the whole area of women's activities from the definition of economics. While military production is priced and perceived as contributing to economic growth, no value is attributed to women's household labour, or to peace, individual and social well-being, or the health of the environment. Value is perceived as arising when (predominantly) men interact with the market. Consequently, the system cannot respond to values it does not recognize (Waring 1989:4).

When the UN institutionalized UNSNA as an economic tool, Western values and economic standards were applied to different realities in Third World economies. One consequence was that the whole area of traditional sustainable agriculture, which was then epitomized as backwardness, did not figure in political decisions as an important factor of economic well-being.

Problems with the UNSNA are not only related to how and what is measured but also to what is not measured, that is, the hidden side of economic growth: poverty and a damaged environment. The paradox of this system is that a Tanzanian woman's eight hour walk to fetch water is seen as an unproductive activity, while the clean-up of chemical spillage or the production and maintenance of nuclear weapons, produce additional value and contribute to economic growth. The UNSNA is by no means an innocent scientific statisitical method. On the contrary, it serves as a tool to perpetuate the reductionist economic values on which it is based and is, therefore, instrumental in producing an economic reality which contributes to the destruction of the environment and the continued subordination of women. The UNSNA is the backbone of the growth model of development. Hence, one of the strategies to change the dominant model of development is to work out alternative accounting systems. Solutions proposed by Marilyn Waring to remedy the system of national accounting include, for example, women's work, environmental accounting, distinction between destructive and creative production, and introduction of economic welfare measurements.

In common with those women scientists and activists who researched and lobbied for recognition of women's work and a redefinition of economics, Marilyn Waring, in her synthesizing efforts, also draws on environmental and ecological economics, both of which see changes in environmental accounting as an important factor in pro-ecological transformations of economics.

Such changes could influence transformations of the system from within but they are not easy to bring about – as Marilyn Waring is very much aware. For instance, the UNDP team which has developed the Human Development Index (HDI),[7] an alternative system of measuring economic performance, recognized the need to account for women's work. An HDI per country provides data separately for the male and female population (UNDP 1990:110-11). But one of the difficulties encountered in showing the true extent of inequalities between women and men was lack of appropriate statistical data concerning women. The United Nations institute INSTRAW has, for example, been actively involved in collecting such data from secondary sources, as well as encouraging these to be collected within national censuses. A fundamental problem with the HDI however, is that it does not take into account the environmental dimension (pollution levels, availability of water, fuel, and so on).[8]

Roefie Hueting (1980, 1990), a Dutch statistician and a precursor in rethinking environmental accounting has, since the early 1960s, been postulating the need for changes in national accounting systems. Though his entry point to the critique of economics differs from Marilyn Waring's, both highlight the fact that the present system of accounting gives partial if not misleading information on the state of the economy. Waring postulates the need to change the value system on which economics is based.

Hueting (1990) questions the assumption that an increase in production, which is defined as economic growth, is beneficial and a condition for an increase in human welfare. In most developed countries growth is achieved by means of increased productivity and technological advancement at the expense of human labour and at the cost of environmental destruction. Therefore one of the solutions proposed by Hueting is to change consumption and production patterns and consequently, to redefine economic growth. He proposes an intermediary step: to include a valuation of the environment in economic accounting. For the purpose of correcting national income in respect to environmental losses he developed the concept of environmental functions (ways of using the environment) as scarce and competing goods which can be validated within a system of shadow prices. Standards for environmental functions are based on their sustainable use. This implies the formulation of measures to meet these standards and that the cash needed to put these measures into practice must be stipulated. In the case of non-renewable resources their valuation would involve an estimation of costs for the development of alternatives, for example, alternative sources of energy.

Hueting thus shows how the concept of sustainability can be made operational in the area of economics. He not only shows the benefits but also the contradictions and disadvantages, and stresses that it is only a second best solution, and cannot be seen as the only remedy to curb environmental destruction.

Proposals for including the environment in national accounting systems are impeded by the fact that the environment's value, by it's very nature, cannot be translated into the mathematical language in which economics operates. Rules for accounting systems do not include the principle of error-friendliness (von Weizsäcker 1986), they are not equipped to accommodate unexpected consequences of environmental changes brought about by humans. And, as already noted, based on the logic of dominant science, the environment is assumed to be a closed and 'knowable' system, a view that is increasingly challenged.

It is important to review other critical positions which point to the deeper roots of the crisis. For example, ideas emerging from deep ecology, social ecology, ecofeminism and the feminist critique of science show that the environment/development crisis also has cultural roots and that the domination of nature is intimately linked with the domination of people.

Population, environment and development

The argument that rapid population growth is one of the main causes of the environmental crisis and that to check population growth, especially in the South, must become a major strategy in order to achieve sustainable development, has gained renewed and increased momentum recently. It was Thomas Malthus who originally propagated the view that the working class in north-west Europe, in the process of proletarianization during the era of industrialization and urbanization in the 19th century, were poor because they had too many children. Therefore, they themselves were responsible for their increasing poverty; the fact of their exploitation was disregarded. The argument that rapid population growth was the main reason for the absence of economic development in the South reappeared in the development discourse of the 'modernization' decades after World War II. Recently, the population growth argument has re-emerged to explain the global environmental crisis. It must be emphasized that this is a vast and complex field and in the short discussion that follows there are, of necessity, omissions and generalizations.

Thomas Malthus (1766-1834) argued that while population increases at a geometrical rate, subsistence, particularly food production, increases only arithmetically. Those who had no opportunity to actively participate in production were seen as surplus population with no right to exist. The poor multiplied faster than they could afford, given their limited resources; they were therefore constructed as a 'threat' to humanity as a whole, by behaving irresponsibly. Within the agricultural mode of production the landed classes saw large families as an asset because the work force was thereby increased. Later, however, the reduced labour requirements within the industrial mode of production, resulted in children being seen as a liability.

Malthus saw as inevitable a 'natural' vicious circle, in that: population growth leads to a crisis of underemployment and higher infant mortality, which in turn leads to stagnation in population growth, resulting in reducing underemployment, which in turn again leads to renewed population growth.

To escape from this dilemma Malthus preached fertility control through abstinence, and the segregation of the workforce into separate quarters for men and women. At the turn of the 20th century neo-Malthusians employed his logic by advocating contraception as a response to the plight of the poor. Neo-Malthusian birth control protagonists developed the family planning ideology for use in the US, targeting the poor: to control their own welfare/well-being they must control their family size. In the US, eugenicists, in collusion with corporate capital, further developed the population control ideology by arguing for the need to control the fertility of 'others': the poor, blacks, and subsequently, people in the Third World.

Malthus employed no data in support of his theory; it thus remained within the realm of ideological construct. But he had set the stage for his argument to resurface within the development context almost a century later as a model to explain the phenomena of underdevelopment, persistent and increasing poverty, especially in the South, and the 'onslaught on the limited resource base'. 'Prophets of doom', for example Paul Ehrlich, reiterated the Malthusian argument and pleaded passionately for stringent population control measures. In his book *The Population Bomb* (1968), a deeply value-laden title, Ehrlich justified coercion to check population growth as it would serve the greater good. In his next book *How to be a Survivor* (1971) (sponsored by Friends of the Earth), Ehrlich called for 'criminal sanctions on overbreeding'. *The Population Explosion* (1991) by Paul and Anne Ehrlich, both biologists, extrapolated findings on animal to human populations: population numbers explode and then crash because of starvation and disease. The Ehrlichs painted the future as involving 'the total collapse of civilization and the disappearance of the United States as we know it' (Ehrlich and Ehrlich, cited after Boyce, 1991:5).

The argument is as simple as it is pervasive and has been given credence by the general public as fact. The neo-Malthusians' simple model explains poverty and consequently environmental degradation as due to population growth, especially in the developing countries. The poor in the South are depicted as having no choice but to destroy their natural resource base in order to survive. This argument is endorsed by many development organizations and environmentalists and put forward to justify intensification of anti-natalist population programmes in the South.

The problem with this line of argument is its simplistic view on cause and effect and the total disregard of other reasons for environmental degradation, such as the North's overconsumption of natural resources (and the problem of aggregating absolute figures of people and resources without quantifying their levels of consumption), trade policies, commodity prices, an so on which create poverty in the South. For example, population growth as a survival strategy of poor families is not analysed, neither is there recognition of the fact that it is induced by poverty, rather than the reverse. In fact, population growth is a symptom of a global economic system that contributes to environmental degradation by forcing poor people to cultivate marginal soils, destroy their own resource base and resort to unsustainable modes of subsistence.

There is, however, no evidence to support the frequent portrayal of poor people as ignorant of the damage they are doing to their own environment (Wiltshire 1992). One example of an analysis that disregards the macro-economic framework, subsumes complex interrelations under mathematically reductionist models and then projects a simple causal relation between poverty and population growth is the Club of Rome report *The Limits to Growth* (1972).

Such oversimplification has a twofold result: it diverts attention from the root causes; and justifies fertility control measures which often are an assault on individuals' rights and well-being, especially of women in the South (Boyce, 1991:6). Many population programmes implemented by development agencies stress the importance of achieving specific numbers of 'family planning' acceptors (of contraception and sterilization). For example, in Brazil's population programme it was officially estimated that in 1986, 45 per cent of all Brazilian women of reproductive age had been sterilized, many without their knowledge, during Caesarean deliveries. By 1991, an estimated of eight out of ten black women in Brazil had been sterilized (Sax 1991).

Some development agencies, for example the World Bank in its World Development Report (1992) and the UN Fund for Population (UNFPA) take a different view of the relations between the environmental degradation and population growth. The analysis by Nafis Sadik (1990), director of UNFPA, included overconsumption in the North, uneven distribution of power, and stressed that the South's poor have no choice but to destroy their environment, particularly in the most vulnerable areas. She outlined three areas for action: a shift to cleaner technologies; an attack on poverty and a slow-down of population growth. The latter was seen as the most urgent and cost-effective measure. This is a recurring argument: population policy interventions and acceleration of family planning services are seen as the least expensive means of dealing with global environmental problems and, as some argue, are among the few that are feasible and offer long-term solutions (Fornos in Popline 1992). The implication is that women are simultaneously the problem – in their role as child-bearers and users of resources – and the solution – as they are able to limit numbers of births and to recover their environment.

Improving women's status and changing men's attitudes towards family size Sadik sees as key factors in reducing birth rates. The goal is to give couples the choice to have fewer children; better spacing of births would also lead to an improvement in the health of women and children. A wide choice in contraceptive is seen as crucial to meet individual couples' needs. Also, as the World Development Report stated: 'Improving education for girls may be the most important longterm environmental policy in Africa and in other parts of the developing world' (World Bank 1992:8).

The instrumental view of people, in particular women, is thus reinforced. Women's empowerment is seen as a cost-effective strategy to achieve sustainable development, not as an end in itself – on women's own terms. People's freedom of choices for contraceptive methods are stressed, but research in the pharmaceutical industry emphasizes long-term, supplier-controlled methods rather than short-term, simple, user-controlled methods which can be discontinued at any time, and do not need close monitoring (often a major bottleneck in areas with insufficient health-care facilities); and this research is directed mainly at women as users, not men.[9] The key issue from development agencies' point of view, albeit in the guise of self-determination and raising women's status, is to control women's fertility. This is achieved with more centrally planned family planning information, education and services.

Paradoxically, procreation in the North is encouraged because it is feared that with longer life expectancy there will be an imbalance of the old over the young, which implies future economic problems, particularly in care for the old. Also, in some Northern countries there is a fear that the white population will soon be outnumbered by the rapidly increasing non-white population.

There are, however, some viewpoints that see no correlation between population growth and environmental degradation; instead the cause of both lies in the prevailing power relations and resulting maldistribution of resources. Keysers (1991) calls this the redistribution view. Overconsumption in the North is a far more important factor in environmental degradation than population numbers in the South. The key strategy to achieve sustainable development is to reduce poverty in the South, by a radical redistribution of wealth from the North to the South, which in itself will bring about a global balance between population and resources. There is evidence in the North to support the view that population growth will slow down with increasing levels of development. This view is subscribed to by the left, some environmentalists, many of them in the South, as well as socialist feminists.

A group of international women scientists and activists (SSRC/ISSC/DAWN 1992) confirm that research findings do not support the contention that population growth is a central variable in environmental degradation. The focus on population growth as a key factor shifts to the dynamics within the global economic system. Extremes of wealth and overconsumption on the one hand, and poverty and erosion of livelihoods on the other, skewed distribution and use of resources as well as patterns of human settlement (urbanization) are seen as more significant factors in relation to environmental degradation. Macro-economic policies affect both people and the environment. Globalization of capital, large-scale technology, subordination of the

South within world markets, and particularly rising consumption levels in the North, are seen as disrupting the relationship between people and their environment. Poor women and children, in particular, are seen as victims in this simultaneous erosion of livelihoods and the environment.

The issue of the population/environment relation has recently become a matter of contention between environmentalists and feminists in view of the fact that many environmentalists endorse the need for strict population control and hence targeting women in the South for population control programmes. Large conservationist-oriented environmental NGOs, such as IUCN, WWF, and the Sierra Club, are launching large-scale efforts to increase and accelerate population programmes in the South. Betsy Hartmann (1991) outlines the positions of some in the environmental movement, the most extreme being that of Earth First!, a group that subscribes to an ecocentric view: 'If radical environmentalists were to invent a disease to bring population back to ecological sanity, it would probably be something like AIDS.'

The Sierra Club is quoted as stating that population growth is a core problem and a major contributary cause of almost all environmental problems: the greenhouse effect, forest destruction, air and water pollution. To control women's fertility is therefore seen as an essential part of the solution. Greenpeace, however, notes that 'Countries that are most often targeted for population control efforts consume far less per capita than the industrialized countries that are doing the targeting' (ibid).

Hartmann argues that to blame environmental destruction on overpopulation obscures the causes of the crisis: corporate irresponsibility, militarism, and elite control over land and other resources. Even though couched in the language of extending women's reproductive choice, population control programmes often hinder the delivery of safe, voluntary family planning services, and damage rather than benefit women's health.

In the NGO Treaty on population produced by women at the Global Forum in Rio de Janeiro, women's empowerment, right to self-determination and full control over their bodies, are seen as central tenets. To achieve these, the need for comprehensive reproductive health care, planned, managed and controlled by women, is stressed. Women present in Rio wanted human-centred and user-controlled reproductive health care. The problems of environmental degradation and parallel impoverishment of the majority of the world's people, the Rio women argue, must be seen in relation to high levels of consumption in the North, excessive spending on military, debt, structural adjustment, and trade policies responsible for perpetuating the inequity of the existing world order. The Population Treaty not only condemns bureaucratic and violent policies for population control, but also criticizes pro-natal policies in the North.

Population growth may not be the central factor in global environmental degradation, to reduce it globally, however, not only in the South, will be important in the long run, but it must be on a voluntary basis. As a short-term strategy in the most vulnerable areas, such as fragile mountain ecosystems, changes in macro policies, land reform, and people-centred, basic-needs oriented development may be more important than concentrating mainly on reducing population growth. Simultaneously, and more importantly, non-sustainable consumption patterns need to be scaled down and excessive military spending discontinued. As Loes Keysers (1991) pointed out, both environmental degradation as well as poverty-induced population growth are integral to a basically unsustainable development model which is based on a wasteful and exploitative consumption system, catering for the needs of the powerful elites globally at the cost of the poor.

Notes

1. See for example Guha (1989) who traces back the origins of the Chipko movement in the Indian Himalayas to local protest movements in the 19th century.

2. For an overview of different positions on the environment see for instance Colby (1990).

3. See also Chapter 6 for Vandana Shiva's understanding of the term sustainable development as seen from the local level in the Indian context.

4. An illustration of attempts to design a new development paradigm is provided by de la Court (1990).

5. See for instance de la Court, op. cit.

6. This critique is based on Colby op. cit; Soderbaum op. cit; and Juan Martinez-Alier (1990).

7. The Human Development Index (HDI) (UNDP 1990) provides an alternative perspective to levels of development. It provides a weighted average of three measures in a particular country: life expectancy at birth, adult literacy rate, and real Gross National Product (GNP) per capita. The USA, for example, the richest nation if conventionally measured by GNP, moves to number 112 out of 130 (occupied by Japan) on the list if categorized within the measures of the HDI.

8. We are indebted to Rachel Kurian for bringing this to our attention.

9. In 1977 the Indian government was forced to resign because its national population programme targeted men to be sterilized. Today, the sterilization programme continues, mainly involving women (80 per cent); they are an easier target because they have less political power.

8. Responses to the Crisis from Deep Ecology, Social Ecology and Ecofeminism

Common to these three fields is a questioning of the epistemological roots of the environmental crisis. The important dialogues and interchanges between them have proved mutually enriching. That is not to say that they do not have their shortcomings and contradictions: carrying over patterns of domination, reversal of hierarchies and reproductions of dualisms are some of the problems inherent in some of these positions, as in others.

Deep ecology

The concept of deep ecology was formulated by the Norwegian philosopher Arne Naess in the early 1970s as a response to the limits of 'shallow ecology' (Naess 1973, 1988, 1989). His view was that in the long run environmental reforms of social and economic systems are not a viable solution to off-set the accelerating destruction of the environment. Warning that the ecological crisis threatens the survival of humanity, Arne Naess identified the deeper roots of the crisis in Western culture and in particular in the cultural values legitimizing the domination of nature.

Since Western culture has given rise to different worldviews, Naess put forward the proposal of deep ecology as an open platform of people coming from different epistemological backgrounds. The unifying factor was the acceptance of transformations in the relationship between humans and nature. Deep ecology has become a powerful counter-discourse to environmental reforms, as the latter tends to reflect the position of governments and business corporations. It has developed into an extensive and differentiated body of theory, with Arne Naess expanding his original proposal into the conceptualization of ecophilosophy. Bill Deval and George Sessions (1985), Michael Zimmerman (1990), Warwick Fox (1990), and Alain Drengson, the editor of *The Trumpeter*, all voices of the Canadian Ecophilosophy Network, are among those who have contributed to further developing the concept.

The common point of departure in deep ecology's critique of Western culture is anthropocentrism, that is, situating human beings in a superior position over nature within value hierarchies. From an anthropocentric view, nature must be dominated, conquered or managed to serve human needs. Assuming a dominating position alienates human beings from the environment on which their survival depends. When human beings ignore natural processes, their antagonistic attitude towards nature leads not only to the destruction of the environment but also to self-destruction.

Deep ecology's critique is targeted not only at anthropocentrism, but also at dualism, hierarchization and fragmentation inherent in Western culture, including the dominant terms for the production of scientific knowledge. Atomistic and hierarchical conceptions of the physical world, as developed in the formative period of modern science, have been extended into the social world and, among others, influenced the concepts of development.

Some deep ecology thinkers criticize the Judeo-Christian religious and cultural tradition for its role in the perpetuation of anthropocentric worldviews and their justification of the domination of nature. Others seek their roots and inspirations in marginalized traditions, for instance in the Franciscan tradition within the Catholic Church, in perennial philosophies which assume interdependence of nature and culture, or in mystic traditions which oppose dominant systems of thought. Eastern religions are an inspiration in the diversified body of deep ecological thinking (see for example Deval and Sessions 1985).

Seeking to overturn the epistemological foundations of Western culture, deep ecologists propose to replace anthropocentric hierarchies with biocentric egalitarianism. In this view 'humanity is no more, but also no less, important than all other things on Earth' (Zimmerman op. cit.).

Deep ecologists see richness and diversity of life as values in themselves and assume that human beings have no right to reduce these, except to satisfy their basic needs. They also stress the need for cultural diversity and diversity in social arrangements as necessary preconditions for the survival of the planet. An essential element in transformations towards an equitable relationship between human beings and nature is the replacement of dualisms (mind and body, nature and culture, subject and object, and so on) with conceptions of self and other formulated in terms of interdependencies and connectedness, which in turn, will stimulate an acceptance of difference. Deep ecologists assert that the transcendence of dualisms leads to the development of a new ecological rationality. Changes in the frameworks of thinking in accordance with an understanding of interdependencies would not only prevent the domination of nature but also domination within human societies. As the concluding part of this chapter shows, this foundational argument of deep ecology is questioned by (eco)feminists in their critique of androcentrism.

For deep ecologists the consequence of this argument is their emphasis on the role of individual human beings. Changes in thinking and lifestyles are emphasized as necessary steps towards ecological transformations of society. By changing their relationship with nature, individuals can attain self-realization and maturity. The emphasis on the role of individual human beings to off-set the ecological crisis has appealed to many people concerned with the degradation of the environment. Since deep ecology offers them an option to be personally involved in transformations, they are no longer disoriented and therefore powerless as to what they can do *vis-à-vis* the magnitude of the crisis. Among other environmental ideas, deep ecology is unique in its stress on changes within, individual responsibility of human beings, and harmonizing lives and beliefs.

During the last 20 years the deep ecology movement has spread across the Northern hemisphere and undergone an internal polarization of positions. The differentiating factors have been soft and radical biocentrism. The latter position has been represented for example by participants of the Earth First! movement in the USA, which postulated a subordination of human beings to nature. Some of them have accepted AIDS and famine as nature's justifiable defensive reaction to population pressure. Among their postulates was the redevelopment of America to the era of BC, where BC stood for Before Columbus. The violent nature of such projects is obvious and may be an outcome of an uncritical reversal of the old hierarchy: from humans over nature to nature over humans. The roots of the ecological crisis are seen in terms of anthropocentrism, which leads to a search for remedies in the reverse: an acceptance of the domination of nature over people. Recently, this radical biocentrist position has been moving to the margins of deep ecology thinking.

The increasingly popular soft biocentrism position within the deep ecology movement aims to abolish all hierarchies. To avoid the accusations of androcentrism, as voiced by some (eco)feminists, Warwick Fox (1989) proposed to replace the notion of biocentrism with that of ecocentrism. In this stream within deep ecology, recognition of the implications of individual human beings in the destruction of the earth remains an important insight, but is correlated with attention to social and political issues within human societies. The views of Michael E. Zimmerman (1990) or David M. Johns (1990) mark an evolution within deep ecology towards learning from and making connections with (eco)feminism as well as Southern alternative development and ecological movements.

One of the contributions of deep ecologists to the rethinking of development has been bioregionalism as, for instance, proposed by Peter Berg and the Planet Drum Foundation or the Bio-Regional Congress, a movement developing in the United States and Europe. Bioregionalism is about re-inhabiting (to borrow a term from Gary Snyder) the earth on new terms. In their critique of the dominant development model bioregionalists propose to reshape and harmonize the human/nature relationship; they see human communities as parts of larger viable planetary ecosystems.[1] The core of the bioregional idea of development is communitarianism, small-scale, self-sufficient development, and a definition of regional boundaries by natural features, such as watersheds, soil types, vegetation or climate. The organization of bioregional communities is described as non-hierarchical and participative. Instead of formal hierarchial structures of leadership, bioregional communities thrive on networking and organic change.

In the early stage of the movement, in the 1980s, bioregionalists refrained from entering politics and focused on the development of their own communities and changes from within; now, they are increasingly concerned with global issues. The depletion of the ozone layer and wider climate changes damage planetary ecosystems, threaten the survival of humanity and the existence of bioregionalism itself. There is, therefore, a new tendency among bioregionalists to join other citizens' movements which oppose multinationals, states, intergovernmental organizations, the General Agreement on Tariffs and Trade (GATT) negotiations and their respective roles in the destruction of the earth. Representatives of the Bio-regional Congress were active in the preparatory process towards UNCED and the Global Forum in 1992. One of their inputs into the NGO idea of sustainable (= re-inhabitory) development was their proposal for a new language. They contributed new formulations to the 'Agenda Ya Wananchi: Citizen's Action Plan for the 1990s', a comprehensive NGO document on environment and development, worked out at the Global NGO conference in Paris in December 1991. Their input made a substantial difference because many of the NGO documents express new radical ecological and emancipatory ideas in the language of conventional hierarchical politics. 'Ya Wananchi' was written from both the brain and the heart.

Another interesting stream within deep ecology has emerged under the influence of the Gaia hypothesis,[2] formulated by James Lovelock and Lynn Margulis (Lovelock 1979). In the mid-1960s Lovelock, a specialist in atmospheric chemistry, was employed by the NASA in its Mars project where he was involved in working out computer simulations of the atmospheric conditions which would make life on a 'barren' planet possible. The success of these computer models led Lovelock to the conclusion that life on Earth has produced itself and keeps on maintaining itself in a constant disequilibrium. The biocenosis of the Earth is viewed as an organic whole – Gaia – with powerful self-regulatory characteristics. Lynn Margulis' contribution to the Gaia hypothesis comes from her work (together with Dorion Sagan in 1988) on symbiosis and mutualism as primary regulatory forces in the history of life on earth. The major efforts of Lovelock and Margulis are to establish Gaia as a legitimate, 'respectable' scientific hypothesis.

In an attempt to quantify deep ecology, Edward Goldsmith (editor of the influential journal, *The Ecologist*) developed the social and epistemological consequences of the concept of Gaia (Goldsmith 1988), and worked out 67 principles for an ecological (Gaian) world view. The following characteristics largely refer to his contribution to Gaia: the major tenet of the Gaia hypothesis is the assumption that Gaia is a total self-organizing and self-reproducing, organic, spatio-temporal and teleological system with the goal of maintaining itself. The focus is on the primary role of a constant disequilibrium (equilibrium would mean death), but at the same time, stability maintained by diversification, co-operation, and mutualism. Gaia and its sub-systems are organized hierarchically with mutualism between the different levels of hierarchies. Competition is attributed a secondary role in the evolution of life. Man (sic), though Gaia's integral part, is of little importance. When humanity outlives its purpose of maintaining life, other life forms will become more useful for the stability of life and will take over.

Man's development of the technosphere is viewed as a threat to the survival of Gaia. Therefore adherents to the Gaia hypothesis present a total critique of techno-bureaucratic development, because it fundamentally alters essential ecological regulatory mechanisms. Monoculture and uniformity are the enemies of Gaia. Rural development, eco-development, sustainable development, and appropriate development are seen as 'euphemisms adopted by the development industry to placate its critics' (Goldsmith, 1988:165). This critique of the dominant mode of development allies 'Gaians' with radical critics of development in the South (de la Court 1990).

Edward Goldsmith points out the roots of the ecological crisis in the reductionist Newtonian paradigm of knowledge which pretends to produce an objective truth but in fact hides its inherently subjective ways of arriving at knowledge. Hidden is the desire to control and regulate nature. In his critique of the Newtonian paradigm of knowledge Goldsmith proposes new ways of practising ecology (and science) which are subjective and intuitive. This involves the restoration of subconscious, unverbalized knowledge. Goldsmith sees ecology as an emotional knowledge based on love and sympathy. It is a qualitative knowledge, with 'events explained in terms of their role within the spatio-temporal gaian hierarchy and not in terms of one event that triggered them off', for example, an event may not be caused by a disease or bacteria only but by 'the local reduction in the critical order of Gaia' (Goldsmith, 1988). This new knowledge is based on a different, ecological way of understanding reality and truth. Opposed to scientific truth (which, as has been argued by Feyerabend and Kuhn,[3] is conforming to the dominant paradigm), true is what 'fits with the largely subconscious and subjective world-view of ecology' (Goldsmith op. cit.).

The Gaia hypothesis has caught the imagination of the ecological movemement and has contributed to replacing the image of the 'Earth as a machine' with the image of the 'Earth as an organism'. The contribution of the Gaia theory was to highlight interdependencies within and among the organic and inorganic world and to focus on Gaia-centrism instead of on anthropocentrism, competition, and individualistic aggression typical of some other biological and social theories. The theoretical underpinnings of the Gaia theory touch upon the biocentric position: the survival of the earth, Gaia, is the foundational image of the newly emerging ecocratic rationality.

Although 'Gaians' share the critique of science and postulate a reworking of science in common with (some) feminists (as outlined in Chapter 3) there are points of disagreement. Lovelock's and Goldsmith's conceptualizations of Gaia reveal their position of privileged (god-like) readers, interpreters of Gaia's order; thus Gaia is readable, open to their scrutiny, simulated in computer models and therefore amenable to control, which is reminiscent of the Newtonian desire to control nature. This is a consequence of the origins of the Gaia hypothesis in system theory. Unlike other reductionist theories, system theory approaches reality from the point of view of interdependencies and holism rather than fragmentation and linearity. But by reducing its objects to the confine of mathematical models and thereby implying their full readability and hence predictability, system theory is an attempt to improve on Western science as it is, without addressing the problem of its in-built epistemological tools of domination. Thus the Gaia hypothesis has recently become the basis for a newly arising type of ecocratic rationality. The Gaia hypothesis rests on the borders of two paradigms of knowledge.

Deep ecology has evoked some criticism. (Eco)feminists for example criticize its claim that the destructive and antagonistic relationship of humans with nature is the prototype of other forms of aggression. Instead, they point out that a conceptualization of the conflict between Humanity and Nature in the singular obscures other forms of domination, for example, patriarchy. (Eco)feminists point out that deep ecology is not free. of a patriarchal bias and hence reproduces androcentrism (Saleh 1984). The radical biocentric stream of deep ecology to which the Earth First! movement, for example, subscribes is criticized by women working in the reproductive rights movements because (see Chapter 7) it implies a justification of coercive population control programmes aimed at women in the South.

Another ecofeminist reaction to deep ecology comes from the realization that the 'new consciousness' of the movement has embraced traditional 'female' values of caring, relatedness and wholeness without connecting these values with women's struggles. Deep ecologists see the need for paradigmatic shifts in thinking, and for man (sic) to transform himself. Sharon Dubiago unmasks deep ecology's patriarchal bias by asking deep ecologists: 'why then are you not feminists? . . . Why is the ecology movement so utterly bereft of any and all knowledge of the vast work that has been done in the past 15 years on the irrefutable connection between misogyny and hatred of nature?' (Dubiago in: Plant 1989:42).

Deep ecologists are fascinated by tribal societies and non-Western religions, and their reciprocal relationship with nature and sustainability in-built in vernacular economies. Seen in an a-historical and a-political fashion such societies seem to embody an ideal model of mutualism and holism. But, as feminists point out, women's position in these societies has been one of subordination to men. With the advent of developmentalism (as we have illustrated earlier) women's status has been constantly deteriorating, a fact overlooked by deep ecologists. Furthermore, deep ecologists echo an overall romanticization of the South and promote the Western idea of the noble savage. The latest change within deep ecology is the increasing interest in an ecological reconstruction of the North.

Development critics have displayed mixed attitudes towards deep ecology. On the one hand they are attracted by its condemnation of the technocratic growth model of development and welcome its role as an ally in demands to change the dominant development mode in the West, in the centres of its dispersion. On the other hand, they distrust deep ecologists because some of them stress the role of population growth as a key factor in the global destruction of nature. While population growth is seen as a problem of the South, other causes for ecological destruction like high energy consumption in the North are not given equal attention. This critique, however, does not acknowledge the internal differentiation of positions within deep ecology on these issues, for instance of those who identify themselves with the Bio-Regional Congress.

Paradoxically, even though criticism aimed at deep ecology is manifold it reflects the importance of the perspective of deep ecology itself. Deep ecology has become a point of reference in establishing positions for other ecological streams of thinking. Among the positions engaged in dialogue with deep ecology are social ecology and ecofeminism.

Social ecology

Social ecology is a stream of thinking which developed in the 1960s in response to the ecological crisis perceived as a crisis of our civilization. An important contribution to the emergence of social ecology as a new science and social practice was made by Murray Bookchin (1971, 1982, 1984, 1990). Social ecologists seek the roots of the crisis in the domination of people as intimately linked with the domination of nature. Both in theoretical investigations as well as social praxis, they aim to uncover structures of domination and to replace the model of society based on domination with an ecological type of society based on the recognition of co-evolution of nature and humanity along the principles of equity, mutuality and unity in diversity. This approach integrates social and ecological concerns and thus corresponds with the imperatives of sustainable modes of development.

Social ecologists, like deep ecologists, seek the roots of their thinking in indigenous cultures. They understand the relationship between human societies and nature as one of co-evolution.

Traditional societies are socialized to existence in a specific place ... they believe they belong to the space they occupy, be that a desert, a rainforest, or a hardwood forest of the northeast United States. Generation after generation expends energy thinking about what it means to be a people of a forest or a desert, and that thinking process develops a conservatism about the ecology which is both healthy and, in the long term, necessary for survival. It is not difficult to contrast that result with a people who spend their time thinking about what it means to be a Nation-State which claims hegemony over deserts and seashore alike, between river systems of vastly different compositions and high plains. (Mohawk in: Clark 1990:94).

Social ecologists draw from different emancipatory traditions. John Clark (1990), for example, claimed the utopian socialism of Fourier as a source of inspiration. Mutual exchanges are taking place between social ecology and feminism, for example in the work of Karen Warren, Chiah Heller and Janet Biehl. Eduardo Gudynas, a social ecologist from Uruguay, connects social ecology with liberation theology (Gudynas in: Engel and Engel 1992: 139-49).

Social ecology's founding father and leading figure is Murray Bookchin who traces his roots to the anarchist tradition and its critique of both socialism and capitalism. This tradition is gaining new currency in the search for alternative forms of social organization based on non-hierarchical social arrangements, on community scale, and the practice of mutual aid and co-operation. Bookchin's published works include *Post-scarcity Anarchism* (1971), *Ecology of Freedom: The Emergence and Dissolution of Hierarchy* (1982), and *Remaking Society: Pathways Towards a Green Future* (1990).

In the words of Bookchin, social ecology is a new science based on a new ecological consciousness and sensibility, integrated with poetry and imagination. This new integrative science is closely connected with reconstructive social practice. In his work Bookchin deals with what he sees as the roots and implications of the key problem of modern civilization, the divorce of humanity from nature and the conception of the two as conflicting opposites. Bookchin challenges the mechanistic and necessitarian view of nature as passive and ruled exclusively by a set of unchangeable physical rules, as it was propagated by scientific theories developed in the 18th and 19th centuries. Freedom was then seen as the prerogative of human societies which are capable of transcending the constrictions of and dependence on nature. Technology, in turn, has been a tool to achieve freedom. The assumption of superiority of human beings over nature justified the domination of nature.

Bookchin challenges this necessitarian view of nature and its implications on three counts. First, his conception of nature radically departs from the mechanistic view. Bookchin perceives nature in terms of continually on-going and mutually interdependent processes towards the emergence of new levels of complexity and diversity. The logic of these processes is participation, mutualism and symbiosis, and the aim of evolution is ever-increasing diversification. Differences are not a basis for conflict but for creative integration. The second and interrelated point is Bookchin's perception of nature as the realm of freedom. In his understanding freedom means self-determination and is expressed in a preservation of identity and difference. As Clark explains, freedom 'is found to some degree at all levels of being: from the self-organising and self-stabilising tendencies of the atom, through the growth and metabolic activities of living organisms, to the complex self-realisation process of persons, societies, ecosystems, and the biosphere itself' (Clark 1990:6). The third point is that Bookchin perceives nature and society not as conflicting opposites but in terms of continuities and interdependencies. In his view a misconception of nature, and the rift between nature and society, account for a deep crisis of modernity. Consequently, he postulates a reconciliation of humanity with nature and proposes to work towards an ecological society modelled on freedom, mutualism and unity in diversity, which according to him are also key organizing principles in nature.

The backbone of Bookchin's theoretical work is that hierarchy is the basic structure of domination. Hierarchy emerged in pre-recorded history, when elder males in warrior tribes claimed for themselves the socio-political sphere of life which then became the basis for their tribal division of labour. This phenomenon in turn triggered off dualistic and antagonistic conceptions of self and society. Hierarchical societies over time replaced organic societies and gave rise to patriarchal and then class societies. 'Hierarchy developed into complex systems of command and obedience in which elites enjoy varying degrees of control over their subordinates without necessarily exploiting them' (Bookchin 1982:78). Bookchin perceives hierarchy as an epistemological practice, interrelated with dualism and reductionism and applied to ordering feelings, thoughts and reality. As the constitutive factor in what Bookchin calls the epistemologies of rule, hierarchy permeates frameworks of meaning and sense in most sophisticated ways and is by no means exclusively attributed to male members of society. In his richly illustrated work *The Ecology of Freedom* Bookchin points out that in early hierarchical societies older women enjoyed a position of power while young men were oppressed.

Bookchin's work reveals connections between the domination of nature and the domination of people, including the hierarchical construction of gender relations, and therefore allows for connections between ecological and feminist projects.[4]

Bookchin points out that there are no innocent victims; women and men alike have been implicated in the epistemologies of rule and hierarchical constructions of social reality. All of us have been socialized within hierarchical frameworks of thought and practice. At stake is how not to reproduce hierarchical and dualistic practices in new ecological and emancipatory projects. This can take place only when practices of domination are carefully thought through and made visible in all their sophistication and at all levels of human existence.

This task unites the different approaches to social ecology. While Bookchin has focused on an epistemological and social analysis of modernity, a number of authors like Kovel and Heller (in Clark, 1990) investigate the practices of domination as implicated in the construction of self. Other authors, for example, Clark (1990), but also Bookchin in his late work, emphasize connections between hierarchies and dualism. Another topic which has been given much attention in the work of social ecologists is the critique of modern technologies. Alternative proposals range from Bookchin's early conceptualization of liberatory technologies, to the development of a web of qualifiers for appropriate technological projects, which would include criteria from the fields of ecological, feminist, and participatory democratic thinking. 'A technological choice is not an isolated one. We are not simply choosing a thing, we are choosing a self, a way of relating to nature, a politics, a society, a way of being and becoming' (Simon, in Clark, 1990:114).

A large body of work on social ecology has been devoted to the development of a new reconstructive social practice. But, at least according to Bookchin, these new projects are seen in terms of improving the project of modernity. Bookchin's critique of the dominant industrial bureaucratic growth model of development aims primarily at the means used to implement the originally emancipatory goals of modernity. Bookchin wants to revive these ideals of human emancipation and to unite social movements, like the feminist, women's, ecological, consumer, and Third World development movements, around the issues of ecology, the survival of the Earth and human livelihood.

Bookchin and other social ecologists postulate the need for radical changes towards ecological transformations of society. These changes include the adoption of small, community-scale social arrangements, decentralization, participatory democracy and decision-making based on consensus, whereby ultimate authority is at the community level, the level of lived experience. An important part of this reconstructive practice of social ecology is the development of new appropriate technologies, in tune with the communitarian scale of life and non-aggressive towards nature. Social ecologists work on technologies which allow for minimalization of the use of natural resources based on renewable forms of energy. Decisions about types of technologies employed are made by the respective communities.

One illustration of reconstructive social practice as postulated by social ecologists is the community development project in Loisaida, the Puerto Rican section of New York's Lower East Side, where local inhabitants have taken over empty and dilapidated lots and turned them into gardens, gyms and community centres.

> The initiative came from within the community, from an indigenous leadership which analyzed the problem and sought a utopian (i.e. reconstructive) solution. They did not look to the city for the solution; they created their own. They contested with the city for the material base of their community, the land; and, in most cases, they gained either legal leases to the lots for token amounts of money, or outright title. Several community land trusts were created to remove particular lots from the real estate market forever, and to guarantee their continued use as a community resource... Owing to a holistic approach, a number of other elements in the community development process grew out of these simple actions. A problem was turned into a resource, and the health of the community benefited as a result. The people involved in the work gained a sense of pride and accomplishment (Chodorkoff, in Clark, 1990:77-8).

Another example of social ecology as a new science and a reconstructive social practice is the Latin American Network of Social Ecology (CLAES) founded in 1989 and based in Uruguay. It involves people who work in governments, NGOs, academia and grassroots groups in several Latin American countries. The network is open to anyone who supports its ideas. Members may join or leave, as they please. Graciela Evia and Eduardo Gudynas, who play a leading role in CLAES, have developed their vision of social ecology. The aim of CLAES is to help communities recover the value of their environments as experienced by people, whether peasant, aboriginals or academics. The network seeks to recover an integrated perspective of the human-human and human-nature relations. A distinct feature in this process is the use of media in a horizontal, participatory way. In stressing the use of media and the power relations involved in the generation of knowledge, the network tries to bridge scientific and subordinated local people's knowledge. It seeks to give an equal voice to all and especially encourages indigenous people and peasants to join in a process of networking and communications. CLAES publishes a bulletin named *Teko-ha*, a Guarani aboriginal word which refers to the natural environment as inseparable from culture and ways of life. Without a *teko-ha* it is impossible to develop a self, a *teko*.

CLAES wants to strengthen NGOs as genuine representatives of local communities who take up responsibility for their problems in a bottom-up process of development. Their aim is to foster South-South exchanges and search for solutions to common problems. The present bias towards the North in NGO relations is seen as disempowering because the Southern partners often respond to Northern priorities as part of funding mechanisms.

Graciela Evia and Eduardo Gudynas of CLAES are not the only development critics from the South seeking an application of the principles of social ecology in their local and regional contexts. Ramachandra Guha (1990), from India, has also put forward an interesting proposal to use social ecology as a framework for cross-cultural environmental ethics.

From the point of view of sustainable development, the idea of social ecology, both as a new science and a reconstructive social practice, appears to be an interesting proposal, as it links social and ecological aspects of sustainability. Bookchin's idealistic vision of nature and society as founded on mutualism, equity and unity in diversity may, however, be debated and challenged as another universalist and utopian project. Yet, among the new streams of thinking which developed in the 1960s with the aim of analysing and transcending the roots of the ecological crisis, so far it is one of the most comprehensive proposals for remaking societies and human/nature relations. Bookchin's notion of hierarchy as interrelated with dualism points to the epistemological roots of the crisis of environment and development. It can be usefully applied as an analytical tool not only for a critique of the dominant development model but also to expose and prevent the reproduction of structures of domination in the new proposals for sustainable development.[5]

The principles of social ecology correspond with new visions for sustainable development which were worked out by a large variety of citizens' movements globally in preparation for UNCED and during the International NGO Forum. These movements did not propose a unitary vision of sustainable development but rather a collage of different but corresponding ideas. The documents worked out by the groups[6] point out the need to dismantle patterns of domination on all levels. Their new proposals connect ecological sustainability with equity, participatory democracy, bottom-up direction of changes, and community scale development. They emphasize the need for developing new technologies friendly to both people and the environment. Furthermore, they aim at replacing violence and domination embedded in the dominant development model with principles of mutualism and unity in diversity. A strong point of social ecology is its role as both a critical science and a reconstructive social practice. As such it is well suited to help citizens' movements in the new challenges they face after UNCED and in putting their proposals into practice.

Ecofeminism: challenges and contradictions

The term ecofeminism was introduced in the mid-1970s by the French feminist writer Françoise d'Eaubonne. She blamed 'the two most immediate threats to our survival', that is 'overpopulation and the destruction of our resources' on what she called 'the Male System' (d'Eaubonne 1980, orig. 1974: 66). In her view the only way out would be women's destruction of this male power. Then 'the planet in the feminine gender would become green again for all' (ibid: 236). The term ecofeminism now refers to a significant stream within the feminist movement, containing a range of theoretical positions which rest on the assumption that there are critical connections between the domination of nature and of women. Ecofeminism points to the interconnections between feminist and ecological concerns.

Though it is one of the youngest responses to the crisis of our civilization, ecofeminism has a rich history. When it emerged, it promised to expose, to challenge and to change dominant power structures whether within the frameworks of meaning, in gender relations, or in economic systems. These promises have been expressed in the first anthologies of ecofeminist writings: *Reclaim the Earth: Women Speak Out for Life on Earth*, edited by Leonie Caldecott and Stephanie Leland (1983); *Healing the Wounds. The Promise of Ecofeminism*, edited by Judith Plant (1989); *Reweaving the World: On the Emergence of Ecofeminism*, edited by Irene Diamond and Gloria Orenstein (1990).

These promises have been largely based on the idea of merging the critical and transformative potentials of ecology and feminism which were expected to create a new, powerful movement for cultural and social change. A number of ecofeminist writers and feminist critics of science hoped that ecofeminism would bring about an epistemological shift.

Ecofeminism is not only a theoretical position. It has also become a new and a rather diversified and decentralized social movement with a number of groups, consisting not only of women but also of men. One of them is the Women's Environmental Network (WEN) in Britain (see Chapter 5). Their main strategy is to campaign for green consumerism. Aiming at a holistic analysis of the life cycle of products, the women (and the few men) in WEN investigate and publicize the social and environmental costs, from the extraction of resources, through production and marketing, to problems with the dumping of waste. Another illustration, from the USA, which is the biggest stronghold of the ecofeminist movement, is the Women's Pentagon Actions organized in 1980 and 1981 by participants of 'Women and Life on Earth:

Ecofeminism in the 1980s', a conference held in Amherst, Massachussetts. The Unity Statement, which was then issued by women who surrounded the Pentagon, covered a wide range of issues, such as the call for an end to the arms race, an end to the exploitation of resources, people, and the environment and the call for social, economic and reproductive rights (see also Lahar 1991). This document can be seen as a predecessor of the Women's Agenda 21, one of the most comprehensive and radical documents on sustainable development.

A common platform for the different positions within ecofeminism is that all of them derive from a critique of patriarchy and patriarchal epistemological frameworks. The male-centred (androcentric) ways of knowing, which account for the antagonistic, dualistic and hierarchical conceptions of self, society and cosmos, are perceived to be at the roots of oppression. Most ecofeminists contrast dualisms, such as the subject/object split associated with patriarchal epistemologies, and the oppression of women and nature, with connectedness and mutualism perceived to be inherent in women's ways of knowing.

Beyond this common ground there is a vast area of differences. Perhaps there are as many ecofeminisms as there are ecofeminists. Initially this diversification was celebrated and different versions of ecofeminism coexisted with each other. At present the lack of a unitary vision and conceptual clarity is perceived as a problem. In the meantime some of the promises of ecofeminism have faded and the theoretical debates are now in the stage of highlighting contradictions and shortcomings within the new theory. One such devastating critique of ecofeminism has been recently provided by Janet Biehl, who calls it 'an agglomeration of contradictory ideas' (1991:3) and terminates her own identification with this position.

Cultural and social ecofeminism and ecofeminist dialogue with other streams of ecological thought

In line with Val Plumwood (1992) we present the two distinct streams within ecofeminism as cultural and social ecofeminism. Some of the most powerful inputs to develop ecofeminism have come from cultural feminism (also labelled nature feminism). By now this stream within the feminist movement is largely known under the name of ecofeminism; this adds to the confusion in the debate.

Located within the essentialist tradition, nature/cultural feminists accept the association of women with nature. A substantial contribution to this position has been made by authors such as Mary Daly, Susan Griffin and Starhawk, who attempts to revive a new pro-woman religion. These ecofeminists condemn male culture for its aggression, individualism, and hierarchical thinking. They see both women and nature as oppressed and subjugated, the victims of patriarchal power structures.

Cultural (eco)feminists, criticizing men's privileged position in history, claim that women's essential features, such as empathy, caring, and female ways of knowing which are based on connectedness, can help to develop new, better, less violent and more sustainable ways of living and social relations. This, however, as we will see, is a problematic position.

Susan Griffin, an early ecofeminist, is aware that the 'social beliefs' supporting 'women's mothering and nurturing activities' are 'crucial to the maintenance of women's general subordination and economic independence'. Yet she writes:

> We [women] can read bodies with our hands, read the earth, trace gravity's path. We know what grows and how to balance one thing against another...and even if over our bodies they [men] have transformed this earth, the truth is, to this day, women still dream (Griffin 1983: 5).

So here the link of women with nature is both material and spiritual. Still, however clearcut this position may seem, there is a snag in the argument. Would all women subscribe to the idea that they 'read the earth with their hands'? And how about men, are they not part of nature, too? And if so, how has this relation become so perverted? Griffin concludes that the connection with nature essentially extends to the whole of humanity, but that men by choice have decided to separate themselves (Christ 1991: 60). In her view the domination of women and nature is the result of a male conspiracy.

There are other writers who depart from a connection between humanity and nature which somehow went wrong. Other writers like Paula Gunn Allen, Starhawk and Javors point to the specific relation of women to the protection of the environment while not denying men their share of humanity's link with nature. Their venue is spiritual, and they are very close to the adherents of goddess worship. Allen speaks with the voice of the dispossessed indigenous people of the Americas: 'We are the land...The earth is the source and being of the people and we are equally the being of the earth... The earth is not a mere source of survival, distant from the creature it nurtures and from the spirit that breathes in us . . .' (Allen, cited in Christ 1991:65).

Starhawk, who is involved in the 'old Religion of the Goddess, called witchcraft', as her biography says, bases her involvement with ecofeminism on the premise that the Earth is alive, part of a living cosmos, and thus spirit. This realization, she writes, '. . . causes us to do something, viz to preserve it' (Starhawk 1990: 74). Here the special link of women with nature fades away to women's greater (innate?) sense of responsibility towards preserving the earth. In this view ecofeminism is not so much fuelled by women's innate powers, but because it is simply the most holistic theory and practice of liberation: all relations of domination are attacked. Where the ecological and environmental movements neglect women, and the women's movements are too little concerned with the issue of the environment, ecofeminism combines it all. Regrettably, though, issues of race and class hardly receive any attention in her article; gender, too, is dealt with very briefly.

In a slightly different vein, Javors writes about her encounters with the Goddess in New York City. Her confrontation with the beggars in that city made her realize that disease and death are part of life and that the Goddess of destruction, whether she is named Hecate or Kali, is everywhere. This experience taught her that 'we can heal ourselves and become whole when we reunite with the cycles of nature', for: 'The Goddess in the metropolis dances amidst the concrete and garbage, embracing us all' (Javors, in Diamond and Orenstein 1990:214). A beautiful sentence, but the problem in her analysis is that race, class and even gender disappear completely. Women's concern with ecofeminism is linked to the sex of the great mythical goddesses.

The gap between the spiritual encounters of these white, Western, middle-class writers and the struggles of poor women in the South is enormous. A recent collection of narratives of struggles by women, in 70 countries, to construct a sustainable way of life is dealing with issues very far removed from the above analyses. Instead, the issues at stake here are concerns such as deforestation, structural adjustment, fertility control, toxic gas leaks and irrigation (Women's Feature Service, 1992).

Janet Biehl, a prominent ecofeminist, supports the ecofeminist critique of feminism, speaking from the position of social constructivism. She highlights the contradictions within ecofeminism by pointing out that the identification of women with nature means the return to regressive social definitions from which feminists have fought long to emancipate women (Biehl 1991:3). Though theoretically her critique may be viable, Janet Biehl ignores the fact that this line of thinking has led to powerful forms of social praxis and strategizing for change. As Carolyn Merchant has noticed, 'turning the perceived connection between women and biological reproduction upside down becomes the source of women's empowerment and ecological activism' (Merchant, in Diamond and Orenstein 1990:102) (see also Chapter 5).

Because this approach reverses patriarchal power structures and places women at the top of new gynocentric value hierarchies, it has attracted and mobilized many women to work towards changing their every day and global realities. This has been, as already pointed out in Chapter 5, a widespread approach at Planeta Femea, the women's gathering at the Global Forum in 1992, where the key message was that women are caring, non-violent, concerned with their local and practical issues, and therefore have the right to be involved in debates on the environment. It was implied that women know better than men how to save the Earth and themselves. This assumption was not really questioned and was presented as if all women, world-wide, agreed to it.

Despite its powerful mobilizing potential, this approach may become a self-defeating strategy, in particular as it has marginalized other approaches in ecofeminism and led to the disenchantment of many women in the environmental movement with associating themselves with ecofeminist positions.

In contrast to cultural ecofeminism, social ecofeminism which is based on the recognition of the social construction of gender (as discussed in Chapter 4), plays only a marginal role and is largely contained within academia. This stream within ecofeminism attempts to draw from and to transform the socialist-feminist tradition and to provide it with the tools to analyse the degradation of the environment. Stress is on developing the conceptual tools for working towards ecological and social change. The work of Karen Warren, Carolyn Merchant and others illustrate the attempts to enrich the socialist-feminist tradition with environmental perspectives. 'The fidelity to the social aspects of women's lives found in socialist-feminism makes a crucial contribution to ecofeminism' (King 1989:131). Ecofeminists such as Chiah Heller, Ynestra King or Janet Biehl claim their roots in social ecology. Self-classified as a radical ecofeminist, Chiah Heller (1990) has criticized cultural feminists for reproducing dualism and reversing hierarchies in their project of a gynocentric culture and has come with her vision of an ecofeminist culture and politics and a new spiritual sensibility which embodies the complexity and diversity of the natural world. Chiah Heller has been inspired by Murray Bookchin. Freedom, mutualism and diversity of nature are seen by both Bookchin and Heller as examples for the organization of free human societies.

Another ecofeminist suggestion to transcend the crisis in development is bioregionalism, that is contextualizing development in the social and natural environment (as we have already described). Bioregionalism as the basis of ecologically sustainable human culture is connected with the decentralization of power, with moving towards self-governing forms of social organization in an attempt to rebuild human and natural communities. As seen by Judith Plant the meaning of bioregionalism is 'to become a native to a place and not to fit the place to our predetermined tastes' (Plant 1989: 157).

A Southern voice trying to reconcile ecofeminism and socialism is that of Corinne Kumar D'Souza (1989). The position she speaks from is that of a Third World feminist who challenges both the androcentrism of her own culture and that of the universalized mode of development based on the patriarchal, mechanistic (dualistic and reductionist) scientific world view which equates both nature and women with 'other'. In her critique of science she draws from the work of Evelyn Fox Keller and Brian Easlea who demystified modern science as a gender-biased project. She also uses the insights of the Indian philosopher and psychologist, Ashis Nandy, who highlights authoritarianism and violence inherent in the project of development and rooted in modern science. The major contribution of Corinne Kumar D'Souza to the ecofeminist debate is her proposal for an epistemological framework which stems from the experience of those who are excluded from the dominant scientific patriarchal knowledge systems. According to her, these new epistemologies should respect the plurality of different cultures and traditions, make it possible to transform the existing exploitative social order and discern a greater human potential. The name she gives to this proposal is 'the Wind from the South':

> The South as movements for change in the Third Worlds; the South as women's movements, wherever the movements exist; the South as development of new frameworks, seeking a new language to describe what it perceives, rupturing the existing theoretical categories, breaking the mind constructs, challenging the one, real, objective reality. The South Wind must reclaim both the subjective and the objective ways of knowing, creating a wider and deeper structure of knowledge in which the observer is not distanced from the observed, the researcher from the researched, the dancer from the dance. The new cosmology will move away from Eurocentric and androcentric methodologies which only observe and describe, methodologies which quantify, percentify, class-ify, completely indifferent to phenomena which cannot be contained or explained through its frames. The South Wind invites us to create a new spectrum of methods which depart from the linear mode of thought and perception to one that is more complex, holistic. It urges us to discover more qualitative methodologies – oral histories, experiential analysis, action-research, poetry metaphor – which perhaps would reveal the complexities of reality more critically, more creatively, to place together the fragments, to discern the essence, to move into another space, another time, recapturing submerged knowledge, generating new spaces (Kumar D'Souza 1989:36).

What is most problematic in Kumar D'Souza's work is her quest for yet another universalism, but one 'that can combine dialectically the different cultural and civilizational idioms of the world...that will not deny the accumulated experience and knowledge of all past generations, . . . that will not accept the imposition of any monolithic, 'universal' structures . . . that will respect the plurality of different societies . . . ' (ibid:35-6).

Whether ecofeminism will be able to invoke the generation of new spaces as envisaged by Corinne Kumar D'Souza depends on its ability to critically approach the reproduction of dualism within its theory and practice. The attempts to overcome dualism are fraught with contradictions and ambiguities. The central paradox within ecofeminism is the question whether the effort to grant women a specific responsibility in the process of safeguarding the environment can be sufficiently legitimized by pointing to women's subordination in patriarchal culture. For then, once women's subordination will have been deconstructed (both in the symbolic as in the political realm) there will no longer be a socio-historical empirical entity called woman. Differently put, how to reconcile women's biological particularity while affirming women as agents of their history? Should women's special relation with nature be seen as a temporary phenomenon or as an immanent source of power? The ultimate consequence of stressing the socio-historical development of women's subordination is hardly ever drawn by most ecofeminist writers. Mostly, references are made to women's specific affinity with processes in nature. This means that dualism and essentialism are elements which will have to be accommodated theoretically. An exception are ecofeminists like Biehl and Heller who draw from social ecology for their theoretical work.

This is one of the challenges posed by the debate between deep ecology and ecofeminism. While ecofeminists accuse deep ecologists of not being deep enough because of the failure to face the androcentrism within their own position, deep ecologists charge ecofeminists with representing themselves as privileged actors in the struggle to reconcile humanity with nature. In this way ecofeminists simply reverse hierarchies. Though most evident in the gynocentric project of cultural feminists (nature feminists), other streams in the ecofeminist movement are also prone to the reproduction of dualism and hierarchies. According to Michael Zimmerman, the explanation of this reversal is an inability to acknowledge that not only men but also women have been distorted by effects of patriarchies (Zimmerman 1990: 154).

To realize the transformative potential of both ecofeminism and deep ecology their mutual links should be stressed. The proposals put forward by Ynestra King (1990) or Michael Zimmerman (1990) are important steps in this direction. In order to facilitate this process, women, children and men have to work together, accepting the need to acknowledge each other's equitable inputs, to recognize the suppressed longing of many men to be caring and to express feelings, and to recognize that women have not only emulated patriarchal strategies of domination but that at times they have also internalized them. This requires a careful process of building transformative politics while at the same time deconstructing existing knowledge systems which reproduce structures of domination.

Notes

1. Source: *The Bulletin*. Ideas for Tomorrow Today (n.d).

2. Gaia is the name of the Goddess of the Earth in Greek mythology.

3. Feyerabend, Paul, 1977, *Against Method*, London: New Left Books ; Kuhn, T.S., 197O, *The Structure of Scientific Revolutions*, Chicago University Press, 2nd edition

4. The social stream in ecofeminism (see Chapter 8) with such authors as Chiah Heller, Janet Biehl and also Karen Warren, point out the value of the framework of social ecology for making connections between ecology and feminism.

5. For an elaboration of the argument of the epistemological roots of the crisis in environment and development and on the epistemologies for transition towards non-violent and sustainable development from the point of view of social movements see Charkiewicz (1990) and Chapter 3 of this book.

6. For example, the Agenda Ya Wananchi, The Women's Agenda 21 and the various NGO treaties ratified at the NGO Forum in Rio de Janeiro 1992.

9. Conclusions

The threat of global environmental holocaust makes imperative a fundamental rethinking of the premises on which the dominant Western model of development is based and to work towards transformations of an unsustainable world order. Urgent actions for transformations on different levels and in different fields need the long-term visions of all those involved. Donna Haraway, in common with an increasing number of black feminist theorists argues that 'the need for unity of people trying to resist worldwide intensification of domination has never been more acute' (1991:154). The implication of increasingly sophisticated technologies and new forms of domination is that all those concerned to facilitate pro-environmental changes have a political and historic responsibility to critically analyse their own position in the wider power structure in order to identify points of leverage from their respective position. This could be as a member of the board of an industrial company, a scientific institution, a citizen's movement or as a consumer. This strategy of 'situating oneself' is the basis for a new type of micro-scale politics, which relies on temporary and mobile coalitions with other social actors or groups, not on the basis of identity, but of affinity of world views and a shared sense of ecological ethics.

This strategy also provides for a new political consciousness by linking together the subjugated knowledges of oppressed people, which we have analysed as marginal subjectivities within dominant patterns of subjectivity, such as those institutionalized in white, post-industrial cultures. This was the aim of our project to develop a theoretical framework for Women, the Environment and Sustainable Development. What seems most urgent, practically and theoretically necessary and feasible is to create multicultural alliances among women, and between women and environmentalists and other social movements, across institutional and disciplinary boundaries, on the basis of respect for each other's identities, specific struggles and different analytical positions.

In this book we have described, discussed and analysed some of the different positions and fields of knowledge which together contribute to a theoretical framework for our theme. Methodologically, as a coalition topic, WED has been very useful in indentifying the connections between a large variety of social actors participating in transformations towards sustainable development. We also attempted to show the strengths, weaknesses, shortcomings and contradictions within the different positions held and how they inform each other by enhancing their respective transformative potential.

The examples we used to illustrate the contributions that emerged from these different positions do not fully reflect the variety of views encompassed in each of the fields we discussed. We would therefore like to offer some concrete suggestions to demonstrate how the different positions inform each other.

Feminist critics of science make some of the most challenging propositions for change as they question rationality as one of the foundational myths of Western thinking. Their contributions to a more fundamental understanding of the political stakes of theoretical debates and of their implications for the future are important. Post-colonialist and black feminists have fruitfully informed these positions. Feminist critics of science share their quest for new epistemologies with groups as diverse as deep ecologists, social ecologists, ecofeminists, and some of the alternative development and WED positions; most agree about the violent and ethno-centric nature of the present dominant model of development. Many of those from within these groups advocate the need for new scientific frameworks, based on an integration of affectivity and reason, in search of more adequate accounts of the structures and aims of technological and scientific progress.

The positions that inform the notion of alternative development highlight the question of values: what is poverty? And what is perceived as poverty, progress and development in a comparative cultural perspective? Our argument is that locally sustainable lifestyles, participatory democracy and recovery of dominated peoples' subjugated knowledge are important contributions to a reconstruction of locally adapted sustainable development styles in both South and North. Among the problems involved we have emphasized the idealization of tradition, blindness to local power structures and to specific issues related to women's subordination.

Environmental reforms from within governments, mainstream political, economic and development institutions are important contributions to the transformation and to 'greening' the dominant model of development from within. But clearly, these positions reflect an impulse to sustain the status quo and the prevailing power structures, with some – often only minor – improvements. Most unacceptable from a women's point of view is a politically uncritical advocacy of more population control programmes targeted at women in the South. Increased support for such programmes has recently come from within some environmental NGDOs.

Internal reform of development is also fostered by WID and NGDOs, many of which are committed to people-oriented development. But they, too, advocate change within the system of present economic and political power structures.

Deep ecology also presents valuable criticism of Western culture and science. It's strengths lie in the questioning of the human/nature relation in general and, in particular, its links to different non-Western cultures and spiritual traditions. Biocentrism, taken to the extreme, manifests totalitarian features when, for example, AIDS and famines are interpreted and tolerated as nature's means of recovery from and revenge for human overbreeding. Recent changes within deep ecology thinking, however, represent a departure from this position. In common with some alternative development groups and ecofeminists deep ecology offers an important cultural critique of the West, as well as the sometimes problematic tendency to over-idealize local tradition. The rethinking of development and recently emerging proposals for bioregionalism as a contribution to the reconstruction of the North are significant inputs from deep ecology.

Social ecology's contribution to environmental thinking is also relevant in its stress on the interconnections and the co-evolution of human societies with nature; it also emphasizes the role played by hierarchical thinking habits in the subjugation of both people and nature. Social ecology is politically differentiated and also more practice oriented. Murray Bookchin, its founding father and most prominent protagonist, does not oppose modernity but instead wants to improve upon its originally emancipatory potential. Social ecology's strength is its holistic and simultaneous understanding of human emancipation and natural cycles. Potentially, it provides a promising basis for action and new ways of people living in harmony with each other and with nature that is of relevance for different movements that are searching for alternative lifestyles.

Most positions within environmental reforms and deep ecology fail to account for women's interests and needs in their own theory. Deep ecology idealizes women's nurturing and emotional capacities but does not make the link to real-life women's specific problems. Social ecology implies the abolition of all forms of hierarchy, including patriarchy. We wonder, however, to what extent is this ideal translated into practice by the groups which have been inspired by social ecology? Many developmental and environmental NGOs, NGDOs and movements are only just beginning to take women's interests more seriously; so far, they remain male-dominated. It must also be noted, however, that feminist and women's movements worldwide have been so preoccupied fighting the effects of patriarchy on their own lives, that only recently have concerns for environmental recovery been moved high on their agendas. Within the UNCED process, environmental, alternative developmental, women's and other citizens' movements understood – at least in theory – that they should link up and respect each others' struggles as part of their own. In the next few years, however, this recognition must also be worked out in practice.

New feminist epistemologies provide the ground for a new, radically differentiated female-embodied materialism. We have redefined feminist subjectivity as a network of simultaneous power formations which define women along the axes of sex, class and race differences. The situated, specific, embodied nature of this feminist view of the human female subject is opposed to both psychic and biological essentialism. The crucial challenge to feminism today is not to uphold the static formulated truths of readily available counter-identities but rather to embrace the living process of transformation and the redefinition of women in their cross-cultural alliances.

We profited greatly from non-Western feminist criticisms of the ethnocentrism, racism and 'whiteness' of most feminist thinking; this is also a way to highlight the shortcomings of Northern feminism in general, feminist criticism of science and the feminist post-modern positions which do not always manifest an awareness of race, ethnicity and ethnocentrism. The critique of dualism and of essentialistic definitions of women as 'naturally' more attuned to the earth and the environment have received our special attention. Discussions within feminism provided some insights which helped highlight the dangers of equating women with nature. We emphasized that, at times, the argument for women's 'closer' connection to nature can serve concrete struggles, while at others it may be a self-defeating strategy. We concluded that the question of which positions on the woman/nature connection are most fruitful for women must remain unanswered. At the same time, however, we take the point from Bina Agarwal (1991) that possibly this question and its bearing on women's understanding of their struggle around environment related issues may not be the most important one to ask. As Agarwal has shown, what is at stake is not to idealize our own position as women, but to deconstruct the power structure that sustains a specific patriarchal ideology which has assigned women a closer relationship to nature, and specific sexual division of labour.

In general, WID has tended to reproduce the misperception that development is a problem located in the South, that women need to be integrated into mainstream development and that better development policy can truly help to benefit women in the South. Even the gender and development approach, the latest stage of WID thinking, works within the framework of developmentalism. But this approach supports, if only in theory, the transformation of all unequal relations: of men towards women and the North towards the South, etc. Indirectly, WID experts – together with women in environmental professions and movements, and Southern women's and alternative developmental movements – contributed to the emergence of WED and eventually to a breach between Northern and Southern women's position on developmentalism as outlined in the Miami Women's Action Agenda 21. WED positions from within development agencies tend to reproduce the problem of WID by arguing that more environmental projects for women would redress the problem of the parallel phenomena of environmental destruction and feminization of poverty in the South. But Joan Davidson (in OECD/DAC Expert Group on WID 1989), for example, made clear that if women are to be involved in environmental projects they must also benefit from them and not be exploited as cheap labour. Melissa Leach (1991) shows how environmental degradation in the South affects different groups of women and men in different ways. She contributes to reforms from within development agencies by illustrating the urgent need for participatory planning for development projects.

Bina Agarwal (1991) points out how women, especially, but not only, in the South, do suffer in gender specific ways from environmental destruction; the increasing number of testimonies of women who have moved to the forefront of environmental struggles at the local level is impressive. But Agarwal demonstrates quite convincingly that women in India have been active in environmental movements not because of their 'natural' relation to their environment, as Vandana Shiva (1989) would have us believe, but simply because their position in society is such that they are the most affected by environmental decline, and consequently most interested in resisting it. Agarwal's proposal for a feminist environmentalism seems to us a very useful proposition of a direction for WED to move towards in the future.

Vandana Shiva (1989), Ashis Nandy (1987 and 1988) and many other development critics fundamentally question the Western bias in values of progress, prosperity and well-being. Shiva shows convincingly that developmentalism has been violent for many people, especially women in the South, as well as local environments, which have been ruthlessly exploited and incorporated into global markets.

From Northern women we learned how they have been struggling around environmental issues in their own locations, for example, the Greenham Common women and the Women's Environmental Network in the UK. Feminist criticism of science and the contributions of women scientists (mostly from the North) yield important insights; the work of Rachel Carson, for example, even though she may not have considered herself a feminist. Her influential book *Silent Spring* (1962), the story of DDT, as well as her later works, sparked off the beginnings of the North's environmental movement.

The DAWN network's strength is their critique of development, including WID and the global economy, from the viewpoint of women in the South. But this strength is simultaneously a weakness: the upholding of an idealized vision of the poor, Third World woman as the source for an alternative vision of development. Non-Western, post-structuralist activists, such as Chandra Mohanty, have strongly warned against such a constructed idealization of the Third World Woman.

Ecofeminism, the feminist position most explicitly concerned with environmental destruction, is also a project for new epistemologies. Ecofeminism has provided important insights into the roots of the ecological crisis, but it may, however, have reached an impasse in its project of thinking its way out of the dualisms and hierarchies on which the Western frame of mind is founded. The issue at stake here is how to postulate effective grounds for action in the post-modern condition? We drew important insights from the feminist critique of science in this respect. We argued that an understanding of the body as a site of power helps avoid an essentialist understanding of women while arguing for their empowerment as political agents. Hence, our understanding of embodiedness differs from that of ecofeminists. We see the body as a construct, an interface between symbolic and material forces: a morphological reality where multiple codes of power and culture are inscribed. The body is not an essence, it is one's situation in reality and one's primary location in the world. The embodiment of the subject is the political standpoint which allows for a critique of dualism as a form of violence, that is to say, an oppositional form of thought which has the effect of psychic warfare. Embodiment of the subject is not a one-way road towards an essentialized female self, but a bio-cultural situation which leads to the deconstruction of a naturalistic basis for female or human identity.

We have emphasized that, as it has evolved historically, the WED debate has both strong and weak points. One of its strong assets is that its origins are firmly rooted in the context of the life experience of mainly poor women in the South. The powerful voices of Southern women leaders emerged on the international scene as important development critics. Speaking on behalf of poor women in the South, these women, together with their Northern counterparts, managed to create a space in international development and environment fora for women to be heard and, as a result, more women joined discussions on WED. During the early years, WED as a topic was situated within the development debate, which in turn saw development problems as located in the South, the 'developing world'. WED was segmented into disciplinary fields of development practice: women and forestry, women and agriculture, women and water/sanitation; and so on. The fact that (mostly Northern) women development experts have moved into these fields has been important in sensitizing the development industry to its male bias. We hope it will eventually help to improve development project procedures as a whole.

This segmentation, however, obscured the potential challenge that WED poses to development in general, by confining the debate within disciplinary boundaries without questioning the underlying assumptions of development itself. After the 1991 Miami Conferences, this segmentation became clearly transcended when women accross all divides entered the WED discourse and raised their voices against a globally unsustainable model of development, as reflected in the Women's Action Agenda 21. This document made clear that the environment and development crisis is a global problem, that we need to fundamentally rethink the very premisses upon which development is built, and that women involved in a multiplicity of struggles were willing to stand up for these views.

Women and UNCED: successes and failures

Within the UNCED process women who had promoted WED positions joined with some feminists, women ecologists, environmentalists, women from development agencies, critics of reproductive technologies and advocates for women's reproductive rights from the North and South, and arrived at a synthesis of women's positions globally. A major problem of this coalition is the stress on women's 'special' relation to nature which gives them a 'special' voice in solving the crisis. At least this position was the basis for the unprecedented unitary statement of women across the board in the Women's Action Agenda 21.

Despite women's great achievement in the UNCED process, the belief in a global sisterhood based on women's 'special' role in saving the planet, encompasses some problems and pitfalls which became clearer at Planeta Femea during the Global Forum 1992. It became apparent that often and in subtle ways women's interaction and politics suffer from reproducing prevailing structures of omission and objectification. Feminist politics reflected broader and more pervasive tendencies, which it is committed to dismantling: patterns of domination, relations of hierarchies and dualisms; epistemological violence; and symbolic exclusion. In this respect, we have emphasized the idea of clearing the theoretical ground for more effective political alliances between women of different cultures, beliefs and orientations. But much remains to be done to problematize the issues of power between women and women's politics.

Another problem is emerging after UNCED: it is becoming increasingly clear that the WED movement was fuelled mainly by individual women in development institutions, and environmental and consumer organizations and movements and was not really carried by WED movements at the grassroots level. WED protagonists were either individual women acting in their capacities as professionals, women from different women's movements, or those who were part of women's groups within ecological, environmental, consumer and other movements. Specific local women's struggles were used to illustrate the need to hear women's voices on environmental issues. Two points are important here. First, a methodological one: many women in UNCED spoke 'on behalf' of others to push for consideration of women's perspectives on sustainable development. This touches on the question of difference between women as indicated above. Secondly, women within the environmental, ecological, developmental, consumer and other movements dominated by male participants must, within their own movements, address both the issues of ecological destruction and the male bias inherent in much of their movements' thinking.

The preparatory process for UNCED thus marked a significant shift, but this shift must reflect a new political practice. This has been a central point we have tried to highlight in our work, namely: the need to increase political coalitions and alliances between all those concerned, more systematically and more widely than in the past. It seems to us that there is a need to also forge stronger coalitions and alliances between women of different origins and orientations and across institutional and ideological borders, in order to address collectively the male bias in ecological and environmental thinking at large. The various positions outlined in this book have yielded valuable insights into the complexities involved in the multiple and shifting processes of transformation. It needs to be stressed, however, that making such alliances involves a number of dilemmas; nevertheless, to resolve these dilemmas is not a precondition for striking alliances and undertaking co-operation.

WED as a coalition theme: some proposals for future action

Those points highlighted in this book, which are of relevance to everyone interested and participating in challenges and transformations of the dominant mode of development, are summarized below:

- The notion of development itself needs to be deconstructed; and recognition of the connections between the destruction of nature globally and the violation of especially women's and other marginal groups' rights constitute a fruitful theoretical perspective from which to view the violence inherent in the dominant Western mode of development.

- On a theoretical level, deconstruction of development discourse should develop much stronger links with the feminist critique of science, post-colonial and black feminist theory, as well as various ecological and environmental thinkers' criticisms of science and knowledge. None of these can establish a privileged claim to truth, but they all make fruitful contributions to an analysis of the multiple nature of the global crisis and to suggestions for change. We have argued that there can be no sustainable development without considering women's roles and input, but we stress that neither women alone nor any other single group involved in the transformations can be made responsible for recovering the environment or have privileged access to 'a truth' about sustainable development.

- On the question of epistemology we have drawn from many positions which provide a critique of Western science, but mainly from feminist critics. These provide important insights into the roots of the crisis. Changes on the level of epistemology towards non-dominating ways of producing knowledge are crucial points of departure for transformations of development.

- Fundamental as well as more subtle structures of domination may survive in the processes of change taking place within all of these positions. One of the main tasks ahead is to reveal these structures by challenging them in an ongoing process of transformations which is inevitably full of contradictions, because it takes place on constantly shifting grounds. As Spivak, Haraway, Harding and Foucault each in their different ways warn us, the same tools can be used for emancipation as for oppression. Today holism, mutualism, diversity, integration may seem to be liberational principles but they also contain new and possibly more pervasive tools of domination. In this context we have questioned the call for 'an alternative paradigm' in the singular as rooted in the modernist mode of linear and teleological thinking. Instead, we take from feminists the imperative for a living process of transformation of self and other, based on an understanding of how the post-modern subject works.

- At UNCED the polarization of positions *vis-à-vis* pro-environmental changes became quite pronounced. Reformative attempts to green the global, political and economic system clashed with more radical visions for a sustainable global future. As a result, powerful citizens' movements worldwide, disenchanted with the way the global environmental crisis is addressed by the international political community, are taking responsibility for change into their own hands. These diverse movements are determined to implement alternative ways of living and relating to each other and to nature. Groups committed to alternative lifestyles also interact increasingly on a global level. Such initiatives may yield important insights into new forms of practice.

- Post-modernist rainbow politics as proposed by black feminist theorists and summarized by Harding (1992a), in our view offer a productive mode of action for social change. The politics of coalitions between different groups interested in fundamental political, economic, and ecological changes requires an acceptance of difference in positive terms. For example, specific struggles on one particular issue may be most fruitfully conducted by a temporary coalition of a certain group, whose individual interests may even be different. Such temporary coalitions could be successful between different groups of women, between ecological and environmental groups and women, between animal rights activists and critics of biotechnology, and so on.

- At the same time, coalitions between social movement groups, especially women's and environmental/alternative developmental groups, need to be strengthened in order to further experiment with alternative, non-hierarchical forms of living and relating with each other and nature on the basis of mutuality and complementarity. Part of this project is the further creation of alternative spaces where such alternative realities can be lived.

- Coalitions and strategic alliances are necessary, not only between marginal individuals and groups outside the mainstream organizations with actors. Coalitions across institutional boundaries, between individuals in mainstream developmental, political, and industrial organizations, and scientific institutions and social movement groups interested in transformations of development are necessary to speed up transformations of the dominant mode of development from within. The differences in institutional investment between different actors poses the question of differences in power and epistemic privilege, which make real exchanges difficult, as not everyone enters the scene on equal terms. The subtleties of co-optation mechanisms need ongoing self-critical analysis. It is untenable to hold up old enemy images of the 'good' social movements and NGOs and the 'bad' governments and development agencies or vice versa. There may be individuals within mainstream organizations who clearly see the possible spaces for transformations within their organizations and need to work together with citizen's groups to provide the necessary pressure. On the other hand, there may be NGOs who have been specifically founded to represent the interests of political parties, transnational capital, pro-life lobbies etc.

- New strategies of power and cooptation mechanisms cut right through institutional and ideological divides. Therefore the terms of alliances and coalitions need to be carefully thought through. The subtleties of co-optation mechanisms need on-going self-reflexive analysis.

- Development critics outside mainstream organizations need to obtain access to fora where decisions are made, otherwise decisions will be made without them. Therefore, strategic information must be circulated between individuals in positions within mainstream organizations and those outside. Mutual accountability of people within and outside the mainstream institutions is essential. Possibly, an important role can be played by people moving between different institutions and disciplines, or between theory and practice: these are the de-professionalized intellectuals as described by Esteva (1987), who are willing to take a holistic view of the problems with which they are dealing. People within scientific institutions, who are in an epistemologically privileged position to participate in formulating scientific discourse, need to enter coalitions with social and political movements. Important lessons can be drawn from the different movements' experiences of struggle throughout the last decades.

The WED movement post-UNCED

From our positions of women committed to social change we offer some ideas for possible directions for WED after UNCED. During the 1991 Miami Conferences, women across regional, institutional and disciplinary divides saw the urgent need to join in a collective critique of the dominant development model from their perspective as women. Translating into practice such a vision is by no means an easy task; it requires a careful analysis of how power works, taking into account the issue of difference among women; it also needs new epistemologies and new types of politics for action, as we have pointed out above.

Apart from entering coalitions with environmental, peace, developmental, and other movements, development organizations and scientific institutions, women who are committed to social change across the board, need to be much more aware than in the past, of the connections between all our separate struggles and the survival of the planet. As we have argued, women's identities *per se* are not necessarily a 'special' basis for coalitions between women, but we need to develop a long-term vision and to radically increase networking between women across institutional boundaries.

As already noted, women's input into UNCED was provided by a relatively select group already interested in environmental change who did not always represent grassroots level constituencies. Within the UNCED preparatory process outstanding women leaders used their personal influence in pointing out the connections between women, the environment and sustainable development and to promote women's cause in the environmental debates surrounding UNCED. However, practical proposals on how to proceed after UNCED are yet to be worked out. The absence of such concrete strategies for the future became obvious at Planeta Femea.

The WED movement so far has been carried on mainly by women leaders and professional women from educated, middle-class backgrounds working in development agencies, scientific institutions, environmental, consumer and reproductive rights movements. It is now entering into a new stage after UNCED. One of the main tasks ahead is how to carry to the grassroots level what has happened at UNCED and, together with the women working on that level, develop concrete strategies for pro-environmental change. The other challenge is for women across institutions and divides of race and class to form coalitions and relate to each other on an equal footing. Coalitions must especially be sought with the feminist movements that were under-represented within the UNCED process.

The shadow side of women's involvement in the WED discussions was that some women have become part of the international 'WED jetset' and have built fashionable careers on the topic of WED. We do not mean to imply that this is necessarily negative; some of it may be the inevitable off-shoot of the institutionalization of environmental issues. There are, however, inherent dangers of co-optation of the issues involved and of competition between women. WED is the first issue that has the potential for women across the South/West/East divides to act together and make a change. We must be well aware of the power dynamics involved in this process, in order to avoid its worst pitfalls. Hence, the issue of power between women is crucial. How can we work closely together as women from different backgrounds and different cultures without reproducing old patterns of domination? We suggest that women across institutional boundaries work together much more closely on specific issues, exchange strategic information and commit themselves to making each other accountable for their actions. Global sisterhood is by no means a given: the privilege of situated and therefore partial perspectives may be much more fruitful in the long-range.

Northern women are taking up the challenge from women from the South to criticize the unsustainable modes of production and consumption within their own societies. The DAWN network initiated two working groups of Northern and Southern women. These groups are developing a much needed alternative economic framework, which considers both women's unpaid labour and the costs of environmental destruction as well as a concerted North/South action on women and reproductive rights. Another potential area for collective and complementary North/South action that has been taken up focuses on consumer issues. Women who are in the position to produce and influence scientific discourse, especially on environment-related topics, can develop feminist critiques of their own fields of knowledge. All the changes that will be introduced after the governmental as well as the non-governmental UNCED processes need to be evaluated from a women's point of view. Women need to develop further their expertise and develop feminist positions on those complex issues in order to be able to influence the post-UNCED decisions taken by governments.

Changes have to be introduced not only at the consumer level, but even more urgently at economic, industrial and business levels. Criticism on the practices of TNCs, global economic processes, the politics of science, and so on needs to be sustained and intensified. One of the important roles for women in mainstream institutions and networks in both North and South, is to make clearer these highly complex and interrelated issues for those women who have no access to such information, and foster exchanges of strategic information between women across the board.

Feminist critics of science bring to our attention how research methodologies themselves support patterns of domination. We believe that a radical feminist epistemology based on the positivity of differences and on post-modern situated perspectives can contribute to forms of networking and resistance for women across cultures. More especially, radical feminism provides some important clues about how to transform the institutions where scientific knowledge is articulated and legitimated, by changing research practices from within. By taking into account the power relations at work not only at the practical but also on the epistemological level, feminist epistemology provides a positive political challenge.

We need also to question research policies: who funds research? what questions are asked? whose questions are they? Who teaches who and what? Are those who teach accountable and do they live up to what they teach? The role of educational systems as formidable vehicles for the spread of domination need to be disclosed and criticized, and less hegemonic forms of pedagogy must be further developed.

The challenge is open for women globally to work out these issues as they prepare for the 1995 Women and Development Conference in Beijing.

Proposals for policy changes on WED in development co-operation

Centralized policy-making by Northern agencies for development programmes and projects to be implemented in the South has been part of the problem of developmentalism. Despite development agencies' continued stress on local people's participation in project formulation, the reality of development co-operation lags far behind such aspirations. In principle we are opposed to centralized policy-making, because it cannot take into account local specificities and needs of various groups; nevertheless, we see the danger of purism and therefore do not risk jeopardizing our potential influence for positive changes within development agencies' project practice.

Our previous discussions highlight the fact that development is by no means a problem only for the South. Development is a global problem. Internationally, there is a growing recognition of this fact. Industrialized Northern countries must rethink their own use of the environment and can no longer serve as a global model. All involved — state apparatuses, national and international governmental and non-governmental development agencies, industry, business, and the military establishment — must fundamentally rethink their own use of the environment and the dominant model of development. Development cannot be seen in isolation from the global economy, militarism, and the changing international economic relations in the 1990s. Changes on national, international, and even global level are needed (in market and exchange rate mechanisms, in GATT, and stringent control mechanisms applied to TNCs if local development projects and initiatives are to become effective.

Policies are guidelines for action that particular organizations agree to implement. People affected by these policies must have a voice in their formulation; in turn, it is essential that development organizations are made accountable to those affected. Development policies must reflect people's, including women's, interests. There should be no project without an expressed need by those to be affected, including women.

A transformative rather than a welfarist approach to development is imperative if people's right to self-determination is to be respected. One major task for development institutions is to change themselves and their own procedures in order to make room for people's input. Part of development co-operation in general has to be a firm commitment by the North's governments, NGOs, and NGDOs to transform the dominant model of development in the North itself.

New strategies of co-optation are, however, already emerging. The new trend in mainstream governmental agencies as well as NGDOs is to favour 'people's voices from the South'. This a simple reversal of the old hierarchy: the new 'truth' about sustainable development is seen to lie in the South. This may be true to some extent, but many of the South's new NGOs and NGDOs do not necessarily reflect the perceptions of local people, as they are run by urban middle-class individuals who are now representing 'the people's voice'. The idealization of the 'poor, Third World woman's' voice is a case in point. What is really needed is a transformational approach to development based on exchange – aimed at equitable relationships between 'donor' and 'receiver' of development assistance. In this respect we commend a small initiative taken by the Dutch Minister for Development Co-operation, Jan Pronk, who has invited Dutch NGOs to join in an experimental programme for developing such equitable development co-operation with the governmental and non-governmental sectors of Costa Rica, Benin and Bhutan. An important element in this initiative is the commitment by the Dutch side to not only teach, but also to learn from their partners in the process.

Policy suggestions for change depend on political feasibility and space that is often absent. Hence, we have to acknowledge the political nature of the development process. Political questions should not be cast in the language of needs for better policy, more technology and more funds and so on. There must be sufficient political space to accommodate local initiatives based on indigenous methods of resource use and locally controllable types of appropriate technologies. Such types of technology must also be appropriate for women and relieve their work burden.

In large bilateral projects consideration needs to be given to the role of the national implementing agencies of environment-related projects, such as ministries, forest, agriculture, and irrigation departments and their extension workers, as they often have their own vested interests, and work in collusion with local elites. Truly sustainable development cannot be implemented by repressive governments.

Gender training in development agencies should become imperative, but with the long-term vision of transforming not only gender but all other relations: North/South, class, caste, ethnic and so on. As was also stressed in the Women's Action Agenda 21 and Chapter 24 of the UNCED Agenda 21, more women need to be involved in decision-making structures in the development process on all levels.

Environmental and women's impact assessments within development projects need to be connected and integrated from the inception of projects and programmes. There needs to be more dialogue between sector specialists than in the past rather than them operating in isolation from each other. In the long run, the checklist approach to measuring the impacts of projects on the environment and women must become integral parts of development projects.

From a women's point of view we acknowledge that population growth is a problem but that population control programmes that overtly or covertly operate in a coercive fashion must be rejected. Much more than in the past, population control should be discussed with and administered by local, regional and national women's organizations. Population programmes must be oriented towards the needs of contraceptive users, and this implies a radical rethinking of the nature of approaches to population programmes.

Environmental projects in the South must ensure that the women involved also benefit from them. This may include making provisions for wider social changes, such as giving women access to decision-making bodies and land ownership. Projects that only instrumentalize women as a cheap labour force for environmental recovery need to be rejected.

Before projects are planned there must be a local level analysis, together with all local groups affected of what are the local needs, how natural resources are used by different groups in society and how these have changed over time. Resource use is often determined by local power structures. The conflicts over the use of resources must be worked out in a democratic process. It is not enough simply to distinguish between women and men without specifying the particular interests and needs of women and men from different ethnic groups and classes.

Bibliography

Published sources

Adams, Parveen and Beverly Brown (1979) The feminine body and feminist politics, in: M/F, 2, pp. 43-61.

Aiken, Susan Hardy, Karen Anderson, Myra Dinnerstein, Judy Nolte Lensink, Patricia MacCorquodale (eds) (1988) *Changing Our Minds. Feminist Transformations of Knowledge*, New York: State University of New York Press.

Afshar, Haleh and Bina Agarwal (eds) (1989) *Women, Poverty and Ideology in Asia — Contradictory Pressures, Uneasy Solutions*, Basingstoke and London: Macmillan.

Afshar, Haleh and Carolyne Dennis (eds) (1992) *Women and Adjustment Policies in the Third World*, Basingstoke: Macmillan.

Agarwal, Anil and Sunita Narain (1985) Women and Natural Resources, in: *Social Action* Vol. 35, October/December, pp. 301-25.

Agarwal, Bina (1986) *Cold Hearths and Barren Slopes: the woodfuel crisis in the Third World*, London: Zed Books.

———(1988) Who Sows? Who Reaps? Women and Land Rights in India, in: *The Journal of Peasant Studies* 15, 1, pp. 531-81.

———(1989) Rural Women, Poverty and Natural Resources. Sustenance, Sustainability and Struggle for Change, in: *Economic and Political Weekly*, 28.10, pp. 46-65.

———(1991) Engendering the Environmental Debate: Lessons Learnt from the Indian Subcontinent, *CASID Distinguished Speakers Series* Monograph No.8, Michigan State University

———(1992) The Gender and Environment Debate: Lessons From India, in: *Feminist Studies* 18/1, pp. 119-58.

Anderson, Lorraine (ed.) (1991) *Sisters of the Earth. Women's Prose and Poetry About Nature*, New York: Vintage Books.

Albrecht, Lisa and Rose M. Brewer (eds) (1990) *Bridges of Power. Women's Multicultural Alliances*, in Cooperation with National Women's Studies Association, Philadelphia: New Society Publishers.

Antipode (1984) Women and the Environment, Vol.16/3, A Radical Journal of Geography. Oxford: Blackwell Publishers.

Antrobus, Peggy (1988) Women and Human Development, in: *Rethinking Caribbean Development*, George W. Schujler, Henry Veltmeyer (eds) (Issues in International Development Series; No. 2), Halifax: International Education Centre.

———(1989) The Empowerment of Women, in: R.S. Gallin, A. Aronoff and A. Ferguson (eds) *Women and International Development Annual*, Boulder: Westview Press.

Apffel, Frédérique and Stephen A. Marglin (eds) (1990) *Dominating Knowledge: Development, Culture, and Resistance*, Oxford: Clarendon Press.

Asian and Pacific Development Centre (APCD) (1992) *Asian and Pacific Women's Resource and Action Series: Environment*, Kuala Lumpur.

Atkinson, Adrian (1991) Environment and Development: Concepts and Practices in

Transition, in:*Public Administration and Development*, Vol. 11, pp. 401-13.

Awekotuku, Ngahuia Te (1982) He Wahine, and He Whenua (1982) Maori Women and the Environment, in: *New Zealand Environment*, 33/30, Autumn.

Bahuguna, Sundarlal (1988) Chipko: The People's Movement with a Hope for the Survival of Humankind, in: *IFDA Dossier* 63, January/February, pp. 4-14.

Bandarage, Asoka (1991) In Search of a New World Order, in: *Women's Studies International Forum* 14/4, pp. 345-55.

Banks, Olive (1981) *Faces of Feminism*, Oxford: Robertson & Co.

bell hooks (1990) *Yearning. Race, Gender and Cultural Politics*, Toronto: Between the Lines.

————(1991) Sisterhood, Political Solidarity between Women, in: Gunew, Sneja (ed.) *A Reader in feminist knowledge*, London and New York: Routledge.

————(1992) *Feminism: Theory as Liberatory Practice*, Anna Maria van Schuurman Centrum, oration held on May 15, Utrecht: Arts Faculty, University of Utrecht.

————and Mary Childers (1990) A conversation about race and class, in: Marianne Hirsch and Evelyn Fox-Keller (eds) *Conflicts in Feminism*, New York and London: Routledge.

Beneria, Lourdes and Gita Sen (1981) Accumulation, Reproduction and Women's Role in Economic Development: Boserup Revisited, in: *SIGNS* 7/2, Winter, pp. 279-98.

————(1982) Class and Gender Inequalities and Women's Role in Economic Development, in: *Feminist Studies*, Vol..8/1 Spring, pp. 157-76.

Benhabib, Seyla and Drucilla Cornell (1987) *Feminism as Critique*, Minneapolis: Minnesota University Press.

Benjamin, Jessica (1990) *The Bonds of Love*, New York: Routledge.

Bennholdt-Thomsen, Veronika (1980) Investment in the Poor: An Analysis of the World Bank Policy, in: *Social Scientist*, Vol.. 8/7 & 8, February/ March.

Berman, Marshall (1983) *All That is Solid Melts into Air: The Experience of Modernity*, London: Verso.

Bernal, M. (1987) *Black Athena. The afroasiatic roots of classical civilization*, London: Vintage.

Bertell, Rosalie (1985) *No Immediate Danger: Prognosis for a Radioactive Earth*, London: The Women's Press.

Biehl, Janet (1991) *Rethinking Ecofeminist Politics*, Boston: South End Press.

Bleier, Ruth (1984) *Gender and science*, New York: Pergamon Press.

————(1986) *Feminist Approaches to Science*, New York: Pergamon Press.

————(1987) *Science and Gender. A Critique of Biology and its Theories on Women*, The Athene Series, New York: Pergamon Press.

————(1991) Science and Gender, a critique of biology and its theories on women, in: Sneja Gunew (ed.) *A Reader in Feminist Knowledge*, London: Routledge.

Bondestam, Kars (1980) The Political Ideology of Population Control, Laws of Population, in: Lars Bondestam and Staffan Bergström, *Poverty and Population Control*, Academic Press.

Bono, Paola and Sandra Kemp (1991) *Italian Feminist Thought*, Oxford: Oxford University Press.

Bookchin, Murray (1971) *Post-scarcity Anarchism*, Berkeley: Ramparts Press.

————(1982) *The Ecology of Freedom. The Emergence and Dissolution of*

Hierarchy, Paolo Alto: Cheshire Books.

———(1984) The Radicalization of Nature, in: *Comment*, July.

———(1990) *Remaking Society: Pathways to a Green Future*, Boston: South End Press.

Bordo, Susan (1986) The Cartesian masculinisation of thought, in: *Signs*, 11/3, pp. 439-56.

Boserup, Ester (1970) *Women's Role in Economic Development*, New York: St. Martin's Press.

Bourdieu, Pierre (1979) *La Distinction*, Paris: Minuit.

Boyce, James K. (1991) The bomb is a dud, in: *WGNRR Newsletter* 35, April-June, pp. 5-7.

Bradford, George (1989) *How Deep is Deep Ecology?* Ojai: Times Change Press.

Braidotti, Rosi (1989) The politics of ontological difference, in: Teresa Brennan (ed.) *Between Feminism and Psychoanalysis*, London and New York: Routledge, pp. 89-105.

———(1991) *Patterns of Dissonance.*, Cambridge: Polity Press and New York: Routledge.

———(1992) Essentialism, in: Elizabeth Wright (ed.) *Dictionary of Feminism and Psychoanalysis*, Oxford: Blackwell.

Brennan, Teresa (1989) Introduction, in: Teresa Brennan (ed.) *Between Feminism and Psychoanalysis*, London and New York: Routledge, pp. 1-23.

Brock-Uttne, Birgit (1988) Formal Education as Force Shaping Cultural Norms on War and Environment, in: Arthur Westing (ed.) *Cultural Norms, War and Environment*, Oxford: Oxford University Press, pp. 3-100.

Brower, Christien (1990) Hierarchie of Harmonie? Gender in de Wetenschapelijke Ondervraging van de Natuur, in: *Tijdschrift voor Vrouwenstudies*, 11/3, pp. 260-72.

Brown, Lester et al (1992) *State of the World 1992*, London, New York: W.W. Norton.

Brown, Rosemary (1991) Matching Women, Environment and Development, in: *Women and Environments*, WEED Foundation Quarterly, Winter/Spring, Vol. 13/2, pp. 37-41.

Brownmiller, Susan (1975) *Against Our Will*, London: Penguin.

Bunch, Charlotte (1990) Making Common Cause, Diversity and Coalitions, in: Lisa Albrecht and Rose M.Brewer (eds) *Bridges of Power. Women's Multicultural Alliances*, in Cooperation with National Women's Studies Association, Philadelphia: New Society Publishers.

Bunyard, Peter (1989) Gaia in Crisis. Is Sustainable Development Feasible?, in: *The Ecologist*, Vol. 19/1.

———and Edward Goldsmith (eds) (1989) *Proceedings of the Second Annual Camelot Conference on the Implications of the Gaia Thesis*, Bodmin, Cornwall: Abbey Press.

Butler, Judith (1990) *Gender Trouble,* London and New York: Routledge.

Caldecott, Leonie and Stephanie Leland (eds) (1983) *Reclaim the Earth: Women Speak Out for Life on Earth*, London: The Women Press.

Capra, Fritjof, and Charlene Spretnak (1984) *The Green Politics: The Global Promise*, New York: Dutton.

Capra, Fritjof (1987) Deep Ecology: A New Paradigm, in: *Earth Island Journal*, Autumn.

Carson, Rachel, (1962), *Silent Spring*, Greenwich, Connecticut: Fawcett Publications.

———(1962), *Of Man and the Stream of Time*, Scripps College Bulletin, July 5-10.

Cecelski, Elisabeth (1987) Energy and rural women's work: Crisis, response and policy alternatives, in: *International Labour Review* 126, 1, pp. 41-64.

Centro Información Mujer, CIM (1992) Mulher e Meio Ambiente, special issue *CIM*, March, Sao Paulo.

Chai, Michael (1992) The "Other Indigenous" Peoples of Sarawk, in: *Development*, Journal of the Society for International Development 2, pp. 56-60.

Chambers, Robert (1986) *Sustainable Livelihoods: An Opportunity for the World Commission on Environment and Development*, Sussex: Institute of Development Studies (IDS).

———(1987) Sustainable Livelihoods, Environment and Development: Putting Poor People First, in: *IDS Discussion Paper* No 240, University of Sussex.

Chay, Deborah G. (1991) Reconstructing Essentialism, in: *Diacritics* 21, 2/3, pp. 135-47.

Cheney, Jim (1987) Eco-feminism and Deep Ecology, in: *Environmental Ethics*, 9, pp. 115-45.

———(1989) Postmodern Environmental Ethics: Ethics as Bioregional Narrative, in: *Environmental Ethics* 11, pp. 117-34.

Chodorow, Nancy (1978) *The Reproduction of Mothering*, Berkeley: University of California Press.

Chowdry, Kamla (1988) Poverty, Environment, Development, in: *Daedalus*, Vol. 18/1, pp. 141-58.

Christ, Carol P. (1991) Why Women need the Goddess, phenomenological, psychological and political reflections, in: Sneja Gunew (ed.) *A Reader in Feminist Knowledge*, London: Routledge.

Christian, Barbara (1988) The race for theory, in : *Feminist Studies* 14/1.

Cixous, Hélène (1985) *L'histoire terrible main inachevée de Norodom Sihanouk roi du Camboge*, Paris: Théatre du Soleil.

———(1987) *L'Indiade ou l'Inde de leurs reves*, Paris: Théatre du Soleil.

———(1988) *Manne: aux Mandelstams aux Mandelas*, Paris: des femmes.

Clark, John (ed.) (1990) *Renewing the Earth. The Promise of Social Ecology. A Celebration of the Work of Murray Bookchin*, London: Green Print.

Code, Lorraine (1988) Experience, Knowledge, and Responsibility, in: M. Griffith and M. Whitford (eds) *Feminist Perspectives in Philosophy*, London: Macmillan.

———(1991) *What Does she Know?* Ithaca: Cornell University Press.

Cole, Sam (1990) Cultural Diversity and Sustainable Futures, in: *Futures*, Vol. 22/1, December.

Collard, Andree with Joyce Contrucci (1988) *Rape of the Wild: Man's Violence Against Animals and the Earth*, Bloomington: Indiana University Press.

Conroy, Czech and Miles Litvinoff (1988) *The Greening of Aid, Sustainable Livelihoods in Practice*, London: Earthscan Publications Ltd with the International Institute for Environment and Development (IIED).

Conway, Gordon R. and Edward B. Barbier (1990) *After the Green Revolution:*

Sustainable Agriculture for Development, London: Earthscan.

Coole, Diana H. (1988) *Women in Political Theory, from Ancient Misogyny to Contemporary Feminism*, Sussex: Wheatsheaf.

Corea, Gina (1986) *The Mother Machine: Reproductive Technologies from Artificial Insemination to Artificial Wombs*, New York: Harper and Row.

Cornell, Drucilla (1991) *Beyond Accommodation: Ethical Feminism, Deconstruction and the Law*, New York and London: Routledge.

Cornia, Giovanni Andrea, Richard Jolly and Francis Stewart (1987) *Adjustment with a Human Face*: A Study by UNICEF, Oxford, Clarendon Press.

Coward, Rosalind (1983) *Patriarchal Precedents, Sexuality and Social Relations*, London: Routledge & Kegan Paul.

Crosby, A. (1986) *Ecological Imperialism: The Biological Expansion of Europe, 900-1900*, Cambridge: Cambridge University Press.

Dahlerup, Drude (ed) (1986) *The New Women's Movement, Feminism and Political Power in Europe and the USA*, London: Sage.

Daines, V. and David Seddon (1991) *Survival Struggles, Protest and Resistance: Women's Responses to 'Austerity' and 'Structural Adjustment"*, Norwich: University of East Anglia.

Dallery, Arlene B. (1989) The Politics of Writing (the) Body: Ecriture Féminine, in: Alison M. Jaggar and Susan R. Bordo (eds) *Gender/Body/Knowledge, Feminist Reconstructions of Being and Knowing*, New Brunswick and London: Rutgers University Press.

Daly, Herman E. (1989) Sustainable development: from concepts and theory to operational principles, in: *Population and Development Review*, Hoover Institution Conference.

———(1990) Towards an Environmental Macroeconomics, in: *Revista de Análisis Económico*, Vol.5/2, pp19-31, November.

Daly, Mary (1978) *Gyn/ecology, the metaphysics of radical feminism*, Boston: Beacon Press.

———(1984) *Pure Lust, Elemental Feminist Philosophy*, London: The Women's Press.

Dankelman, Irene and Joan Davidson (1988) *Women and Environment in The Third World -Alliance for the Future*, London: Earthscan.

Davies, Donald Edward (1989) *Ecophilosophy: A Field Guide to the Literature*, San Pedro, California: R. & E. Miles.

Davis, Elisabeth Gould (1971) *The First Sex*, New York: G.P. Putnam.

Davies, Katherine (1987) Historical Associations: Women and the Natural World, in: *Women and Environment*, 9/2, pp. 4-6.

D'Eaubonne, Françoise (1980) Feminism or Death, in: Elaine Marks and Isabelle de Courtivron (eds) *New French Feminisms, An Anthology*, Brighton: The Harvester Press.

de Beauvoir, Simone (1949) *Le Deuxieme Sexe*, Paris: Gallimard; English edition.

Deckard, Barbara Sinclair (1979) *The Women's Movement, Political, Socioeconomic and Psychological Issues*, New York: Harper & Row.

de la Court, Thijs (1990) *Beyond Brundtland. Green Development in the 1990s*, London: Zed Books.

———(1992) Critique of the Dominant Development Paradigm, in: *Development* Journal of the Society for International Development 2, pp. 42-45.

de Lauretis, Teresa (1984) *Alice Doesn't,* Bloomington: Indiana University Press.

———(ed.) (1986) *Feminist Studies Critical Studies,* Bloomington: Indiana University Press.

———(1987) *The Technologies of Gender,* Bloomington: Indiana University Press.

———(1988) The essence of the triangle or, taking the risk of essentialism seriously: feminist theory in Italy, the U.S. and Britain, in: *Differences,* 2 (1989) pp. 3-37.

———(1990) Eccentric subjects: feminist theory and historical consciousness, in: *Feminist Studies,* 16/1, pp. 115-50.

Deleuze, Gilles, and Felix Guattari (1984) *Anti-Oedipus: Capitalism and Schizophrenia,* London: Athlone Press.

———(1980) *Mille Plateaux,* Paris: Minuit.

Delphy, Christine (1984) *Close to Home: a materialist analysis of women's oppression,* London: Hutchinson.

Derrida, Jacques (1978) *Writing and Difference,* Chicago: University of Chicago Press.

———(1987) *The Post-Card: From Socrates to Freud and Beyond,* Chicago: University of Chicago Press.

Deval, Bill and George Sessions (1985) *Deep Ecology. Living as if Nature Mattered,* Peregrine, Utah: Smith Books, Layton.

Diamond, Irene, Gloria Orenstein (eds) (1990) *Re-Weaving the World. The Emergence of Ecofeminism,* San Francisco: Sierra Club Books.

Dietrich, Gabriele (1988a) *Women's Movement in India. Conceptual and Religious Reflections,* Bangalore: Breakthrough Publications.

———(1988b) Development, Ecology and Women's Struggles in: *Social Action* Vol.38, January/March. pp. 1-13.

———(1990) The Development Debate and Gender Implications, in: *Lokayan Bulletin* 8/1.

di Leonardo, Micaela (ed.) (1991) *Gender at the Crossroads of Knowledge, Feminist Anthropology in the Postmodern Era,* Berkeley: University of California Press.

Dodson Gray, Elizabeth (1982) *Green Pradise Lost,* Wellesly, Mass: Round Table Press.

Donovan, Josephine (1990) Animal Rights and Feminist Theory, in: *SIGNS,* 15/2, pp. 350 -75.

Dovers, Steven (1989) Sustainability: Definitions, Clarifications and Contexts, in: *Development* 2/3, Journal of the Society for International Development.

Dubiago, Sharon (1987) Deeper Than Deep Ecology: Men Must Become Feminists, in: *The New Catalyst Quarterly,* No. 10, Winter 1987/88, pp. 10-11.

DuBois, Marc (1991) The Governance of the Third World, in: *Alternatives* 16/1, pp. 1-30.

Duc, Aimée (1984) (orig. 1901), *Onder Dames,* Amsterdam: Sara.

Duchen, Claire (1986) *Feminism in France,* London: Routledge and Kegan Paul.

EARTHWATCH, special issue on Women and Environment (1989) 4th Quarter, No. 37, IPPF, IUCN, UNFPA joint publication published quarterly with IPPF's *People* magazine, ISSN 0301-5645.

Easlea, Brian (1980) *Witch-Hunting, Magic and the New Philosophy. An Introduction to Debates of the Scientific Revolution 1450-1750,* New Jersey: Harvester Press.

———(1981) *Science and Sexual Oppression: Patriarchy's Confrontation with*

Women and Nature, London: Weidenfeld & Nicholson.

Ecoforum (1985) Issue on Women and Environment, Vol.10/2, A Journal of the Environmental Liaison Centre, Nairobi.

Ecologist, The (1988) Rethinking Men and Nature: Towards an Ecological Worldview, special issue Vol. 18, 4/5 .

Ecologist, The (1992) Feminism, Nature, Development, special issue Vol. 22/1.

Eisenstein, Hester (1984) *Contemporary Feminist Thought,* Sydney, Australia: Allen & Unwin.

Ekins, Paul and Manfred Max-Neef (1992) *Real Life Economics*, London and New York: Routledge.

Elson, Diane (ed.) (1990) *Male Bias in the Development Process*, Contemporary Issues in Development Studies, Manchester.

Enloe, Cynthia (1990) *Bananas, Beaches and Bases: Making Feminist Sense of International Politics*, Berkeley: University of California Press.

Escobar, Arturo (1984-85) Discourse and Power in Development: Michel Foucault and the Relevance of his Work to the Third World, in *Alternatives* X, pp. 377-400.

Esteva, Gustavo (1987) Regenerating People's Space, in: *Alternatives* XII, pp. 125-52

Esteva, Gustavo and Madhu Suri Prakash (1992) Grassroots Resistance to Sustainable Development: Lessons from the Banks of the Narmada, in: *The Ecologist,* Vol. 22/2, pp. 45-51.

Etsuko, Kaji (1989) Asian Feminism – Confronting the four Ps: Poverty, Prostitution, Patriarchy and Pollution, in: *AMPO*, Vol. 21/2-3.

Evia, Graciela and Eduardo Gudynas (1990) Strength through ecology network, in: *Media Development* 37/2, pp. 21-2, London.

Featherstone, Mike (1991) *Consumer Culture and Postmodernism*, London: Sage.

Feder Kittay, Eva (1988) Woman as Metaphor, in: *Hypatia* 3/2, pp. 63-87.

Feldenstein, Hilary Sims and Susan V. Poats (eds) (1990) *Working Together: Gender Analysis in Agriculture*, Vol. 1, West Hartford, CT: Kumarian Press.

Fernandes, Walter and Geeta Menon (1987) *Tribal Women and Forest Economy*, New Delhi: Indian Social Science Institute.

Firestone, Shulamith (1970) *The Dialectic of Sex, the case for feminist revolution*, New York: Bantam Books

Flax, Jane (1987) Postmodernism and gender relations in feminist theory, in: *Signs*, 12/4, pp. 621-43.

————(1990a) *Thinking Fragments. Psychoanalysis, Feminism & Post-modernism in the Contemporary West,* Berkeley: University of California Press.

————(1990b) Postmodernism and Gender Relations in Feminist Theory, in: Linda J. Nicholson, *Feminism/Postmodernism*, New York and London: Routledge.

Fortmann, Louise P. (1986) Women in Subsistence Forestry, Cultural Myths Form a Stumbling Block, in:*International Forestry. Journal of Forestry* 84/7,July.

Foucault, Michel (1971) *L'ordre du discours,* Paris: Gallimard.

————(1977) *Discipline and punish.* London: Allen Lane.

————(1980) *Power/Knowledge*, New York: Pantheon Books.

————(1988) *Politics, Philosophy, Culture. Interviews and Other Writings 1977-1984* (ed.) D.Kritzman, New York and London: Routledge.

Fox, Warwick (1989) The Deep Ecology–Ecofeminism Debate and Its Parallels, in: *Environmental Ethics*, Vol. 11 Spring.

————(1990) *Towards Transpersonal Ecology. Developing New Foundations for Environmentalism*, Boston and London: Shambala Publications.

Fox-Keller, Evelyn (1982) Feminism and science, in: *Signs*, 31/7.

————(1983a) *A feeling for the organism*, New York: N.H.Freeman.

————(1983b) The mind's eye, in: Sandra Harding and Meryl Hintikka (eds) *Discovering reality*, Dordrecht: Reidel.

————(1985a) *Reflections on Gender and Science*, New Haven and London: Yale University Press

————(1985b) *Reflections on Gender and Science*, New Haven and London: Yale University Press.

Fraser, Nancy (1992) The Uses and Abuses of French Discourse Theories for Feminist Politics, in: *Theory, Culture & Society*, Vol. 9.

French, Hilary (1992) After the Earth Summit: The Future of Environmental Governance, Washington, DC: *Worldwatch Paper* 107.

French, Marilyn (1985) *Beyond Power: Women, Men and Morality*, New York: Summit Books.

Fuss, Diana,(1989) *Essentially Speaking*, New York and London:Routledge.

Gallop, Jane (1991) *Around (1981)* New York: Routledge.

Gandhi, N. (1987) Gender and Housing, in: *Economic and Political Weekly*, 22, pp. 1995-97.

Giddings, Paula (1984) *When and Where I Enter, The Impact of Black Women on Race and Sex in America*, New York: Bantam Books.

Goldsmith, Edward (1988) The Way: An Ecological World-view, in: *The Ecologist*, Vol. 18/ 4/5, pp. 160-85

Goonatilake, S. (1983) *Aborted Discovery: Science and Creativity in the Third World*, London: Zed Books

Gould Davis, Elisabeth (1971) *The First Sex*, New York: G.P. Putnam.

Groot, Joanne de (1991) Conceptions and misconception: the historical and cultural context of discussion on women and development, in: Haleh Afshar (ed.) *Women Development & Survival in the Third World*, London and New York: Longman.

Grossmann, Angela (1992) Investing in Women, in: *Stadtblatt* 23, Berlin: 4, June.

Griffin, Susan (1979) *Women and Nature: The Roaring Inside Her*, San Francisco: Harper & Row.

————(1983) Introduction, in: Leonie Caldecott and Stephanie Leland (eds) *Reclaim the Earth, Women Speak out for Life on Earth*, London: The Women's Press.

Griscom, Joan (1981) On Healing the Nature/History Split in Feminist Thought, in: *Heresies #13: Feminism and Ecology* 4/1, pp. 4-9.

Gronemeyer, Marianne (1991) Hilfe, Wo Geholfen Wird, da Fallen Späne, in: D. Dirmoser, M. Gronemeyer and G.A. Rakelmann (eds)*Mythos Entwicklungshilfe. Entwicklungsruinen: Analysen und Dossiers zu einem Irrweg*, Giessen, Germany: Focus: Ökozid Extra, Focusverlag.

Gudynas, Eduardo (1992) The Search for an Ethics of Sustainable Development in Latin America, in: J.R. and J.B.Engel (eds) *Ethics of Environment and Development*, London: Belhaven Press, pp. 139-49.

Gudynas, Eduardo and Graciela Evia (1991) *La Praxis por la Vida. Introduccion a las Metodologias de la Ecologiaa Social*, Montevideo, Uruguay: CIPFE, CLAES, NORDAN.

Guha, Ramachandra (1989) *The Unquiet Woods. Ecological Change and Peasant Resistance in the Himalayas*, New Delhi: Oxford University Press.

———(1990) Towards a Cross-Culural Environmental Ethics, in: *Alternatives*, Vol. XV, pp. 431-47.

Gulati, Leela (1984) *Profiles of Female Poverty*, New Delhi.

Halpin, Zuleyma Tang (1989) Scientific Objectivity and the Concept of "the Other", in: *Women's Studies International Forum*, Vol. 12/3, pp. 285-94.

Haraway, Donna (1989a) Monkeys, aliens and women: love, science and politics at the intersection of feminist theory and colonial discourse, in: *Women's Studies International Forum*, Vol, 12/3, pp. 295 -312.

———(1989b), *Primate Visions. Gender, Race and Nature in the World of Modern Science*, New York and London: Routledge.

———(1989c), The biopolitics of postmodern bodies: determinations of self immune system discourse, in: *Differences*, 1/1, pp. 3-44.

———(1991) *Simians, Cyborgs and Women. The Re-invention of Nature*, London: Free Association Books.

Harding, Sandra (1986) *The Science Question in Feminism*, Ithaca: Cornell University Press.

———(1987) *Feminism and Methodology*, London: Open University Press.

———(1989) The Instability of the Analytical Categories of Feminist Theory, in: Micheline R. Malson, Jean F. O'Barr, Sarah Westphal-Wihl and Mary Wyer (eds) *Feminist Theory in Practice and Progress*, Chicago and London: The University of Chicago Press.

———(1990) Feminism, Science and the Anti-Enlightenment Critiques, in: Linda J. Nicholson (ed.) *Feminism/Postmodernism*, New York and London: Routledge.

———(1992a) Subjectivity, Experience and Knowledge: An Epistemology from/for Rainbow Coalition Politics, in: *Development and Change*, Vol. 23/3, pp. 175-93.

———(1992b) *Whose Science? Whose Knowledge?*, Milton Keynes: Open University Press.

———and M.B. Hintikka (eds) (1983) *Discovering Reality. Feminist Perspectives on Epistemology, Metaphysics, Methodology and Philosophy of Science*, Dordrecht, Holland: D.Reidel.

Hargrave, Eugene C. (1989) *Foundations of Environmental Ethics*, Englewood Cliffs, N.Y.: Prentice Hall.

Harrison, Paul (1991) Population and Degradation: The View from the Village, in: *People*, Vol. 18/3.

Hartmann, Betsy (1987) *Reproductive Rights and Wrongs: The Global Politics of Population Control and Contraceptive Choice*, New York: Harper.

———(1991) The Ecology Movement: Targeting Women for Population Control, in: *Women in Action* 4/24.

Häusler, Sabine (1992) Reformulating Social, Cultural and Ecological Sustainability, in: *Development* 2, Journal of the Society for International Development, pp. 46-50.

Hecht, Susanna and Alexander Cockburn (1989) *The Fate of the Forest. Developers, Destroyers and Defenders of the Amazon*, London and New York: Verso.

Held, Virginia (1985) Feminism and Epistemology: Recent Work on the Connection between Gender and Knowledge, in: *Philosophy and Public Affair*, 14, pp. 296-307.

————(1988) Gender as an Influence in Cultural Norms Relating to War an Environment, in: Arthur Westing (ed.) *Cultural Norms, War and Environment*, Oxford: Oxford University Press.

Heller, Chiah (1990) Toward a Radical Eco-Feminism, in: Clark, John (ed.) *Renewing the Earth. The Promise of Social Ecology*, London: Green Print.

Henderson, Hazel (1984) The Warp and the Weft – The Coming Synthesis of Eco-Philosophy and Eco-Feminism, in: *Seeds of Change* 4, pp. 64-8.

————(1981) *Politics of the Solar Age, Alternatives to Economics*, New York: Anchor Press.

Heyzer, Noeleen (ed) (1987) *Women Farmers and Rural Change in Asia – Towards Equal Access and Participation*, Kuala Lumpur: Asian and Pacific Development Centre.

Hill Collins, Patricia (1991) *Black Feminist Thought*, London and New York: Routledge.

Hubbart, Ruth, Mary Sue Henifin, and Barbara Fried (eds) (1979) *Women Look at Biology Looking at Women: A Collection of Feminist Critiques*, Cambridge, MA: Schenkman.

————(eds) (1982) *Biological Woman, the Convenient Myth*, Cambridge, MA: Schenkman.

Huby, Meg (n.d) *Where You Can't See the Wood for the Trees. Extension Methods in Rural Woodfuel Development*, Kenya Woodfuel Programme, Institute for Environmental Technology & Managment, Box 2142, S-103 14 Stockholm, Publ. by Beijer Institute, York, England: William Sessions Ltd., The Ebor Press.

Hueting, Roefie (1980) *New Scarcity and Economic Growth. More Welfare Through Less Production*, Amsterdam: North Holland Publishing Company.

Hull, Gloria *et al* (1982) *But Some of Us Are Brave,* New York: Feminist Press.

Huston, Perdita (1979)*Third World Women Speak Out*, New York: Praeger.

Hynes, Patricia H. (ed.) (1989) *Reconstructing Babylon: Women and Technology,* London: Earthscan.

————(1989) *The Recurring Silent Spring*, New York etc: Pergamon Press

Hypatia (1991) Vol.6/1, Issue on Ecofeminism.

Hyvrard, Jeanne (1988) *La pensée corps*, Paris: des femmes.

IDOC Internazionale (1989) 3, Issue on Women and Nature.

Irigaray, Luce (1974) *Speculum*, Paris: Minuit.

————(1977) *Ce sexe qui n'en est pas un*, Paris: Minuit.

————(1984a) *Ethique de la difference sexuelle*, Paris: Minuit.

————(1984b) *Sexe et parente*, Paris, Minuit.

ISIS International (1991) Women Speak out on the Environment, Special issue 4/91.

IUCN/UNEP/WWF (1991) *Caring for the Earth – A Strategy for Sustainable Development*, London: Earthscan.

Jagentowicz Mills, Patricia (1991) Feminism and Ecology: On the Domination of Nature, in: *Hypatia*, 6/1, pp. 162-79.

Jain, Devaki (1991) Can We Have a Women's Agenda for Global Development? in *Development*, 1, pp. 74-9, Rome: Society for International Development.

Jaggar, Allison (1983) *Feminist Politics and Human Nature*, Totowa, New Jersey: Rowman & Ackenheld.

Jameson, Frederic (1984) Postmodernism or the Cultural Logic of Late Capitalism, in: *New Left Review* 146, pp. 53-9.

Jansz, Ulla (1990) *Denken over sekse in de eerste Feministische Golf,* Amsterdam: Sara/Van Gennep.

Jaquette, Jane S. (ed.) (1989) *The Women's Movement in Latin America, Feminism and the Transition to Democracy,* Winchester: Unwin Hyman.

Jayawardena, Kumari (1982) Feminism and Nationalism in the Third World in the Early 19th and 20th Centuries, The Hague: *Lecture Series History of the Women's Movement,* Institute of Social Studies.

Jeffreys, Sheila (1985) *The Spinster and her Enemies, Feminism and Sexuality 1880-1930,* London: Pandora.

Johns, David M. (1990) The Relevance of Deep Ecology to the Third World: Some Preliminary Comments, in: *Environmental Ethics,* Vol. 12, Fall, pp. 233-53.

Johnston, Diane (1991) Constructing the Periphery in Modern Global Politics, in: C.N. Murphy and R. Tooze (eds) *The International Political Economy,* Boulder: Lynne Rienner.

Johnston, Jill (1973) *Lesbian Nation, the Feminist Solution,* New York: Touchstone.

Jokes, Susan P. (1987) *Women in the World Economy* (INSTRAW Study), New York: Oxford University Press.

Jonas, H. (1984) *Imperative of Responsibility: In Search for an Ethic of the Technological Age,* Chicago: University of Chicago Press.

Jordanova, Ludmilla (1989) *Sexual Divisions. Images of Gender in Science and Medicine between the Eighteenth and Twentieth Centuries,* New York/London: Harvester/Wheatsheaf.

Journal of Society for International Development (1989) Human Development, in *Development* 2/3.

Journal of Society for International Development (1990) Human Centred Economics, Global Sustainability, in *Development,* 3/4.

Kabeer, Naila (1992) Evaluting Cost-Benefit Analysis as a Tool for Gender Planning, in: *Development and Change,* Vol. 23/2, pp. 115-39.

Kahn, S. A. and F. Bilquess (1978) Environment, Attitudes and Activities of Rural Women, -Case Study of Jhok-Sayal, in: *Sociologia Ruralis,* Vol. 18/2-3, Pakistan Institute of Development Economics.

Kaoru, Oshima (1989) PP21 Indigenous People Spreading a Spirituality of Hope, in: *AMPO,* Vol. 21/2-3.

Keysers, Loes (1991) Population-and-environment from women's perspective, in: *WGNRR Newsletter,* July-September.

Kheel, Marti (1987) Animal Liberation is a Feminist Issue, in: *New Catalyst Quarterly,* No. 10, Winter 1987/88, pp 8-9.

Khor, Martin (1992a) Third World Begins to Assert Itself in UNCED, in: *Third World Resurgence* 14/15.

————(1992b) What to do, now it's over..., in: *Third World Resurgence* 24/25, pp. 4-5.

Ki-Zerbo, J. (1981) Women and the Energy Crisis in the Sahel, in: *UNASYLVA* (FAO) Vol. 33, p. 133.

King, Ynestra (1981) Feminism and the Revolt of Nature in: *Heresies #13:Feminism and Ecology,* Vol. 4/1, pp. 12-16.

————(1983a) Toward an Ecological Feminism and a Feminist Ecology, in: J. Rothschild (ed.) *Machina ex Dea. Feminist Perspectives on Technology,* New

York and Oxford: Pergamon Press.

———(1983b) The Eco-feminist Imperative, in: Leonie Caldecott, Stephanie Leland (eds) *Reclaim the Earth. Women Speak Out for Life on Earth*, London: The Women's Press.

———(1989) Healing the Wounds: Feminism, Ecology and Nature/ Culture Dualism, in: Jaggar and Bordo (eds) *Gender, Body and Knowledge. Feminist Reconstruction of Being and Knowing*, Rathgurst: Rathgurst University Press.

———(1990) Healing the Wounds: Feminism, Ecology, and the Nature/Culture Dualism, in: Diamond, Irene and Gloria Feman Orenstein (1990) *Reweaving the World. The Emergence of Ecofeminism*, San Francisco: Sierra Club Books.

Klein, Hilary Manette (1989) Marxism, Psychoanalysis, and Mother Nature, in: *Feminist Studies*, Vol. 15/2, pp. 255-78.

Kothari, Rajni (1981-82) On Eco-Imperialism, in: *Alternatives* Vol. VII/3.

Koonz, Claudia (1986) Some Political Implications of Separatism: German Women between Democracy and Nazism 1928-1934, in: Judith Friedlander et al. (eds) *Women in Culture and Politics, a Century of Change*, Bloomington: Indiana: University Press.

———(1987) *Mothers in the Fatherland, Women, the Family and Nazi Politics*, London: Methuen.

Kristeva, Julia (1982) Women's time, in: N.O. Keohane et al. *Feminist Theory: a critique of ideology*, Chicago: Chicago University Press.

Kuhn, Annette (1982) *Women's Pictures. Feminism and Cinema*, London: Routledge.

Kumar D'Souza, Corinne (1989) A New Movement, a New Hope: East Wind, West Wind and the Wind from the South, in: Plant, Judith (ed) *Healing the Wounds. The Promise of Ecofeminism*, Philadelphia PA, Santa Cruz, CA: New Society Publishers.

Lahar, S. (1991) Ecofeminist Theory and Grassroots Politics, in: *Hypatia* 6/1, pp. 28-45.

Lal, Deepak (1983) *The Poverty of 'Development Economics'*, Institute of Economic Affairs, UK: Hobart Paperback No. 16.

Lather, Patti (1988) Feminist Perspectives on Empowering Research Methodologies,in: *Women's Studies International Forum*, Vol.II/6, USA.

Lee-Smith, Diana, and Catalina Hinchey Trujillo (1992) The Struggle to Legitimize Subsistence: Women and Sustainable Development, in: *Environment and Urbanization*, Vol. 4/1, April, pp. 77-84.

Leland, Stephanie (1983) Feminism and Ecology: Making Connections, in: Leonie Caldecott and Stephanie Leland (eds) *Reclaim the Earth. Women Speak Out for Life on Earth*, London: The Women's Press.

Levy, Karen (1992) Gender and the Environment: The Challenge of Crosscutting Issues in Development Policy and Planning, in :*Environment and Urbanization*, Vol. 4/1, April, pp. 134-49.

Lloyd, Genevieve (1984) *The Man of Reason*, London: Methuen.

Longino, Helen L. (1987) Can there be a feminist science?,in: *Hypatia* 2/3, pp. 51-64.

———(1989) Feminist critiques of rationality: critiques of science or philosophy of science? in: *Women's Studies International Forum*, Vol. 12/3, pp. 261-70.

———(1990) *Science as Social Knowledge*, Princeton: Princeton University Press.

Lorde, Audre (1980) Poetry is not a luxury, in: Hester Eisenstein and Alice Jardine (eds) *The Future of Difference*. Boston: G.K.Hall, pp. 125-7.

————(1984) *Sister Outside*, Trumansberg: N.Y.Crossing.

Loutfi, Martha F. (1987) Development with Women: Action, not Alibis, in: *International Labour Review* , Vol.126/1, January/February, pp. 111-24.

Lovelock, James (1979) *Gaia: A New Look on Life on Earth*, London: Oxford University Press.

Luke, Tim (1988) The Dream of Deep Ecology, in: *TELOS*, No. 76, Summer, pp. 65-92.

Lycklama à Nijeholt, Geertje (1987) The Fallacy of Integration, in: *Netherlands Review of Development Studies*, Vol. I, pp. 23-37.

————(1992) Women and the Meaning of Development: Approaches and Consequences, *ISS Working Papers, Sub-series on Women's History and Development*, No. 15, February.

————, Armida Testino, Virginia Vargas and Saskia Wieringa (forthcoming) *The Triangle of Empowerment; Policies and Strategies related to Women's Issues*.

MacCormack, Carolyn and Marilyn Strathern (eds) (1980) *Nature, Culture, and Gender*, New York: Cambridge University Press.

McAllister, Pam (1982) *Re-weaving the Web of Life. Feminism and Non-Violence*, Philadelphia: New Society Publishers.

McCormick, J. (1989) The Global Environmental Movement. Reclaiming Paradise, London: Belhaven Press.

McStay, Jan and Riley E. Dunlap (1983) Male-Female Differences in Concern for Environmental Quality, in: *International Journal for Women's Studies*, 6/4, pp. 291-302

Margulis, Lynn and Dorion Sagan (1988) *Microsmos*, Allen & Unwin.

Martin, Michael (1990) Ecosabotage and Civil Disobedience, in: *Environmental Ethics*, Winter (1990) Vol. 12/4, pp. 291-310.

Martinez-Alier, Juan (1990) *Ecological Economics. Energy, Environment and Society*, Cambridge: Basil Blackwell.

Mathur, G.B. (1989) The Current Impasse in Development Thinking: The Metaphysics of Power, in: *Alternatives*, XIV, pp. 463-79.

Max-Neef, Manfred A. (1982) *From the Outside Looking in: Experiences in 'Barefoot Economics'*, Dag Hammarskjold Foundation.

Merchant, Carolyn (1982) Isis' Consciousness Raised, in: *ISIS* 73/268, pp. 398-409.

————(1983) *The Death of Nature. Women, Ecology and the Scientific Revolution*, London: Harper and Row.

Mies, Maria (1986) *Patriarchy and Accumulation on a World Scale. Women in the International Division of Labour*, London: Zed Books.

———— and Vandana Shiva (1993) *Ecofeminism* London and New Delhi: Zed Books and Kali for Women.

Miller, Nancy (1985) *The Poetics of Gender*, New York: Columbia University Press.

————(1991) *Getting Personal*, New York: Routledge.

Mische, Patricia (1989) Ecological Security and the Need to Reconceptualise Sovereignty, in: *Alternatives*, Vol. XIV/4, October, pp. 389 -428.

Mitchell, Juliet and Jacqueline Rose (eds) (1982) *Feminine Sexuality: Jacques Lacan and the école Freudienne*, London: Macmillan.

Mitlin, Diana (1992) Sustainable Development: A Guide to the Literature, in: *Environment and Urbanization* Vol 4/1, April, pp. 111-24.

Momsen, H. and J.F. Townsend (eds) (1987) *Geography of Gender in the Third World*, London: Hutchinson.

Mohanty, Chandra (1987) Feminist Encounters: locating the politics of experience, in: *Copyright*, 1, pp. 30-44.

———(1988) Under Western Eyes: Feminist scholarship and colonial discourse, in: *Feminist Review*, 30, pp. 60-86.

Mohanty, Manoranjan (1989) Changing Terms of Discourse. A Poser, in: *Economic and Political Weekly*, New Delhi: 16 September.

Moi, Torild (1985) *Sexual/Textual Politics*, New York: Methuen.

Monimart, Marie (1989) *Femmes du Sahel. La desertification au quotidien*, Paris: Editions Karthala and OCDE/Club du Sahel.

Moraga, Cherry (1983) *Loving in the War Years*, Boston: South End Press.

———and Gloria Anzaldua (1981) *This Bridge Called my Back*, Watertown: Persephone.

Morgan, Elaine (1972) *The Descent of Woman*, New York: Stein and Day.

Moser, Caroline O. N. (1989) Gender Planning in the Third World: Meeting Practical and Strategical Gender Ne(eds) in: *World Development*, Vol. 17/11, pp. 1799-1825.

———(1988) *Residential Struggle and Conciousness. The Experiences of Poor Women in Guayaquil, Ecuador*, London.

Mowlana, Hamid and Laurie J. Wilson (1991) *The Passing of Modernity. Communication and the Transformation of Society*, New York and London: Longman.

Munslow, B. with Y. Katerere, A. Ferf, and P. O'Keefe (1988) *The Fuelwood Trap: A Study of the SADCC Region*, London: Earthscan.

Murphy, Patrick (ed.) (1988a) Feminism, Ecology and the Future of Humanities, Special issue of: *Studies in the Humanities* 15/2.

———(1988b) Sex-Typing the Planet: Gaia Imagery and the Problem of Subverting Patriarchy, in: *Environmental Ethics* 10, pp. 155-68.

———(1991) Ground, Pivot, Motion: Ecofeminist Theory, Dialogics and Literary Practice, in: *Hypatia* 6/1, pp. 146-61.

Naess, Arne (1973) The Shallow and the Deep, Long-range Ecology Movement: A Summary, in: *Inquiry*, No. 16, p.96.

———(1988) Deep Ecology and Ultimate Premises, in: *The Ecologist*, Vol. 18/ 4-5, pp. 128 -131.

———(1989) *Ecology, Community and Life Style*, Cambridge University Press.

Nandy, Ashis (1987a) Cultural Frames for Social Transformation: A Credo, in: *Alternatives*, XII, pp. 113-23.

———(1987b) Development and Authoritarianism: An Epitaph on Social Engineering, in: *Journal für Entwicklungspolitik* 1, pp. 43-53.

———(ed) (1988) *Science, Hegemony and Violence. A Requiem for Modernity*, United Nations University, Oxford University Press.

Narayan, Uma (1989) The project of feminist epistemology: perspectives from a non-western feminist, in: Allison Jaggar and Susan Bordo (eds) *Gender/Body/Knowledge*, New Brunswick: Rutgers University Press.

Nederveen Pieterse, Jan P. (1990) *Empire and Emancipation*, London: Pluto Press.

———(1991) Dilemmas of Development Discourse: The Crisis of

Developmentalism and the Comparative Method, in: *Development and Change* 22, pp. 5-29.

Nicholson, Linda J. (ed) (1990) *Feminism/Postmodernism*, New York and London: Routledge.

Nisbet, R. (1980) *History of the Ideas of Progress*, New York: Basic Books.

Norwood, Vera L. (1987) The Nature of Knowing: Rachel Carsons and the American Environment, in: *Signs*, Vol. 12/4.

Oakley, Ann (1981) *Subject Women*, Oxford: Robertson.

O'Connor,James (1989) Uneven and Combined Development and Ecological Crisis: a Theoretical Introduction, in: *Race and Class*, Vol. 30/3, January-March.

Odum, Eugene P. (1989) *Ecology and Our Endangered Life-Support System*, Sunderland, Ma.: Sinaner Associates.

Omvedt, Gail (1990) Women and Ecology, in: *Economic and Political Weekly*, June 2, p. 1223.

————, Chetna Gala, and Govind Kelkar (1988) *Women and Struggle*, Patna: Nari Mukti Sangharsh Sammelan.

Ortner, Sherry B. (1974) Is Female to Male as Nature is to Culture?, in: M. Z. Rosaldo and L. Lamphere (eds) *Women, Culture and Society*, Stanford, California: Stanford University Press.

Pagels, Heinz R. (1982) *The Cosmic Code, Quantum Physics as the Language of Nature*, New York: Simon and Shuster.

Pearce, David, Anil Markandya, and Edward B. Barbier (1989) *Blueprint for a Green Economy*, London: Earthscan.

Pearce, David, Edward B. Barbier and Anil Markandya (1990) *Sustainable Development. Economics and Environment in the Third World*, Hants, UK: Edward Elgar Publishing Limited.

Peterson, Abby and Carolyn Merchant (1986) Peace with the Earth: Women and the Environmental Movement in Sweden, in: *Women Studies International Forum*, 5-6, pp. 465-79

Picq, Françoise (1986) 'Bourgeois Feminism' in France: a Theory developed by Socialist Women before World War I, in: Friedlander, Judith, et al (eds) *Women in Culture and Politics, a Century of Change*, Bloomington: Indiana University Press.

Pietilä, Hilkka and Jeanne Vickers (1991) *Making Women Matter. The Role of the United Nations*, London: ZED Books

Plant, Judith (1987) Searching for Common Ground: Ecofeminism and Bioregionalism, in: *The New Catalyst Quarterly*, 10, pp. 6-7.

————(ed) (1989) *Healing the Wounds: The Promise of Eco-feminism*, Philadelphia: New Society Publishers.

Plaza, Monique (1978) Phallomorphic Power and the psychology of woman, in: *Ideology and Consciousness*, 4, pp. 4-36.

Plumwood, Val (1986) Ecofeminism: An Overview and Discussion of Positions and Arguments,in: *Australasian Journal of Philosophy*, supplement to Vol. 64, June (1986) pp. 120-37.

————(1988) Women, Humanity and Nature, in: *Radical Philosophy*, 48, Spring, pp. 16-24.

————1991: Nature, self and gender: feminism, environmental philosophy and the critique of rationalism, in: *Hypatia* 6/1, pp. 3-27.

————(1992) Feminism and Ecofeminism: Beyond the Dualistic Assumptions of Women, Men and Nature, in: *The Ecologist*, 1.

Popline (1992) 'No Quick Fixes' For Environment, Population Balance, Vol. 14 January-February, p.4.

Porritt, Jonathon and David Winner (1988) *The Coming of the Greens*, London: Fontana/Collins.

Pretty, Jules N. and Irene Guijt (1992) Primary Environmental Care: An Alternative Paradigm for Development Assistance, in: *Environment and Urbanization*, Vol.4/1, April, pp. 22-36.

Prigogine, Ilya and Isabelle Stengers (1979) *La Nouvelle Alliance*, Paris: Gallimard.

Race and Class (1989) Un-Greening the Third World. Food,Ecology and Power, Vol. 30/3, Jan-March.

Radford Ruether, Rosemary (1975) *New Women/New Earth: Sexist Ideologies and Human Liberation*, New York: Seabury Press.

Rahnema, Majid (1988) Power and Regenerative Processes in Micro-spaces, in: *International Social Science Journal*, 117, pp. 361-75.

————(1990) Participatory Action Research: The 'Last Temptation of the Saint' Development, in: *Alternatives* XV, 2, pp. 199-227.

Rapp, Rayna and Ellen Ross (1986) The 1920s: Feminism, Consumerism and Political Backlash in the United States, in: Judith Friedlander et al (eds) *Women in Culture and Politics, a Century of Change*, Bloomington: Indiana University Press.

Redclift, Michael (1987) *Sustainable Development, Exploring The Contradictions*, London and New York: Routledge.

Reinalda, Bob and Natascha Verhaaren (1989) *Vrouwenbeweging en Internationale Organisaties 1868-1986 een vergeten Hoofdstuk uit de geschiedenis van de internationale Betrekkingen*, Nijmegen: Ariadne.

Rich, Adrienne (1976) *Of Woman Born, Motherhood as Experience and Institution*, New York: W.W. Norton.

————(1979) *On Lies, Spectres and Silence*, New York: W.W.Norton.

————(1986) *Blood, Bread and Poetry*, London: Virago.

Riley, Denise (1988) *Am I That Name?* London: Macmillan.

Rocheleau, Dianne E. (1991) Gender, Ecology and the Science of Survival. Stories and Lesson from Kenya, in: *Agriculture and Human Values*, January Vol. 8/1.

Rodda, Annabel (1991) *Women and the Environment*, Women and World Development series, London: Zed Books and the UN-NGO Group on Women and Development.

Rodman, John (1983) Four Forms of Ecological Consciousness Re-considered, in: Donald Sherer and Thomas Attig (eds) *Ethics and the Environment*, Englewood Cliffs, N.Y.: Prentice Hall.

Rose, Hillary (1983) Hand, Brain and Heart: A Feminist Epistemology for the Natural Sciences, in: *Signs* 9/1, pp. 73-90.

Rose, Jacqueline (1983) Femininity and its discontents, in: *Sexuality in the Field of Vision*, London: Verso pp. 83-103.

Rossato, Veronica (1991) Una Vision Ecofeminista del Manejo de los Recursos Naturales, in: *Mujer*, Fempress 115, Mayo.

Rosser, Sue V. (1991) Eco-feminism: Lessons for Feminism from Ecology, in: *Women's Studies International Forum*, 14/3, pp. 143-51.

Rothschild, Joan (ed) (1983) *Machina Ex Dea. Feminist Perspectives on Technology,* The Athene Series, New York, Oxford, Toronto, Sydney, Paris: Pergamon Press.

Rubin, Gayle (1975) The traffic in women; notes on the political economy of sex, in: Rayna Rapp (ed.) *Towards an Anthropology of Women,* New York: Monthly Review Press.

Sachs, Wolfgang (1990) On the Archaeology of the Development Idea, in: *Lokayan Bulletin,* 8, p.1.

———(ed.) (1992) *The Development Dictionary. A Guide to Knowledge as Power,* London and New Jersey: Zed Books.

Sadik, Nafis (1990) The 1990s: The Decade of Decision, in: *Populi,*Vol. 17/2.

Salleh, Ariel Kay (1984) Deeper than Deep Ecology: The Eco-Feminist Connection, in: *Environmental Ethics,* 6, pp. 339-45.

Sarin, Madhu (1991) Improved Stoves, Women and Domestic Energy, in: *Environment and Urbanization* Vol 3/2, October.

Sax, Anna (1991) Bevölkerung 'aufhellen', in: *Pharma Brief,* BUKO Pharma-Kampagne, Health Action International, 7, pp. 2-3, September.

Schor, Naomi (1987) Dreaming dissymetry, in: Alice Jardine and Paul Smith (eds) *Men in Feminism,* New York: Methuen.

———(1989) This essentialism which is not one: coming to grips with Irigaray, in: *Differences,* 2, pp. 38-58.

Scott, Joan (1990) The usefulness of gender as a category of historical analysis, in: *The Politics of History,* New York: Columbia University Press.

———(1988) Deconstructing equality versus difference, in: *Feminist Studies,* 14/1, pp. 33-50.

Seed, John (1988) *Thinking like a Mountain. Towards a Council of All Beings,* London: Heretic Books.

Seddon, Terry ,(1984) The Dangers of Eco-Feminism, in :*Chain Reaction* Oct/Nov.

Segal, Lynne (1987) *Is the Future Female? Troubled Thoughts on Contemporary Feminism* London: Virago Press.

Sen, Gita (1984) Subordination and Sexual Control: A Comparative View of the Control of Women, in: *Review of Radical Political Economics,* Vol.16/1, pp. 133-42.

Sen, Gita and Caren Grown (for DAWN) (1988) *Development Crises and Alternative Visions: Third Women's Perspectives,* London: Earthscan.

Sessions, George (1987) Deep Ecology and the New Age, in: *Earth First!* Sept.23, Vol. VII/8, Radical Environmental Journal.

Shanmugaratnam, N. (1989) Development and Environment: A View from the South, in: *Race and Class,* Vol. 30/3, January-March, pp. 13-30.

Sheth, D.L. (1987) Alternative Development as Political Practice, in: *Alternatives,* Vol. XII, pp. 155-71.

Shiva, Vandana (1988) Reductionist Science as An Epistemological Violence, in: Ashis Nandy (ed.) *Science, Hegemony and Violence: A Requiem for Modernity,* New Delhi: Oxford University Press.

———(1989) *Staying Alive,Women, Ecology and Development,* Delhi and London: Kali and Zed Books.

———(1988b) *The Violence of the Green Revolution. Ecological Degradation and Political Conflict in Punjab,* London: Zed Books.

————and Jayanta Bandyopandhyay (1987) Chipko: Re-kindling India's Forest Culture, in: *The Ecologist*, Vol. 17/1.

Showalter, Elaine (ed) (1985) *Feminist Criticism*, New York: Pantheon.

Skolimowski, Henryk (1984) *Eco-philosophy: Designing New Tactics for Living*, London: Marion Boyers.

————(1988) Eco-philosophy and Deep Ecology, in: *The Ecologist*, Vol. 18/ 4-5, pp. 124-28.

Slater, David (1992) Theories of Development and Politics of the Post-Modern-Exploring a Border Zone, in: *Development and Change* 23/3, pp. 283-319.

Slicer, Deborah (1991) Your Daughter or Your Dog?, in: *Hypatia*, 6/1, pp. 108-25.

Smith, Barbara (1983) *Home Girls: a black feminist anthology*, New York: Kitchen Table Press.

Smith, Barbara (1985) Towards a Black Feminist Criticism, in: Elaine Showalter (ed.) *The New Feminist criticism*, New York: Pantheon.

Smith-Rosenberg, Carroll (1985) *Disorderly Conduct: Visions of Gender in Victorian America*, New York: Alfred A. Knopf.

Sontheimer, Sally (ed) (1991) *Women and the Environment: A Reader*, London: Earthscan.

Snitow, Ann (1991) Gender Diary, in: M. Hirsch and E. Fox-Keller (eds) *Conflicts in Feminism*, New York: Routledge.

Spelman, Elizabeth (1989) *Inessential Woman*, Boston: Beacon Press.

Spivak, Gayatri Chakravorty (1983) Displacement and the discourse of woman, in: Mark Krupnick (ed.) *Displacement: Derrida and After*, Bloomington: Indiana University Press, pp. 169-95.

————(1987) *In Other Worlds*, New York and London: Methuen.

————(1988a) Can the Subaltern Speak? in: Nelson (ed.) *Marxism and the Interpretation of Culture*, Chicago: University of Chicago Press.

————(1988b) In a Word. Interview with Ellen Rooney, in: *Differences* 2, pp. 124-54.

————(1990) *The Postcolonial critic*, New York and London : Routledge.

————(1991) Feminsm in Decolonization, in: *Differences* 3/3, pp. 139-71.

Spretnak, Charlene (1988) Our Roots and Flowering, in: *The Elmswood Newsletter*, Winter, Solstice.

Stamp, Patricia (1989) *Technology, Gender and Power in Africa*, International Development Research Centre Ottawa, Canada: Technical Study 63e.

Stanton, Donna (1980) The Franco-American disconnection, in: Hester Eisenstein and Alice Jardine (eds) *The Future of Difference*, Boston: J. K. Hall.

Starhawk (1990) Power, Authority and Mystery: Ecofeminism and Earth-based Spirituality, in: Diamond, Irene and Gloria Feman Orenstein (eds) (1990) *Reweaving the World. The Emergence of Ecofeminism*, San Francisco: Sierra Club Books.

Strathern, Marilyn (1980) No Nature, no Culture: the Hagen Case, in: Carol MacCormack and Marilyn Strathern (eds) *Nature, Culture and Gender*, Cambridge: Cambridge University Press.

Teitelbaum, Michael S. and Jay M. Winter (eds) (1989) *Population and Resources in Western Intellectual Traditions*, Cambridge: Cambridge University Press.

Theweleit, Klaus (1987) *Male Phantasies*, Minneapolis: University of Minnesota Press

Tinker, Irene and Michele Bo Bramsen (eds) (1976) *Women and World Development*, Washington: Overseas Development Council.

Timberlake, Lloyd and Laura Thomas (1990) *When the Bough Breaks...Our Children, Our Environment*, London: Earthscan.

Thuilier, Pierre (1984) La cause des femmes et l'ecologie, in: *La Recherche*, 15, p. 151.

Thurow, Lester C. (1980) *The Zero-Sum Society*, New York: Penguin Books

Tisdell, Clem (1988) Sustainable Development: Differing Perceptions of Ecologists and Economists, and Relevance to LDC's, in: *World Development*, 16/3, pp. 373-84.

Tomorrow (1992) Ten Trends in Corporate Environmentalism. Putting it all Together, Vol. 2/2.

The Tribune (1991) Women, Environment and Development. Newsletter 47, September.

Trinh Minh Ha (1989): *Woman, Native, Other*, Bloomington: Indiana University Press.

———(1991) *When the Moon Waxes Red: Representations, Gender and Cultural Politics*, New York: Routledge.

Tristan, Flora (1977) *Unión Obrera*, Barcelona: Fontanara.

The Trumpeter (1987) Voices from the Canadian Ecophilosophy Network, Vol. 4/3, Summer, Issue on: Ecofeminism, Science, Magic, Technology and Self-Realisation.

Turner, R. Kerry (1988) *Sustainable Environmental Management. Principle and Practice*, Boulder, Colorado: Westview Press.

Vallely, Bernardette (1991) Green Living: Consumer Clout, in: *Women and Environments*, WEED Foundation Quarterly, Winter/Spring, Vol. 13/2, pp. 54-7.

van Vliet, Willem (ed.) (1988) *Women, Housing and Community*, London: Gower.

Verhelst, Thierry (1989) *No Life Without Roots*, London: Zed Books.

Vickers, Jeanne (1991) *Women and the World Economic Crisis*, London: Zed Books and the UN/NGO Group on Women and Development.

Viola, E. (1988) The Ecologist Movement in Brasil (1974-1986) from Environmentalism to Eco-politics, in: *International Journal of Urban and Regional Research*, Vol. 12/2, June, pp 211-18.

Visvanathan, Shiv (1987) From the Annals of the Laboratory State, in: *Alternatives* XII, pp. 37-59.

———(1990) Mrs. Brundtland's Disenchanted Cosmos, in: *Alternatives*, Vol. XVI/3, pp. 377-84.

von Werlhoff, Claudia, Maria Mies, Veronika Bennholdt-Thomsen (1983) *Frauen, die Letzte Kolonie,* Reinbek: Technologie und Politik 20,"Die Zukunft der Arbeit" Bd.4. English-language edition *Women: the Last Colony* (1988) London: Zed Books.

Walker, Alice (1984) *In Search of Our Mothers' Garden*, London: The Women's Press.

Wallace, Tina with Candida March (eds) (1991) *Changing Perceptions. Writings on Gender and Development*, Oxford: OXFAM.

Ward, Nicole (1991) *White Woman Speaks with Forked Tongue*, London: Routledge.

Warren, Karen J. (1987) Feminism and Ecology: Making Connections, in: *Environmental Ethics* 9, pp. 3-21.

———(1988) Toward an Ecofeminist Ethic, in: *Studies in Humanities* 15, pp. 140-56

———(1990) The Power and the Promise of Ecological Feminism, in: *Environmental Ethics*, 2.

———(1991) Ecological Feminism, in: *Hypatia* 6/1.

———and Jim Cheney (1991) Ecological Feminism and Ecosystem Ecology, in: *Hypatia* 6/1, pp. 179-98.

Waring, Marilyn (1988) *If Women Counted. A New Feminist Economics*, London: Macmillan.

Whitehead, Ann (1990) Food Crisis and Gender Conflict in the African Country-side, in: H. Bernstein et al (eds) *The Food Question: Profits versus People?* London: Earthscan.

Whitford, Margaret (1991) *Luce Irigaray: philosophy in the feminine*, London and New York: Routledge.

WIDE Bulletin (1992) Special Issue on Women and Environment (1992) 1.

Wieringa, Saskia, *Sub-versive Women: Women's Movements in Historical Perspective*, (forthcoming).

Wichterich, Christa (1992) Für alle etwas, für niemanden genug, ein Rückblick auf das Frauen-Forum in Rio de Janeiro, in: *TAZ* 19.6.

Wittig, Monique (1975) *The Lesbian Body*, New York: William Morrow.

———(1991) *The Straight Mind*, London and New York: Harvester/Wheatsheaf.

Women and Environments (1991) Charting out a New Environmental Course (Special Issue Winter/Spring) Toronto, Canada: Quarterly published by Women and Environments Education and Development Foundation.

Women's Feature Service (1992) *The Power to Change, Women in the Third World Redefine Their Environment*, New Delhi: Kali for Women; and (1993) London: Zed Books.

Women's Health Journal (1990) Take Back the Earth – Women, Health and the Environment, No. 20, Latin American and Caribbean Women's Health Network, ISIS International.

World Commission on Environment and Development (WCED) (1987) *Our Common Future* (Brundtlandt Report), Oxford, New York: Oxford University Press.

Worster, Donald (ed) (1988) *The Ends of the Earth*, Cambridge: Cambridge University Press.

———(1990) *A History of Ecological Ideas*, Cambridge: Cambridge University Press.

Wylie, Ann et al (1989) Feminist critiques of science: the epistemological and methodological literature, in: *Women's Studies International Forum*, 12/3, pp. 379-88.

Wyman, Miriam (1987) Exploration of Ecofeminism, in: *Women and Environments*, Spring, pp. 6-7.

Young, Iris (1983) Feminism and Ecology and Women and Life on Earth: Eco-Feminism in the 80s, in: *Environmental Ethics*, pp. 173-80.

Young, Iris (1985) Humanism, Gynocentrism and Feminist Politics, in: *Women's*

Studies International Quarterly, 8.

Zimmerman, Michael E. (1987) Feminism, Deep Ecology and Environmental Ethics, in: *Environmental Ethics* 9, pp. 21-44.

———(1990) Deep Ecology and Ecofeminism: The Emerging Dialogue, in: Diamond, Irene and Gloria Feman Orenstein (eds) (1990) *Reweaving the World. The Emergence of Ecofeminism*, San Francisco: Sierra Club Books.

Zwerdling, D. (1977) The Pesticide Treadmill, *The Environmental Journal*, 15-18 September.

Unpublished Documents, Reports and Other Publications.

Alliance of Northern People for Environment and Development, ANPED (1992) *Ya Wananchi*, Citizens Action Plan for the 1990s, Global Conference of NGOs Paris, 17-20 December 1991.

As, Berit (1988) *Our Common Future: The Brundtland Report Seen From Women's Perspectives*, The Feminist University of Norway, Box 130, N-2340 Loten, Norway.

Baines, James and John Peet (1990) Sustainable Development and Stock Resources: Is There a Contradiction? (Energy Policy Within a Framework of Sustainable Development), paper presented at The Ecological Economics of Sustainability Conference, The World Bank, Washington, DC May 21-23.

Batie, Sandra S. (1989) *Sustainable Development: Challenges to the Profession of Agricultural Economics*, Presidential Address, AAEA Summer Meeting, Baton Rouge, 30 July-2 August.

Bauvinic, Mayra and Rekha Mehra, *Women in Agriculture. What Development Can Do* International Centre for Research on Women, 1717 Mass.Avenue, NW Suite 302, Washington, DC 20036.

Bhavani, Kum-Kum (1992) Towards a Multi-Cultural Europe? Talk delivered at the Bennadijn ten Zeldam Stichting, Amsterdam.

Boesveld, Mary (1986) *Towards Autonomy for Women. Research and Action to Support a Development Process*, The Hague: RAWOO.

Boserup, Ester and Christina Liljencrantz (1975) *Integration and Women in Development: Why, When and How*, New York: UNDP, May.

Brandt, Willy (1990) Need for a Radical Change in International Co-operation, in: *Ein Besseres Leben für Zukünftige Generationen. Die Erklärung von Amsterdam*, DGVN-Reihe No.25, Bonn: Deutsche Gesellschaft für die Vereinten Nationen.

Brown, Valerie A. and Margaret A. Switzer (1991) Engendering the Debate. Women and Ecologically Sustainable Development, Australia: *Centre for Resource and Environmental Studies*, Australian National University, Canberra.

Bruchhaus, Eva-Maria (1990) *Women as Pioneers and Managers of Knowledge and Skills*, Workshop Report, 16-29 August 1988, Bonn: Evangelische Zentralstelle für Entwicklungshilfe e.V.

Buechner, Gregor et al (1990) Gender, Enviromental Degradation and Development: The Extent of the Problem. Paper presented at Environment and Development Seminar, University College London: MSc. Course in Environmental and Resource Economics, Dept of Economics.

———(1991) Gender, Evironmental Degradation and Development.: Modifying the New Household Economic Model, in: *Gender Environmental Degradation and*

Development: The Extent of the Problem, George Buchner et al, London Environmental Economic Centre.

Burgess, Joanne C. (1991) Land Management and Soil Conservation in Malawi: A Case Study in Gregor Buechner et al *Gender, Environmental Degradation and Development: The Extent of the Problem*, London Environmental Economic Centre.

Canadian Council for International Co-operation, CIDA, MATCH int. Center (1991) *Two Halves Make a Whole: Balancing Gender Relations in Development*, Ottawa.

Cecelski, Elizabeth (1985) *The Rural Energy Crisis, Women's Work and Basic Needs: Perspectives and Approaches to Action*, Geneva: ILO.

Centre for Information on Women and Development (1991) *Women and Sustainable Development*. A Report from the Women's Forum in Bergen, Norway, 14-15 May 1990 (Fr. Nansenspl. 6 0160 Oslo 1, Norway).

Centre for Our Common Future (1991) (1992) Independent Sectors Network '92, Geneva: Briefs for UNCED.

Centre for Science and Environment (CSE) (1991) *The CSE Statement on Global Democracy*, Draft, New Delhi.

Chambers, Robert (1987) Sustainable Livelihoods, Environment and Development: Putting Poor Rural People First, IDS Discussion Paper 240, December.

Charkiewicz-Pluta, Ewa (1991) *Ecology and Emancipation. From the Dominant Mode of Development to Sustainable Alternatives – The Perspective of Social Movements*, MA Thesis, The Hague: Institute of Social Studies.

———and Sabine Häusler with Rosi Braidotti and Saskia Wieringa (1991) *Remaking the World Together*, A state-of-the-art-report and a proposal for a reassessment of the topic, Institute of Social Studies, the Hague and University of Utrecht.

CILSS, Club du Sahel (n.d.) Women in the Fight Against Desertification, *IIED Publications* No. 12.

Commonwealth Secretariat (1989) Engendering Adjustment for the 1990s, Commonwealth Expert Group on Women and Structural Adjustment, London.

———(1991) *Sustainable Development – An Imperative for Environmental Protection*, Report by a Group of Experts on Environmental Concerns and the Commonwealth (Chapter 6, on Women, Environment and Development) London, August.

Colby, Michael E. (1990) Environmental Managment in Development: The Evolution of Paradigms, *World Bank Discussion Paper* No. 80, Washington: World Bank.

Daines, Victoria and David Seddon (1990) Survival Struggles, Protest and Resistance: Women's Responses to 'Austerity' and 'Structural Adjustment', paper presented at the Social Movements Studies Seminar No. 11, Institute of Social Studies, The Hague.

Dankelman, Irene, Rachel Kurian and Els Postel (1992) *Environmental Problems and Their Consequences for Different Sections of Society*, Netherlands, unpublished manuscript, NAR.

Davidson, Nicol and Margaret Croke (eds) (1978) *The United Nations & Decision Making: The Role of Women*, Vol.II, UNITAR (Sales No. E.78.XV.CR/11).

de Jong-Boon, Caroline, ed (1990) *Environmental Problems in the Sudan*, Reader Part I and II, The Hague: Institute of Social Studies (Chapter on Women and

Environment in Part II).

Dixon, John A. and Louise A. Fallon (1989) The Concept of Sustainability: Origins, Extensions, and Usefulness for Policy, The World Bank Environment Department, Division Working Paper No. 1989-1, Washington: The World Bank.

Dogra, Bharat (1983) *Forests and People. A Report on the Himalayas,* 2nd Edition, published by B.Dogra, A-2/184, Janakpuri, New Delhi-110058, India.

dos Santos, Selene Herculano (n.d.) *On Brundtland Report: Some Questions About "Sustainable Development" and the "New International Economic Order",* Manuscript, Oslo: Feminist University of Norway.

Drake, Victoria C. (1991) The Gender Bias Issue in Environment and Development: Fact or Fiction, in: Gregor Buechner et al, *Gender Environmental Degradation and Development: The Extent of the Problem,* Gregor Buechner et al., London: Environmental Economics Centre.

Dutch Foreign Ministry (1991) A World of Difference. A New Framework for Development in the 1990s, The Hague: Netherlands Development Cooperation Information Department.

Duvvry, Nata (1989) Women in Agriculture: A Review of the Indian Literature, in: *Economic and Political Weekly,* 28 October, pp. 96-112.

E & D files 1991/1992 Briefings for NGOs on UNCED, Geneva: United Nations Non-Governmental Liaison Service.

Environment Liaison Centre International (ELCI) (1986) *Women and the Environmental Crisis. Forum 1985.* A report on the proceedings of the workshop on women, environment and development. Nairobi: 10-20 July, 1985.

――――(1992a) *Justice Between Peoples – Justice Between Generations,* Nairobi: Synthesis of Citizen Movements Responses to Environment and Development Challenges.

――――(1992b) *Agenda Ya Wananchi – Draft Citizens Action Plan for the 1990s,* Nairobi.

ESCAP (1980) *Report of the Expert Group Meeting on Women and Forest Industries,* Bangkok.

Escobar, Arturo (1987) 'Power and Visibility: the Invention and Management of Development in the Third World', PhD dissertation, University of California, Berkely.

FAO (n.d.) *Gender and Development. A Framework for Project Analysis,* W/U0696, Rome.

――――(1984) ECA/FAO Subregional Seminar on Fuelwood and Energy Development for African Women, Lusaka, Zambia: 18 April 1983, Report.

――――(1988) *Women in Fishing Communities. A Special Target Group of Development Projects,* Rome.

――――(1989) *FAO Plan of Action for the Integration of Women in Development,* W/Z4902, Twenty-fifth Session, 11-30 November, Rome.

――――(1989) *Women's Role in Forest Resource Management. A Reader.* Regional Wood Energy Development Programme in Asia, Prepared by Brigitte van der Borg, Bangkok: December, Project Working Paper No.1.

――――and SIDA (n.d.) *Restoring the Balance. Women and Forest Resources,* Rome.

――――(1988) *Experiences of Institutional Changes Concerning Women in Development,* Expert Consultation, 21-23 September, Rome.

――――(1989a) *The State of Food and Agriculture,* Rome.

————(1989b) *Women in Community Forestry. A Field Guide for Project Design and Implementation*, Rome.

————(1989c) *FAO Plan of Action for the Integration of Women in Development*, W/Z4902, Twenty-fifth Session, 11-30 November, Rome.

————(1989d) *Progress Report on the Implementation of the Plan of Action for Integration of Women in Development*, W/Z4959/c, Twenty-fifth Session, 11-30 November, Rome.

————(1990a) *Women in Agricultural Development. Women, Food Systems and Agriculture*, Rome.

————(1990b) *Women in Agricultural Development. Gender Issues in Rural Food Security in Developing Countries*, Rome.

————(1990c) *Women in Agricultural Development*. FAO's Plan of Action, Rome.

————(1991a) *The Role of Women in Fisheries Development*. Committee on Fisheries, W/Z6857, Nineteenth Session, 8-12 April, Rome.

————(1991b) *Integration of Women in Agriculture and Rural Development*. Committee on Agriculture, W/Z6884, Eleventh Session, 22-30 April, Rome.

Gaia Foundation (1991) *The Amazon Development Fund*, UK.

Gameson, Tom (1991) The Gender Issue in the Third World and the Constraints on Economic Theory, in: George Buchner et al, *Gender, Environmental Degradation and Development: The Extent of the Problem*, London Environmental Economics Centre.

Goodland, R.J.A. (1989) *Environment and Development; Progress of the World Bank (and Speculations Towards Sustainability)*, February, Washington DC: The World Bank.

Die Grünen im Bundestag (1987) *Frauen & Oekologie*. Gegen den Machbarkeitswahn, AG Frauenpolitk.

GTZ (1991) Proceedings of Workshop 'Fachgespräch Frau und Umwelt', Eschborn: German Corporation for Development.

Hanrahan, David (1991) Women in Development and Environment: Indicators of the Extent of Bias, in Gregor Buechner et al, *Gender, Environmental Degradation and Development: The Extent of the Problem*, London Environmental Economics Centre.

Hansen, Stein (1988) *Debt for Nature Swaps: Overview and Discussion of Key Issues*, The World Bank, Policy Planning and Research Staff, Environment Department, Washigton DC: Environment Working Paper No. 1.

Harmony, Barbara Helen (n.d.) *A Course Curriculum for Women and Environment* (The Qwater Centre, Route 3, Box 720, Eureka Springs, AR 72632).

Harris, Jonathan M. (1990) *Global Institutions and Ecological Crisis*, Institute for Economic Development, Boston University, Discussion Paper Series No 11, February.

Häusler, Sabine (1990) The Image of Third World Women as 'Environmental Managers' in Development Media, course paper MDC 202, The Hague, Institute of Social Studies, unpublished.

————(1991) *Community Forestry – A Critique, Illustrated by a Case Study of Nepal*, MA Thesis, The Hague: Institute of Social Studies.

Heller, Chiah (n.d.) *Towards a Radical Ecofeminism*, Germinal Freedom, brochure, mimeo.

Hoksema, Jan (1987) *Women and Social Forestry, from Theory to Practice*, Thesis,

University of Amsterdam, Anthropological/Sociological Centre.

Hoskins, Marilyn (1979) *Women in Forestry for Local Community Development*, Washington, DC: US Agency for International Development.

————(1981) *Household Level Appropriate Technologies for Women*, Washington DC: US Agency for International Development, Office of Women and Development.

Hueting, Roefie (1990) Correcting National Income for Environmental Losses: A Practical Solution For a Theoretical Dilemma, paper prepared for the *Conference on Ecological Economics of Sustainability*, Washington, DC: 21-23 May.

INSTRAW (n.d.) *According to statistics, she is not working. Improving statistics and indicators on women*, San Domingo.

————(n.d.) *Women, Water and Sanitation*, Training Kit.

International Labour Organization, (ILO) (1976) *Employment, Growth and Basic Needs: A One-World Problem*, Geneva: Report of the Director-General of the ILO.

————(1988) *The Bankura Story*-Rural Women Organise for Change,by Nalini Singh, New Delhi: ILO.

ISIS International (1990) *Directory of Third World Women's Publications*, Quezon City: The Philippines.

Ivan-Smith, Edda, Nidhi Tandon and Jane Connors (1988) *Women in Sub-Saharan Africa*, London: Minority Rights Group.

Kirdar, Uner (1989) A Review of Past Strategies, in: Khadija Haq and Uner Kirdar (eds) *Development for People. Goals and Strategies for the Year 2000*, by North/South Roundtable and the UNDP Development Study Programme.

Kraus, Florentine (1985) *Energy for Sustainable Development, Part One: The Soft Path Perspective*, IPSEP/ELC.

Kuperus, Siteke (1990) *La Participation des Femmes aux Activites Forestiers au Senegal, Une Etude de la Situation de la Zone d'Intervention du Previnoba* Author's address: Hoogstraat 37A, 6071 Wageningen, Netherlands.

Leach, Melissa (1991) Gender and the Environment: Traps and Opportunities, Paper prepared for Development Studies Association (DSA) Conference, Swansea, UK: 11-13 September.

Lutz, Ernst and Michael Young (1990) Agricultural Policies in Industrial Countries and Their Environmental Impacts: Applicability to and Comparisons with Developing Nations, Policy Planning and Research Staff, Washington DC: The World Bank Environment Department, Environment Working Papers, No. 25.

Lycklama à Nijeholt, Geertje (1992) Women and the Meaning of Development: Approaches and Consequences, Working Paper – Subseries on Women's History & Development, No. 15, The Hague: Institute of Social Studies.

Magrath, William B. and John B. Doolette (1990) Strategic Issues for Watershed Development in Asia, Policy Planning and Research Staff, Washington DC: The World Bank Environment Department, Environment Working Papers, No. 30.

Maguire, Patricia (1984) *Women in Development: An Alternative Analysis*, Centre for International Education, Amherst, MA.: University of Massachussets.

Maathai, Wangari (1987) *The Greenbelt Movement*, Nairobi, Kenya: Environmental Liaison Centre International.

————(1988) *The Greenbelt Movement, Sharing the Approach and the Experience*, Nairobi, Kenya: Environment Liaison Centre International.

Mearns, Robin (1991) Environmental Implications of Structural Adjustment: Reflections on Scientific Method, Sussex: IDS Sussex, Discussion Papers, No. 284.

Ministry of Foreign Affairs, DAEGIS, Netherlands (1990) *Banskantha Women's Rural Development Project, SEWA's Two-Year Ground Work, Project Proposal 1991-1996*, Appraisal of two years linking socio-economic and supportive activities with the Gujarat water and sanitation supply scheme, The Hague: Mission Report 6-20 October, prepared by Loes Schenk-Sandbergen.

Ministry of Foreign Affairs, Directorate General for International Cooperation (1990) *Women, Energy, Forestry and Environment. Policy on an operational Footing: Main Points and Checklists*, The Netherlands, March.

Molnar, Augusta and G.Scheiber (n.d.) Women and Forestry – Operational Issues, Washington DC: World Bank, PPR Working Paper, WPS, No. 183.

Monimart, Marie (1989) Women in the Fight Against Desertification, International Institute of Environment and Development Issues Paper No 12, December.

Netherlands Ministry for Development Cooperation (1991) *A World of Difference. A New Framework for Development Cooperation in the 1990's*, The Hague.

NGO-EC Liaison Centre (1989) *Gender and Development. Combatting Gender Blindness*, Brussels.

OECD/DAC/Expert Group on Women in Development (1989) *Focus on the Future: Women and Environment*, Seminar Report, Paris: May.

Office of the Status of Women Department of the Prime Minister and Cabinet (Australia) (1991) *Engendering the Debate. Women and Ecologically Sustainable Development*, Discussion Paper prepared by Valerie A. Brown and Margaret A. Switzer, Center for Resource and Environmental Studies, Australian National University, Canberra.

Pandey, Shanta (1990) Women in Hattisunde Forest Managment in Dhading District, Nepal, Kathmandu: MPE Series No. 9.

Pela, Giuseppina (1991) Agrochemicals: A Woman's View, Rome: FAO Working Papers Series, No. 1.

Pembinaan Kesejanhteraan Keluarga (PKK) (1987) *Women, Environment and Development. A brief account of women's participation in a human waste disposal program in two urban areas in Indonesia*, Tim Penggerak Pusat.

———(1987) *Women, Environment and Sustainable Development. The inclusion of women in the decision making process regarding potable water supply. An Indonesian experience*, Tim Penggerak Pusat.

Pezzey, John (1989) Economic Analysis of Sustainable Growth and Sustainable Development, Washington DC: *World Bank Environment and Development Department Working Papers* No. 15.

Pietilä, Hilkka (1989) Tomorrow Begins Today. Elements of a Feminist Alternative for the Future of Industrialised Countries, Women's Worlds, Finnish contribution to the Third International Interdisciplinary Congress on Women, Dublin: published by Institute of Women Studies, Abo Aacademy University, Turku, Finland.

———(1991) The Environment and Sustainable Development, in: *Report of the Nordic Conference on Women, Environment and Sustainable Development*, Oslo, Norway: Centre for the Research on Women, University of Oslo and Secretariat for Women and Research at the Norwegian Research Council for Science and

Humanities.

Rocheleau, Diane E. (1990) Gender Complimentarity and Conflict in Sustainable Forestry Development: A Multiple User Approach, paper presented at IUFRO World Congress Quinquennial, Montreal, 5-11 August.

Sadik, Nafis (1989) *Investing in Women: The Focus of the Nineties*, The State of World Population, UNFPA.

Sarkar, Saral (1990) The Green-Alternative Movement in West Germany -A Third World View, Social Movements Seminar Paper No. 90/5, The Hague: Institute of Social Studies.

Sharma, Chandrika and Madhu Sarin (1989) *Local Trees, Local Uses – A Catalogue of Trees of Bicchiwara Block, District Dungapur, Rajastan* Madhu Sarin,48, Sector 4, Chandigarh 160001, India.

Shiva, Vandana (n.d.) *Discovering the Real Meaning of Sustainability*, Dehra Dun,India: Research Foundation for Science and Ecology.

Soderbaum, Peter (1991) *Economic Values for a Sustainable Future*, Uppsala, Sweden: Swedish University of Agricultural Sciences, Department of Economics, 31 January.

Solis, Vivienne and Marta Trejos (1991) *Women and Sustainable Development in Central America*, IUCN and CEFEMINA.

Southgate, Douglas and David Pearce (1988) Agricultural Colonization and Environmental Degradation in Frontier Developing Economies, The World Bank, Policy Planning and Research Staff, Environment Department, Environment Department Working Paper, No. 9, Washington DC.

Sprenger, Ellen (1991) The Greenbelt Movement in Kenya: Two-Edged Environmentalism or a Strategic Dilemma? in: *SAUTY YA SITI*,June, publ. by the Tanzania Media Women's Association TAMWA, Tanzania.

————(1992) *Women, Environment and Development? Gender Focused Social Forestry in Tanzania*, MA thesis, Nijmegen: Third World Centre, University of Nijmegen, Netherlands.

SSRC/ISSC/DAWN (1992) *Policy Statement on Population and the Environment*, Mexico: Workshop on population and the environment, January/February.

Stephens, Alexandra (1991) Women in Conservation and Development, FAO RAPA, Khao Yai, Thailand. Paper presented at: International Workshop on Conservation and Sustainable Development,FAO/ RAPA, 22-26 April.

Stock, Molly, Jo Ellen Force, Dixie Ehrenreich (1982) Women in Natural Resources: An International Perspective, Paper presented at: Conference for men and women, held at the University of Idaho, 8-9 March, sponsored USAID, WID, published in: Forest, Wildlife and Range Experiment Station, Moscow Idaho: University of Idaho.

The Stockholm Initiative on Global Security and Governance (1991) *Common Responsibility in the 1990s*, 22 April.

Tinker, Irene (n.d.) *The Real Rural Energy Crisis: Women's Time*, Washington DC: Equity Policy Centre.

Truong, Thanh-Dam (1992) Human Development: Conceptual and practical issues, paper prepared for: International Forum on Intercultural Exchange, Saitama, Japan: National Women's Education Centere, 30 September - 2 October.

United Nations (1985) The Nairobi Forward Looking Strategies for the Advancement of Women, Conference to Review and Appraise the Achievements of the United

Nations Decade for Women: Equality, Development and Peace, Nairobi, Kenya, 15-26 July, New York: United Nations, Sales Section (States No. E.85. IV.10).

———(1986) *World Survey on the Role of Women in Development*, A/CONF.ii6.4/Rev.1, Sales Section No E.8. IV. 3.

———(1991) World's Women, Trends and Statistics 1970-(1990) UN, UNICEF, UNFPA, UNIFEM, New York.

United Nations Conference on Environment and Development (UNCED) (1991) Women and Children First, Report of Symposium in Geneva 27-30 May (1991) sponsored by UNCED, UNICEF, UNFPA, and Governmrnt of Denmark. Conches, Switzerland.

———(1992) *A Guide to Agenda 21*, Geneva.

United Nations Development Programme (UNDP) (1987) *The Invisible Adjustment: Poor Women and the Economic Crisis*, the Americas and the Caribbean Regional Office, Santiago: Regional Program Women in Development.

———(1990) *Human Development Report*, New York.

———(1991) *NGO Perspectives on Poverty, Environment and Development*, Environment and Natural Resources Group, New York.

———(1992) *Human Development Report*, New York.

United Nations Environment Programme (UNEP) (1980) *Environmental Brief* 4/80, Special Issue on Women and Environment, Nairobi.

———(1991) Success Stories of Women and the Environment, Global Assembly Miami, Washigton DC: United Nations Environment Programme and WorldWide Network.

United Nations Children's Fund (UNICEF) (1987) The Invisible Adjustment. Poor Women and the Economic Crisis, Santiago: *UNICEF The Americas and the Caribbean Regional Office.*

United Nations Development Fund for Women (UNIFEM) (1990) *Women on the Agenda: UNIFEM's Experience in Mainstreaming with Women 1985-(1990)* prepared by Mary B. Anderson.

United Nations Family Planning Association (UNFPA) (1991) World Population Report, prepared by Nafis Sadik.

von Weizsäcker, Ernst and Christine (1986) How to Live with Errors: On the Evolutionary Power of Errors, Bonn, Germany: Institute for European Environmental Policy.

van den Hombergh, Heleen (1992) *Gender, Environment and Development; a Guide to the Literature*, Amsterdam: Institute for Development Research, Amsterdam, (INDRA).

Vrouwenberaad Nederlandse Ontwikkelingsinstanties (1989) *Women,Producers of Development*, New Challenges and Alternatives, The Hague.

Wadehra, Renu and Manab Chakraborty (1987) *Deforestation and Forestation: Women's Response in Uttarakhand (India)*, Netherlands IUCN Committee.

Weekes-Vagliani, Winifred (1992) Lessons from the Family Planning Experience for Community-Based Environmental Education, Paris: *OECD Development Centre Technical Papers* No. 62.

Wichterich, Christa (1984) *Frauen in der Dritten Welt. Zum Stand der Diskussion um die Integration von Frauen in die Entwicklung*, Bonn, Germany: Deutsche Stiftung fur Internationale Entwicklung, Zentralstelle fur Erziehung, Wissenschaft und Dokumentation.

Wiltshire, Rosina (1992) Environment and Development: Grass Roots Women's Perspective, Development Alternatives with Women for a New Era (DAWN), Barbados.

Women in Development Europe, (WIDE) (1992) Special Issue on Women and Environment, *WIDE Bulletin* 1.

Women's Environment and Development Organization WEDO (1992) *World Women's Congress for a Healthy Planet*, Official Report, Miami, Florida, US: 8-12 November 1991.

Women's Environmental Network (WEN) (1988) *Sanitary Protection Scandal*, London.

――――, War on Want, ODA (1989) *Women, Environment and Development, Seminar Report*, 7 March, Rachel Hedley (ed.) IIED.

――――(1990) *A Tissue of Lies? Disposable Paper and the Environment*, London.

――――(1990) *Green Living*, a magazine, ISSN 0957-0012.

Women and Environment in Latin America and Caribbean, Conference Proceedings (1991) Quito: Marc Documento Aprobado Por La Plenaria Del Encuentro Internacional Mujer Y Medio Ambiente En America Latina Y El Caribe.

Women in Fight Against Desertification (1990) a background paper for the Regional Encounter in Segou (Mali) on local level natural resource management CILSS/Club du Sahel, published by IIED.

Women's Health Journal (1990) Latin American and Caribbean Women's Health Network, Take Back the Earth: Women, Health and the Environment. No 20, Oct.,Nov.,Dec.

Women, Water and Sanitation, Journal published by the Centre for Women, Water and Sanitation, P.B.93190, 2509 AD Den Haag, Netherlands.

Wood, D.H. et al (1980) *The Socio-Economic Context of Firewood Use in Small Rural Communities*, Washington DC: US Agency for International Development.

World Bank (1990) *Report on Poverty*, Washington DC.

――――(1991) *The Challenge of Development*, Washington, DC.

――――(1992) *World Development Report (1992) Development and Environment*, executive summary, Washington DC.

World Bank News (1992) Special Issue on The World Bank, The Environment and Development, Washington DC.

World Conservation Union (IUCN) (1989) *Estudio de Caso en Poblacion y Recursos Naturales* Costa Rica.

――――(1989) *Estudio de Caso en Poblacion y Recursos Naturales,* Honduras.

――――(1990) *Resolution on Women and Natural Resource Management*, adopted IUCN General Assembly, Perth, Australia, December.

――――(1991) *Women and Natural Resource Managment: An Overview of the Activities of Canadian Governmental and Non-Governmental International Development Organizations*, presented by Patricia Fay Thomas, Gland, Switzerland

――――/ORCA/CCAD (1991) *Aporte de la Mujer en el Ejecucion de los Planes de Accion Forestal*, Regional Seminar, 24-25, January, El Salvador.

World Health Organization (WHO) (n.d.) Women and Environment, Effects of Environmental Factors on Women's Health, Prepared by Jaqueline Sims, Geneva: Prevention of Environmental Pollution, Division of Environmental Health, WHO.

Index

(ILO), 17, 19, 92
International Monetary Fund (IMF), 19,
    22, 139
International Planned Parenthood
    Federation (IPPF), 89
International Policy Action Committee
    (IPAC), 91, 103
Irigaray, L., 33, 41, 66, 67

Jain, Devaki, 121
Jameson, 11, 54
Johns, David M., 151
Johnston, J., 73

Keysers, Leo, 145, 147
King, Ynestra, 165, 167
knowledge: Newtonian paradigm of, 153;
    organization of, 31; production of *see*
    epistemology; redefinition of, 42;
    scientific, 23; situated, 11, 48, 53;
    vernacular, 10; woman-based, 39
knowledge systems, Western,
    universalism of, 56
knowledge, indigenous environmental, 87
Kristeva, J., 60
Kumar D'Souza, Corinne, 165, 166, 167

language, value placed on, 39
Latin American Network of Social
    Ecology (CLAES), 159
Leach, Melissa, 99, 100, 173
Leland, Stephani, 161
lesbian perspective, 40, 73
Lévi Strauss, C. 38
liberation theology, 156
literary language, as instrument of
    liberation, 36
Loisaida project, 159
Lorde, Audre, 70
Lovelock, James, 152, 154
low external input agriculture, 113, 124
Luzenberger, Jos, 114

Maathai, Wangari, 86, 98
Maclintock, Barbara, 52
male domination, 8, 171
male power, destruction of, 161
male promiscuity, 66
male supremacy, 31
Malthus, Thomas, 131, 142
mankind, definition of, 30
marginality, validation of, 27
Margulis, Lynn, 152
Marxism, 22, 44, 50, 64, 65, 93, 95, 107,
    137; reform, 71
masculine viewpoint, 33, 37
Material Product System, 139

materialism, 49; concept of, 40;
    female-embodied, 172; rereading of,
    50
matriarchies, search for, 65
men, subordination to, 155
menstruation, 70
Merchant, Carolyn, 31, 164, 165
Miami conferences, 7, 77, 96, 102, 103,
    104, 174, 179
micro-politics, 10
middle-class activists, 121
Mies, Maria, 93, 94, 96, 112
militarism, 5, 119
militarization, 19, 109
military spending, 4, 146, 162
Mohanty, Chandra, 173
Mohawk people, 115
Moral Majority, 74
Morrison, Toni, 72
mortality, infant, 142
Moser, Caroline, 78, 81
Mother Nature, 56
motherhood, 40, 68; moral, 62
mothering, 163
mystic traditions, 150

Naess, Arne, 149
Nairobi Conference, 86, 87
Nairobi office, 80
Nandy, Ashis, 109, 112, 166, 173
Narmada dam, 134
nation state, 21; disintegration of, 26
natural resources: consumption of, 4;
    depletion of, 1; misuse of, 26
nature: as brute matter, 33; as realm of
    freedom, 157; domination of, 149;
    subjugation of, 72; utilitarian value of,
    125; women's relationship with, 59-76
Nazi Germany, 62-4
Nazis, Women's Bureau, 63
needs: basic, 17, 19, 134; commodity-
    based, 22; human, 108
neo-fascism, 74
networking, 11
nongovernmental development
    organizations (NGDOs), 2, 113, 170,
    171, 182
nongovernmental organizations (NGOs),
    2, 81, 89, 96, 98, 113, 171, 178, 182;
    role of, 127; strengthening of, 160
NGO Global Forum, 28, 85, 91, 116,
    126-31, 160, 164
NGO treaty on population, 146
Nijeholt, Lycklama, 81
noble savage, idea of, 155
North/South relations, 19, 20, 24, 180
nuclear weapons, 5, 140; testing ban, 128